Sari Says

Sari Says

The REAL DIRT on
Everything from Sex to School

Sari Locker

HARPERCOLLINS*PUBLISHERS*

This book may contain advice and information relating to health care for teenagers and young adults. Any such advice or information is not intended to replace or substitute for professional medical advice or the labeling recommendations of any given product. Rather, any advice and information contained in this book should be used to supplement and elaborate on the advice and regular care given by the teenager's or young adult's medical specialists or the directions of any such product.

Library of Congress Cataloging-in-Publication Data
Locker, Sari.
    Sari says: the real dirt on everything from sex to school / Sari Locker.—1st ed.
        p.   cm
    ISBN 0-06-447306-6 (pbk.)
    1. Teenagers—Life skills guides—Juvenile literature. 2. Interpersonal relations in adolescence—Juvenile literature. 3. Adolescent psychology—Juvenile literature. [1. Life skills.] I. Title.
HQ796.L636 2001   2001024331
305.235—dc21   CIP
                                                                                AC

1 2 3 4 5 6 7 8 9 10
❖
First Edition

Acknowledgments

I am grateful to all the teens who have shared stories about the trials and tribulations of their lives. Your questions provided the foundation of this book, and will surely help other teens.

Thanks to the fabulous team at HarperCollins, including my superb editor Julia Richardson, the excellent designer Alison Donalty, and Elise Howard for her continuing support of this book.

Thanks to others for their contributions: Molly Aboud, Amy Zavatto, and Howard Huang. Special thanks to my amazing agent at William Morris Agency, Mel Berger.

As always, thanks for the wonderful support of my friends and family: Molly Lind, Jeffrey Lind, Larry Locker, Aliza Locker, Murray Siegel, Gert Siegel, Jonathan Siegel, Jodi Sharon, Paul Levy, Erica Peters, Daniel Kaufman, Amanda Carlson, and especially Brian Clinton.

Hi, Reader!

For years, you've been sending me all your questions on just about everything you can think of—friends, parents, school, boyfriends, girl-friends, sex. Thousands of you have mailed handwritten letters directly to me. Even more of you have posted questions to me on the Sari Says area of www.teenpeople.com, as well as on my web site, www.sarisays.com. I've truly enjoyed getting your questions. But I've especially loved answering them. It makes me so happy every time you let me into your world and trust that I can say something to make life a little easier for you.

In this book, I've put together tons of your questions: some that I've answered before and some that are brand-new and totally unique. All of the questions you'll read here are real questions from real teens. I've even included some of the actual original letters for you to check out. I'm thrilled about this book, because it gives me the chance to give you advice about everything you want to know!

You are going through a really great time in your life. There are so many possibilities just waiting for you. But I know that as exciting as life is right now, it can also be confusing and difficult. I am definitely here to help. Keep sending me your questions, and I'll keep giving you my advice. Always remember one thing: This *is* a wonderful time in your life, so have fun!

Sari

Sari Locker

Contents

there's no place like home

Maybe when you were a kid, you were Daddy's little girl or a mama's boy. But now that you're getting older, your home life is probably much more complicated. Even the coolest parents can upset their teen at some point in life. You may think that your parents are too strict, they don't understand you, or they don't fully respect you as the individual you are becoming. Or the difficulties could be caused by the way that your parents' relationship is affecting how they deal with you. It might not just be your 'rents who cause you grief. Your brothers, sisters, grandparents, and cousins can all drive you up the wall. But you know that deep down they all love you, right?! In this chapter, I'll help you learn to deal with all those loving (but sometimes annoying) folks at home.

Parents: You Can't Live With Them, But You Wouldn't Be Alive Without Them

snooping mom

Dear Sari,

My mom reads my email, my journal, and goes through my backpack. She wants to know everything I am doing, and when I don't tell her enough, she tries to find out more on her own. She thinks that I don't know that she snoops, but I'm not stupid. I don't want to confront her because I am afraid that it would just turn into a huge fight. What should I do?

Sari Says:

You have the right to privacy, but you have to remember that you are still living in your mom's house. She worries about you, and she thinks that if she checks up on you, she'll find out if you are safe and sound, or if you are doing things that are dumb and dangerous. Snooping is not the right way for her to do this. The two of you should work out a way that you can trust her to respect your privacy, while she can still feel as if she knows enough about what is going on in your life.

Explain to your mom that you are growing up, and you want more privacy now that you are older. Let her know that you would never do anything bad and try to hide it from her. Promise that if she respects your privacy, then in return, you will tell her more about what's going on in your life. If she agrees to this, make an effort to tell her more about your day at school and your friends—even your crushes.

If she doesn't agree, then you'll have to find privacy wherever you can. When you write down your most private thoughts, hide them somewhere she won't look. You can get a small file box that locks and keep it in your room, or keep your journal in your school locker. As far as email goes, it's easy to type out a message quickly and send it off, without thinking much about it. But email can be forwarded, printed out, and it can remain on someone's hard drive forever. So whether your mom's reading it or not, you should still always be very careful about putting too much personal stuff in email.

I hope that you do not have to go to these extremes of hiding everything, but if your mom insists on snooping, the best you can do is make sure she does not find anything. If she doesn't find anything, she will probably stop on her own.

Fighting with your parents

Dear Sari,

My parents and I fight about everything—my clothes, my friends, my boyfriend, money, you name it. They never let me do anything. It's not fair! Help me!

Sari Says:

To cut down on the fighting, it may help if they understand what you are going through now that you're a teen. Calmly talk with them. Ask them what they were like when they were teens. Ask them to tell you some fun stories about what *their* parents were like at that time. This conversation may help you talk about how you'd like them to treat you.

Then, tell them that you want to meet them halfway between what you want and what they want. If your mom says she only wants you in long skirts and you want to wear mini-skirts, then agree that from now on you'll wear knee-length skirts. Or if they never allow you to go over to your boyfriend's house, then ask if he can come to your place for dinner sometime, so they can get to know him.

If your conversation starts turning into a fight, stay calm and find a way to agree on something—even if it is not exactly what you would ideally want.

Fighting Fairly

It's only natural to fight with your parents at least once in a while. In order to get through it, you need to learn to fight fairly. Here are some things that will help:

- Don't call them names.
  No matter how annoying they are, keep the criticisms to yourself. Words can hurt.
- Don't scream.
  If you get so mad that you want to yell at them, instead take a deep breath and tell them that you need to take a time-out for a few minutes to calm down and collect your thoughts.

- Don't tell them that your friends' parents are not as strict.
  Your parents make their own rules. They won't care about what other parents do.
- Don't worry about "winning" the argument.
  State your point of view and listen to theirs. Maybe you are both right; maybe neither of you are right. All that should matter is that you can reach a compromise.

Expressing Your Individuality

piercing problem

Dear Sari,

I got my bellybutton pierced. The thing is, my parents don't know. They think that I'm a good girl, and they will freak when they find out . . . if they find out! Should I keep this from them?

Sari Says:

It's best to tell your parents that you got pierced, even for the basic reason that your parents should be aware of your general health. (If your belly button piercing gets infected, it could become a serious problem.) Besides, if you don't tell, you'll spend years making sure that you never change in front of your parents, and you will always have to wear a one-piece bathing suit. Find a quiet time to have an uninterrupted talk with the parent who is most likely to be lenient. If you profusely apologize for doing it without asking, and you give great reasons why you got pierced—not just "my friend did it, too"—then your parents may let you keep it. If not, as you know, the hole can close up at any point in your life, so you may decide for your parents' sake that you'll let the piercing close now.

You know how people say that teens are halfway between childhood and adulthood? At this stage in life you want to express your individuality, but sometimes your parents are still treating you like a kid. Your parents aren't trying to make you into a clone of them; they just might not understand all your changes. To help them through it, make every effort to talk with them about who you are becoming. Whether you want to dye your hair green, take up skateboarding, or start studying Shakespeare, telling them about your changes before they notice will help them accept the new you.

religious choices

Dear Sari,

I was raised a Christian, but I have major issues with some of the beliefs and would much rather follow another religion. My parents are saying that I have no choice, and I am only looking into another religion to be difficult. How can I persuade them to let me become another religion, which has similar, but not identical beliefs?

Sari Says:

Part of religion is about carrying on the heritage of your family and passing on the religion to future generations. Of course, your parents want you to hold true to their beliefs because Christianity probably makes great sense to them, and they want to pass on to you all the good things that the religion has brought into their lives. If you are sure that you want to be part of a different religion, then someday you can go along with your individual beliefs. However, I don't think that now is the time for you to switch religions.

Your parents may think that you are just being difficult because you are going through your teen years, a time when so many people rebel against their parents' beliefs and values. Consider your parents' feelings.

They want what's best for you, and they think that Christianity will help your life. While you are still living under their roof, you should give them the joy of accepting and participating in their religion. Then later, when you are living on your own, maybe in college, you can pick up your own exploration of other religions, and if you choose a different religion, then you are making an adult decision without involving your parents.

Your Drinking and Drugging

trusting the party animal

Dear Sari,

I lost my parents' trust big time. I hid beer in my room and they found it. What can I say? I just like to have fun sometimes. I know they did when they were my age. Now they don't let me do anything. My curfew was midnight; now its freakin' 10:00. They have taken away all my privileges like driving and dating. I'm trying my hardest to get their trust back. I clean the house, I'm getting a job, I make dinner, but they still don't trust me.

Sari Says:

You messed up, so of course your parents are going to be mad at you for a while. But you are on the right track to regaining their trust by doing so many good things. After another couple of weeks on your best behavior, sit down with them to talk about what's happened. Tell them that you want them to trust you again, and remind them that you have been working very hard to make that happen. Suggest to them that they gradually let you have more freedom to prove that you are trustworthy. Perhaps at first they will make your curfew 11:00. Then, if you are still behaving well, they will let you drive again. Finally, when they think you are ready for the responsibility, they will let you start dating again. If you are patient, at some point they will be able to trust you again.

Risks of Drinking

Teens who drink occasionally can be putting themselves at risk for getting hurt from alcohol. Even one beer may be enough to impair driving. According to Mothers Against Drunk Driving, the leading cause of injury and death among teens is car crashes, and alcohol is involved in about half of teen auto-related deaths. In fact, during a typical weekend, an average of one teenager dies each hour in a car crash.

Your Dates, Your Sex Life, and Your Parents

permission to date

Dear Sari,
I have never dated before, but now I really want to go out with this guy. The problem is that I don't know how to tell my parents. Shouldn't I have their permission? What if they say I can't go?

Sari Says:
All parents expect that at some point their kids will want to date. Of course, some parents are stricter than others about when their children are allowed to start. The only way to find out how your parents feel is to ask them. Find a time when they are relaxed, in a good mood and available to talk. Tell them something like: "I met a guy I like, and he asked me out. It's not a big deal, we just want to hang out." Tell them a little bit about him, and then tell them what you plan to do: go for ice cream, go to a movie, whatever. Then see what your parents say. Hopefully they'll be cool with it. If not, just spend time with this guy at school, or in groups of friends. Then in a few weeks or a month, bring it up again with your parents. At some point, they will let you start dating.

Dear Sari,

A while ago, I told my mom that I find black guys attractive and she totally freaked out. She told me then that it is fine with her if I am friends with blacks, but I am not allowed to date blacks. She and my dad still call them the "n" word. Now, I do not know what to do because I just started going out with a black guy, and he wants me to be his girlfriend, and my mom is gonna kill me. Should I break up with him, or hide him from my mom, or what?

Sari Says:

Racial discrimination should not keep you and your boyfriend apart. Do you think you are up to the task of helping your 'rents get over their prejudices? Since your mom doesn't mind if you have black friends, have this guy over as a friend—do not tell them that you are going out yet. That way maybe they'll see what a great guy he is, and it will help them understand why you like him. Also, when you talk to your parents about him, do not refer to him only as "my black friend." Instead, say stuff like, "My new friend is so smart and nice." Then they'll think "nice guy" before they think "black guy." Also, explain why you do not discriminate, and why you think they need to stop. Tell them that they must not use the "n" word anymore. In your quest to help educate them about these issues, maybe a teacher or adult friend who understands race issues could come over to your house one night for dinner and just happen to bring up this issue to enlighten your parents. Hopefully you will have a positive influence on your parents.

Dear Sari,

My boyfriend asked me if I would be allowed to stay in a hotel room alone with him after our senior prom. We are very much in love and already have sex (with protection), so I am not worried about that. It's just that my mom isn't too happy about the situation. She thinks that I will ruin my reputation by sleeping in the same room with him with basically the whole senior class knowing. But what she doesn't understand is that most of the people in school assume that we are sexually active and it really doesn't give me a bad reputation. She is being irrational and I don't know what to do about it. Can you help me figure out how to make her realize that I'll be fine?

Sari Says:

Maybe part of the reason why your mom doesn't want to give you permission to stay the night with your boyfriend is because she is trying to be "momlike." Moms are not supposed to say, "Sure, go for it, honey. Enjoy a night of sex in a hotel with your boyfriend!" On that note, is your mom really worried about your rep? Maybe what she's worried about is the fact that you're having sex at all. By telling you that you can't spend prom night with your boyfriend, she may think that she is preventing you from having sex with him.

Explain to your mom that you are being honest with her: many girls fib to their parents on prom night, saying that they are sleeping over at a girl friend's house, when they are actually sleeping with a guy. But you are trying to be responsible by telling her where you'll really be that night. Tell her that you will not be up all night having sex in the hotel room—you'll be talking and hanging out. Explain to her that you and your guy will be discreet about staying at a hotel.

Also, be honest with her about your sex life. Tell your mom about how you love this guy, and that is why you decided to have sex with him. Also, tell her that you use birth control and condoms, so your mother knows you are also being responsible.

If your mom still doesn't want you to stay the night with him on prom night, then maybe she'll let you set a really late curfew, like 4 A.M., so you can stay out almost all night with him. If she will not even allow that, do not let it spoil your night. Have a great time at the prom and forget about this disappointment.

'Fessing Up to Your Parents

For lots of people, the natural inclination is to hide things from their parents for fear that it will make their parents angry. You may think that you're protecting them by not telling them things that might upset them. But the fact is, they want to protect you, and if they don't know what you're really up to, then they have no way of knowing if they can help you. Let your parents help—tell them the truth about yourself.

coming out to mom and dad

Dear Sari,

I am an 18-year-old guy, and since I was 16, I have been sure that I am gay. I have been waiting to tell my parents, but now I think I might be ready. How should I tell my parents that I am gay?

Sari Says:

First, think about how you think your family will deal with the news. You should be prepared for some reaction. Try to assess generally how they would feel about this, based on their beliefs and how they treat you. Next, choose the best time and place to tell them. Never just blurt it out in the middle of some other conversation (or fight!). Pick some time when you know you will have at least an hour of quiet family time to talk.

Before you tell them, tell your parents how much you love them, and that you might be surprising them with what you are about to tell them, but you do not want to upset them, only to tell them more about who you are. Then tell them.

Be prepared for some response, ranging from: "We thought so" to "Are you joking?" to anger. Some parents take time accepting that their child is gay, so you may need to bring it up again in a few days to see how they are coping. If the conversation goes very badly, find someone who you both trust, such as a family friend or clergyperson who can help you talk with your parents again. Try to have that support system in place before you even approach your parents, just so you have people on your side whom you can always call. For more information, call one of the relevant organizations listed in the appendix in the back of this book. Remember about 10 percent of the population is gay, so you are not alone.

talking with parents about sex

Dear Sari,
I am 17 and I want to start having sex with my boyfriend of a year. I want to tell my parents that I am ready to have sex. I know that I am making the right choice about starting to have sex, but I do not know quite how to tell them.

Sari Says:
It's great that you want to talk with your parents about sex. That sort of openness fosters trust, and gives them the chance to help you out if you need assistance getting to a gynecologist for your first exam, or if you need money for birth control, or if you want to ask them anything about sex. Here are some things that may make "the talk" easier:

- Think about what you want to say in advance.

  You do not need a written script or anything, but you should think about what you want to tell them. Do you want to tell them that you are sure you want to have sex, or is it more that you are thinking about having sex? Are you asking for their opinion, or are you telling them that you've made up your mind no matter what they say? Do you want to ask for their help in getting you to a doctor or obtaining birth control? Or are you just telling them about your personal life so that you do not have to lie to them? Try to figure out what you need to tell them, what you want to ask them and your purpose in talking to them.

- Be prepared for a reaction.

  Your parents may be thrilled that you are talking with them about this—or they could be quite angry. They may say that they do not want you having sex (ever!)—or they may say that they will help you make decisions and get birth control. Or, they could have an in between reaction, expressing some of their concerns.

  Have a good idea of how you want to react to each type of response they might give you. For example, if they start freaking out and saying that they forbid you to have sex, you need to keep your cool and say something like, "I was hoping that we could talk calmly about this. I see that this has upset you, so let's talk again in a couple of days." Perhaps next time they will be more open to hearing your point of view. However, if your parents have good reasons why they think you shouldn't have sex at this point in your life, you should listen to them and give serious consideration to what they say—after all, they have more life experience and they probably know you quite well.

- Find a good time and place.

  If possible, pick a time when your parents are not stressed. Perhaps a weekend is better than during the work week. Wait until you can be alone with your parents in a quiet place where you are all comfortable and you have time to talk. Do not start the talk while the TV is on, or too late at night, or in the car, or just before everyone is leaving the house in the morning. Maybe you could sit down with them to talk after dinner. If you are all watching TV, you could say that after the show's over, you'd like to turn off the TV and talk for a while.

• Start with the positive.
Before you lay some heavy news on someone, it always helps to soften the blow a bit by saying some positive (almost corny) stuff. For example, rather than just announcing, "Mom, Dad—I am thinking about having sex," try something like: "Mom and Dad, you are such great parents and cool people, and I always feel like I can talk with you about everything. As you know, I'm really growing up, and now that I am in a serious relationship, we have been thinking about becoming sexual. I wanted to talk with you first, because you are such terrific parents, and I'd like to hear your advice." Compliments may get you far, so give them a few before you get to the heart of the matter.

• Do not tell too much.
Your parents do not need to hear the details of how far you have gone sexually or what exactly you plan to do—that's too much information. Also, they do not need to know the exact day and time you will be doing it. All they need to know is that you are thinking about having sex, and that you want their help so you are prepared and protected if and when you have sex.

• Ask them about their values.
Most parents have some values about sex, such as they think that teens should wait until they are married, or they think that having sex

when you are single is okay as long as you are in love. If you're not completely sure what your parents' values are, then you should ask them. You are not obligated to have the exact same values as your parents, but knowing what they are may help you make decisions about sex for yourself.

- Tell them how much you appreciate their help and support, and tell them you love them. Your parents need to hear that you still love them, and that you are glad that they are there for you. They may always see you as their little girl, so even while you are asking for their support with an adult issue, you can still let them know that in your heart you are their girl and you are grateful for that.

busy with boyfriend

Dear Sari,
My parents think that my boyfriend takes up too much of my time. My mother says she's going to pull the plug on our relationship. How can I convince her that I am not totally obsessed, and that we were meant to be together?

Sari Says:
In order to get your parents to see that you're not obsessed with this guy, you'll need to spend more time with them, more time with friends, and even more time by yourself. If you can let a day or two go by without even mentioning this guy at home, then hopefully your mom will start to see that your life does not revolve around him. Instead, talk about your friends and your other activities and interests. In fact, you may want to start a new activity or hobby to show your mom that you have interests besides this guy.

As far as trying to convince your mom that you and he "were meant to be together," don't bother. Your mom might not agree with you no matter what you say, so don't force the issue. All your mom seems to care about right now is that you spend time doing things other than hanging out with your boyfriend, so if you want to make her happy, that's all you need to do. Plus, it will be good for you if there's more to your life than just this guy.

Your School and Extracurriculars and Your Parents

parents obsessed with grades

Dear Sari,
Every day my parents grill me about if I've done my homework, or what happened in school, or if I got any grades back yet. Why won't they back off? It just puts pressure on me! How do I get my parents to stop being so obsessed with my grades?

Sari Says:
Your parents care that you do well in school. They probably have high hopes for your future. They may already be thinking about where you could go to college. But the fact is that if you are doing well in school, you do not need them bothering you every second. Pressure does not help someone succeed. What helps more is gentle support. Talk with your parents about finding a new way that you can tell them about school, without feeling like they are on top of you about it. Maybe you can tell them each Friday all about the grades you got back during the whole week. Most importantly, tell them that if you are having trouble in school, you will let them know right away. Explain that you just want to have a little less pressure so you can keep doing well.

dealing with an F

Dear Sari,

I need help now! I am a junior in high school. I'm no "goody" but I just got my first F in my life on my report card, and I don't know how to tell my parents!

Sari Says:

Pick a day when your parents are in a good mood, and tell them you want to talk to them about school. Explain your situation in three steps: Start by saying something positive. Then gradually explain the bad news to them. Finally, tell them what you will do about it.

    For example, let's say that you got the F in Math. Step 1: Tell them about the B+ that you got in English! Step 2: Tell them that Math was really hard for you this term, and you got an F. Step 3: Immediately tell them that you are planning to get extra help in Math for the rest of the year. Offer to go with them to talk to your teacher, if they want to. The problem here is not just about a grade; it is that you are having trouble in school. Talk with your parents about how you can work harder and get more help from now on.

chess champ or yahooligan?

Dear Sari,

I go online, and I play chess with people on Yahoo. I am really great at it, and my ranking is like a hundred out of twenty thousand people or something. The problem is my parents. They are always like, "Stop playing games online!" They don't get that this is a thing that I am good at. Why can't they just be proud for me? Instead they say that I am too obsessed with playing games online. Am I? What should I do?

Sari Says:

You may have a bit of an obsession with playing games online. Your parents are probably proud that you are such a great chess player, but they may be very concerned that you spend hours and hours online. Why not compromise with them? Instead of spending so many hours in front of the computer, join the chess club at your school. Most schools have them, but if there isn't one at yours, ask a teacher who knows how to play if you can start one. Or ask your parents if they want to play chess with you sometime. I bet they'd really enjoy spending time with you.

Cars and Driving

driving your parents crazy

Dear Sari,

I only had my license for five hours and I got into an accident. I hit a Wal-Mart store. I am not a bad driver at all, but now my parents won't trust me to drive anywhere without them for three months. It was an accident that could have happened to anyone and I don't know what to do. Help!

Sari Says:

Go along with your parents. It's reasonable that they would worry about you. Even though an accident can happen to anyone, it is still very scary for your parents to think that something bad could happen to you. Let them watch out for you, so they don't worry so much. If you want to compromise, you could ask them to cut down the time to two months. But even if it is three months, it will go by quickly, and having them there may even help your driving improve.

Parents, Money and Getting a Job

Dear Sari,

I want to get an after-school job, but I am 15, and my dad says I am too young. Is that true? Aren't there laws that say that teens can work? Please tell me so I can tell him.

Sari Says:

At 15, you can work legally. The legal age to get a job varies from state to state. It is usually age 13 or 14. To work in a store, or a restaurant, or some other kind of traditional job, the employer will ask for proof of your age. You may also need "working papers" which verify your age. Most of the time you can get these from the main office in your school, otherwise, they can direct you to where you'd have to go in your town to get the paperwork. However, regardless of age, if there are other reasons why your father does not want you to work, then talk it out with him. He should feel comfortable with your decision to get a job, and he should feel as if it will help you, rather than interfere with your schoolwork or anything else that is a priority.

money lover

Dear Sari,

I love money. I always want to buy new stuff. But I spent too much yesterday—I spent $50! I am 16, and I know I am spending too much already. My mom says my friends have a lot of money because "they don't spend it like you do." I tell myself I am not going to spend money again—only if there is a big cause for it. But still, I like to spend it! What can I do to stop?

Sari Says:

Since you spend too much, you need to change your relationship with money. Instead of thinking of it as just something you use to buy stuff, start thinking about how exciting it would be to have a lot of money. In order to have a lot of money, there are two things you can do: save what you have *or* get a job to earn more. In terms of savings, make a deal with yourself that for every dollar you spend, you will save exactly the same amount. If you don't have enough money to put away, don't let yourself buy anything until you do. This way you will still be able to buy some stuff, but you will also have some savings. Ask your parents to go to the bank with you so you can open a savings account. You will feel better about saving when you start seeing the interest that you can make just by letting the money sit there.

How Much Can You Make?

If you want to make enough money so you don't have to get Mom and Dad to pay for everything, how much would you have to work? Well, I did the math for you. If you get a job for minimum wage, then you will get about $5.15 per hour. (Minimum wage goes up every couple of years, so it may even be more by the time you read this!) During the school year, you can get a job where you can work just weekends, or a few hours after school a few days a week, too. That means that during the school year, you could work somewhere between 8 hours and 18 hours a week. So if you were making minimum wage, you would make between $41.20 and $92.70 each week. In the summer you can make even more money, because you can work about 40 hours each week—that's $206 dollars each week. Summer vacation lasts about eight weeks; so that's $1648 for the summer. There are other jobs in the summer where you can make more than minimum wage. For example, if you work as a lifeguard at a summer camp for 6–8 weeks, you may be able to make $2,000 to $3,000 for the summer. You can also baby-sit, or do odd jobs around your neighborhood, like raking leaves, or mowing lawns to make extra money. Usually those sorts of jobs pay between $5 and $10 an hour. Yet I'd have to point out that even teens have taxes taken out when you get a paycheck, so you will get a bit less than all this.

Dear Sari,
I am freaking out, because I'm 17 and my parents say that I have to get a job, and I do not want to. I don't know where to look or what to do! Help!

Sari Says:
Don't get stressed out about having to work—it can be fun! Think of something that you enjoy doing and think of a way to make money at it. For example, if you like to see a lot of movies, get a job in a video store. If you love animals, you could get a job at a pet store or animal hospital. If you love reading, get a job at a bookstore. If you adore fashion, work in a clothing store. Be creative!

If you know where you want to work, go there and ask if they have any openings. If you are not sure what you want to do, look in your local newspaper's "Help Wanted" section for jobs. Or ask your parents' friends if they need any help baby-sitting, dog-walking, raking leaves, lawn-mowing, or other work like that. Also, ask your parents, teachers, or friends if they have any other job ideas for you.

Sisters and Brothers

Dear Sari,
Everything from clothes to makeup seems to be missing from my room, and there have actually been times where I find my sister snooping around in my room. Every time I tell my dad, he always takes her side. I don't know what to do.

Sari Says:

If your dad is taking your sister's side, then I am guessing that your sister must be giving some good reason why she was in your room looking around. Even if there's a reason for your sister to go into your room, however, she should still ask you before she does so. Talk to your dad. Rather than accusing your sister of stealing, explain to him that now your privacy is more important to you, and you'd appreciate it if he makes a new rule that your sister isn't allowed in your room without your permission.

As far as your missing items: Make a list of what is missing, show it to your dad, and ask him to look in your sister's room to see if he finds some of the stuff. If you can't find the stuff in your sister's room, take a good look all around your room—maybe you just misplaced some things—or keep an eye on your friends the next time they come over.

growing apart from sis

Dear Sari,

I'm upset. My sister and I used to be really good friends . . . but now we seem to be growing apart and arguing so much more. She blames all the arguments on me, and it's really making me sad and mad. I wish we could sit down and talk like we used to. She even takes her friends' words over mine about everything! *Plus*, ever since I entered high school and got a senior boyfriend (I'm only a freshman obviously), she's been acting jealous. What do I do about this stuff?

Sari Says:

Sisters can be a pain—I know, because I sometimes hassle my sister for no apparent reason. Sometimes it's about jealousy; sometimes it is simply a quest for more independence. Ask her if you two can do something fun together—shopping, a movie, whatever. Spend some time talking and reconnecting. Because you are both growing up, you're changing a lot, and you might need to take the time to find out what new things you have in common, and what things are different. Hopefully, you'll find out that you can still have fun together, even if you are getting older.

On the other hand, sometimes sisters just need to mellow out and spend time apart. If that happens, don't worry. No matter how hard it gets, remember that your sister loves you, and you love your sister. Even if you seem to fight a lot now, you will probably be best friends again when you're older.

miss my brother

Dear Sari,
My brother just left for college and I miss him so much. What can I do to stop thinking about him?

Sari Says:
Actually, it's okay to think about him—it makes sense: you love him. But when you think about your brother, try not to feel sad. Instead, think of all the good things about him and how happy you are for him. Call or write every week to ask how he is doing and what college is like. This way, when you think about him, you'll have more things to go on, not just old memories. Also, let your brother know everything that's going on with you—he misses you, too, and by letting him know what's happening in your life, it will help him feel close to you.

To feel better, take advantage of the fact that you have the house more to yourself now! Were there things that you two used to disagree on, such as what you'd watch on TV, or who could use the bathroom first? At least now those things are a bit easier. Spend more time with the rest of your family and friends. Finally, after some time has passed, you can ask your parents if you may visit your brother—by yourself—at his college. You'll have a great time experiencing college life, and you'll get to see what he's up to now. A visit will help you feel happy when you think about him afterward, rather than just missing him and feeling sad.

brother's looking at porn

Dear Sari,
I was doing homework on my family's computer, and I came across a file that I thought was mine, and opened it. It was a picture of a naked woman in a sexual pose. I wanted to find out who had put it there, so I checked what folder it was in. It was my younger brother's. From the titles of other pictures, I can tell he has over two dozen porn pictures. I know my parents would not be happy if they found out about this, but I don't want to be a tattletale and don't know how to bring it up.

Sari Says:
Even though you may feel like a tattletale, you should tell your parents. Because you all share this computer, it is perfectly understandable that you would have stumbled onto these files. Tell your parents the way you told me. Then it will become their responsibility to decide if they want to talk to him, or simply activate some "parental controls" on the Internet that can prevent your brother from accessing pornographic sites. If you and your brother have a very close relationship, you might try talking to him directly about this, but he will probably be embarrassed. Many people are naturally curious about naked pictures, but it is something that they may not want to talk about.

hands off!

Dear Sari,
My sister hangs all over my boyfriend every time I bring him home. He doesn't like her, but then again he doesn't dislike her, so he rarely complains about her. She gets me soooo mad. How should I tell my (pardon my French) slutty little sister to stop it?!

Sari Says:
You could talk to your sister, but then again, that might only make her do it more. Ignoring your sister's behavior might be the best way to go. She is probably doing this just to upset you and get attention. She knows you well enough to know how to push your buttons. If your boyfriend is the faithful kind, you do not have to worry that he would do anything about your sister's (or any girl's) advances. Knowing little sisters as well as I do (because I am one), I think that your sister might just stop hanging on him, if she sees that you really don't care at all. Good luck fakin' it.

brother's bothered

Dear Sari,
My sister flirts with any guy with a pulse. All of my guy friends end up drooling over her. I am her big brother, and it pisses me off to see her like this! She's not exactly all innocent about it, either, when she goes running around in her bikini all day. I think I'm gonna kill her! (Not really though, I'm not psychotic.)

Sari Says:
Well, I'm glad you're not psychotic. But maybe you should think of this in a different way: Instead of saying you're going to kill her, stick with real-

ity—*she makes you angry.* Try to figure out why this makes you so mad. Is it because she's stealing your friends' attention away from you? Or is it because you're afraid that she might end up getting sexually involved with guys before she's really ready?

Once you figure out why you get so angry, talk to her about it. You could explain to her that some guys think flirting means they'll get to have sex, so she should be careful. Or explain that you'd like her to leave you alone more when you are with your friends, and ask her to put a cover-up over her bikini when she's around your guy friends. It's okay to be honest with her. She needs to know that she does not have to be the center of attention. Hopefully she'll respect you for having a real talk with her and change her ways.

Divorce and Cheating

in the middle

Hi Sari,
My dad cheated on my mom and moved out, and my parents say they are going to get divorced. Now I'm in the middle. My mom tells me that all men lie like my dad did to her. My dad says that she drove him to it. Then, whenever my dad calls, my mom always asks me what he says and it really ticks me off! Now they are asking me which parent I would rather live with. I don't know what to do!

Sari Says:
Your parents are wrong for putting you in this position. They should be dealing with their marital problems on their own (or with the help of a good therapist). Tell them how uncomfortable it feels to be put in the middle. If either one of them tries to talk to you about their problems again, remind them you're a teen, they're the parents, and it's wrong for

them to be talking to you like this. Also, explain that they can't ask you to choose between them, and tell them that you love them both.

Talking to them will be difficult, but you need to do it to keep your peace of mind. If you need more help deciding what to say and how to say it, then talk to a guidance counselor or a teacher at school. Finally, I want to make sure you understand that someday you can have a great relationship with someone you love and who loves you—someone who would never cheat on you.

Living with Mom, and Still Loving Dad

According to the Department of Health and Human Services, 30 percent of people under age 18 live with one parent, and in eight out of ten homes, it's their mother. If your mom is raising you, but you still see your dad, make an extra effort to get to know him really well. Call him often to update him about all the little things going on in your life. He still loves you! Also, remember, just because your mom and dad couldn't stay married, and maybe they don't like each other now, at some time they loved each other. So their marriage was important, especially because it brought you into the world.

Uncomfortable, Inappropriate, or Abusive Situations

mom's boyfriend is staring

Dear Sari,
My mom and I just moved in with her boyfriend, and I think he's perverted! I am not sure, but a lot of times I think I can see him staring at my chest. I am developing, and it just started majorly speeding up and it shows. When he looks at me it is gross, and I'm afraid that one day he might go further . . . help!

Sari Says:
Sometimes parents notice when their daughter is developing, and she might feel that they are actually staring, because she's so self-conscious about the changes in her body. I know he's not your dad, but if your mom's boyfriend just glanced at you and "noticed," then you probably don't need to worry about it.

However, if you really get a creepy, bad feeling that he is staring at you, then you must tell someone that he makes you feel uncomfortable. You should not talk to your mom's boyfriend about it alone; neither should your mom, her boyfriend, and you sit down and talk about it, because this could be embarrassing for you. Plus, he might deny it and make everything worse. Talk to your mom. After you tell her, you should expect that she can get him to stop. If he doesn't quit it, and your mom won't help, then you should talk to another adult about it—a relative, a friend of your mom's, or a counselor or teacher at school.

SARI,

See, I have this problem. My step father is always calling me a BITCH, and every other name in the book. I don't do anything-seriously I don't. HE does this EVERY day. I don't remember 1 day that has gone by he hasn't done-or said something to me. I tried to RUN-AWAY once, but my mom caught me and told me that she'd rather have me go to jail than live w/ someone else. She knows what he does, but she has stopped saying things to him. I also Had a friend tell her mom, but all she could say was tell someone I trust, and that's you. I believe you're the only one that can help me. I just wonder, why? Why does he do this. I've almost killed myself my OD (over-does) because I couldn't take it!! SARI PLEASE HELP ME. Sincerely,

STANDING ALONE
and LOST

Sari Says:

You are not alone. Thousands of teens are verbally abused every day. You have at least one friend, and her mom, who listen to you. And your mom has tried to help. Now you need more immediate action to be taken. Go to a counselor at your school and see what that person suggests you do. Perhaps they can call your mom and stepfather in so the three of you can talk together about how things at home can change. Maybe you can have weekly family counseling sessions to work on this. If they are not willing to work at it, and things don't get better, then calmly tell your mom that you really think that you would be happier if you could find a relative or a friend to live with. Keep talking with your counselor at school about this until things get better for you. Your stepfather needs to change his behavior, or you need to find a better place to live. Also, you must always remember that he treats you this way because he has a serious problem. You are a good person, and you have not done anything wrong. He is abusive and he is very wrong to hurt you this way.

physically abusive dad

Dear Sari,

I am 15 years old, and my father takes all of his frustrations out on me. Lately it has gotten much worse, and he slammed my face into a wall, and dragged me around by my hair. I tried to fight back, but he punched me until I stopped. My mom won't do anything about it, and my parents won't agree to counseling sessions. What can I do?

Sari Says:

Your dad is severely abusing you, and you must get help! He must be stopped, or you must move somewhere you will be safe. Since you reached out to me, I know that you are ready to take the next step to stop this abuse. Immediately tell a counselor or teacher at school exactly what is happening at home. Or for more information about how to get help, look in the appendix at the back of this book for toll-free teen crisis hot-lines you can call anonymously. Finally, remember that this abuse is not your fault, and you deserve to get help.

Not Your Fault

Abuse is never the victim's fault. As a teen, if you do something "wrong" (such as breaking a house rule, or missing curfew), you may think that you deserve to be punished. But, in a healthy family environment, the parents will give a punishment such as grounding or taking away phone privileges. In an abusive home, a teen who does the same thing may get yelled at or beaten. That is always wrong. Never blame yourself for abuse no matter what you did.

sexual abuse

Dear Sari,

I am 14 and my uncle lives with my family. Every night, he comes into the room that me and my little sister share and starts touching us in all our private parts. My parents never believe anything my sister and I tell them, and they favor my uncle. What can I do? I tell him to stop coming into our room and stop touching us, but he denies it. What can I do? I need help.

Sari Says:

It makes me so sad to hear that you are going through something so scary. Your uncle is sexually abusing you. He is doing something horrible and very wrong. It is not your fault, and he has to be stopped. But when someone is a victim of sexual abuse, like you are, it is very difficult to stop him yourself. Since your parents are not helping, you need to ask some-one else to help you. You should immediately talk to an adult you trust.

Do you have a teacher or counselor at school who you like? Please tell that person what you told me. Also, right now, call one of the sexual abuse hotline numbers listed in the appendix in the back of this book. I know you can get through this, if you ask for help!

kissing cousins

Dear Sari,

I have always thought that my first cousin is cute, and since he and I are both 16, we have a lot in common. One night we were watching some TV and sharing a blanket. We were play-fighting over the remote and I ended up on top of him. Then he started kissing me. The same encounter happened tonight when we were alone again, except it went a little bit farther and it happened on my parents' bed! Ahh! I know I have made a terrible mistake! I know that it is wrong! But the most horrible thing is that . . . I enjoyed it :(.

Sari Says:

Since you two are the same age this is not abusive incest, but it is actually still considered incest. Kissing a cousin is not dangerous in itself, but if your families ever found out (which they could at the rate you're going), then they would most likely be really upset. Don't worry about what already happened, since the past is in the past. Also, stop blaming yourself—you both kissed each other. But from now on, do not kiss your cousin. Tell him that you know that what you've been doing could hurt your families, so you can never do it again. Finally, while you should not kiss him again, you should not feel guilty that it physically felt good; that is just something your body automatically responded to. You will feel a million times better when you kiss someone who is *appropriate* for you to be involved with.

Dear Sari,

My dad's a drug addict. He smokes weed and I want him to quit. What could I say to him?

Sari Says:

Often, when people have been smoking marijuana for many years, it becomes a habit or an addiction and it's very hard to quit. Bring up this subject with your dad to get things out in the open. Discuss this with him when he's sober, at a time when you both have time to talk alone. Tell him that you feel worried and sad when he smokes. Explain that you want him to stop because you don't like the way he acts when he's stoned. Also, you could tell him that marijuana smokers actually have a greater risk of getting lung cancer than cigarette smokers (since marijuana smoke is unfiltered), and that you want him to be healthy and live for a long, long time. If you tell your dad that you want him to stop, it may motivate him to get help. If he needs professional help, such as a therapist or a drug treatment center, you or he can get more information by calling the drug abuse hotlines listed in the appendix in the back of this book.

Adoption Issues

dad versus "real" dad

Dear Sari,

I'm adopted. I just found out one year ago. How can I get over my anger toward my "foster parents," so that I can love them as I had loved them my whole life before? How do I love this new family, my "birth parents," that has rushed too quickly into my life?

Sari Says:

The people who you have considered your parents your whole life—the people who have been raising you—*are* your real parents. They love you and have taken care of you. Nothing changes that. Talk with them about your feelings, so you can work on your anger.

Your birth parents also feel a connection to you, and when you feel ready, you might want to get to know them, but only if you can deal with it. The issues you are coping with are very tough, and it is important for you to know that you are not alone. To find other people who are having similar experiences, look for a support group for people who have been adopted, or see a therapist who deals with adoption. Perhaps you can bring your parents or birth parents with you to see the therapist. To find a therapist in your area, call a local adoption agency and ask if they have counseling for teen or adult adoptees.

looking for birth mom

Dear Sari,

When I was 7 my parents told me that they adopted me on the day I was born. I never really cared who my birth parents were, since my parents had me my whole life. But now I am 17, which is the age that my parents said that my birth mother was when she gave me up. Now I think about it all the time, and I would like to find her. How can I do this?

Sari Says:

First, before you start searching for your birth mom, seriously think about how this could change your life. What if you search for years, using all your free time and money, and never find her? What if you find her but she is dead, in jail, or simply does not want to see you? Not all birth mothers want to be found. Also, consider how this could affect your parents. It could be an uncomfortable situation for everyone. Of course, it is possible that you could have a positive experience. Think about all the possibilities, both positive and negative, before you start searching.

Since you are under 18, you'll need your parents' permission to have access to the information about your birth mother. Talk with your parents and have them agree to let you start the search. Next, they can tell you if they have any information that could help you find her, such as the name of the adoption agency that they used. If your parents refuse to help you, then you will have to wait until you are 18 before you can start looking.

If your parents do not have your birth mother's name, then the agency that they went through to adopt you may have it, but they can only give it out in states that have "open" adoption laws. If you can get her name, then you just need to try to find out where she is living. If you have trouble doing that, then if your parents can help you financially, you may be able to hire a private investigator to help. If you cannot find her name, or if you reach a dead end when you try to track down your birth mother, then you may want to list yourself in adoption registries. These are lists of adoptees and birth parents who are looking for each other. Read the appendix in the back of this book for contact information for those organizations.

Gay Parents

mom's a lesbian

Dear Sari,

My mother is gay. She figured out that she is a lesbian a year after she and my dad got divorced, when I was 14. And now I don't know whether I should stay with her or not, because I've overheard people talking about how it's not a healthy place for me to be living. Help!

Sari Says:
Just because your mother is a lesbian, it does not change how she feels about you, and it should not affect your relationship with her. She still loves you just as much. A lesbian is as good a mom as any heterosexual mom. Ask her to help you understand why people are talking about you two and her personal life. Ask her how you can deal with those people—does she think you should ignore them, or say something back to them? If you want someone else to talk to about this, look in the appendix in the back of this book for the information about support groups for family members of gays, lesbians, and bisexuals.

Illness and Death in the Family

bulimic sister

Dear Sari,
My sister takes a shower every night at the same time right after dinner, and I always hear the toilet flush. She is very obsessed about her weight, so I had my suspicions that she was making herself vomit. One night I looked under the door and saw that she was, indeed, making herself throw up. I was thinking of "accidentally" walking in on her while she was doing it, and I've also considered telling my mom. I'm really scared that I'm going to lose my sister. What should I do?

Sari Says:
Bulimia (an eating disorder in which someone forces herself to throw up after eating) is a very serious problem that worsens the longer it continues. Bulimia can harm your sister's body and mind in many ways; it can even be life-threatening. Your sister needs to get help as soon as possible. You really need to tell your mom. Also, you can talk with your sister about what you suspect she is doing. You don't have to walk in

on her, but if that makes it easier for you, then that's your choice.

Try to get her to be honest with you about this. Be supportive: explain that she can get help and completely get over this. Your sister will need therapy and maybe medication in order to get past this. For more information, or to help your sister find a referral to a therapist or support group, contact an eating disorder organization listed in the appendix in the back of this book. Finally, tell your sister that you love her, because she needs your support now more than ever.

grandmother has cancer

Dear Sari,

My mom has just found out that her mother, my grandmother, has cancer. My mom's really sad, and I don't know what to do to make her feel better. Please help me deal with it.

Sari Says:

Ask your mom what you can do for her and for your grandma. Your mom may need you to help out more around the house if she needs to spend extra time with her mom, or maybe she'll need you to cheer her up every once in a while when she is feeling blue. Suggest to your mom that you and she make a card or bake some cookies to bring to your grandmother. This will give you and your mom some time together to talk more about this, while you do something nice for her mom.

When you talk to your mom, ask her how she feels: Is she scared that her mom might die? Does this make her worry about her own health? What will her mom have to go through during treatment? Ask as many questions as you want to try to understand what your mom and grandma are going through. Fighting cancer takes time and requires a great support system. You are part of that support.

brother's death

Dear Sari,

My brother died last year, and it is really hard for me to deal with it. People said that it is supposed to get easier, but it just gets harder every day. Sometimes I feel that he has not really died, and he will be at home when I get home from school. What can I do to get over this?

Sari Says:

I am so sorry that your brother passed away, and that you are going through this. While the pain usually does go away somewhat over time, most people who have had a sibling die will tell you that they will always feel the sadness.

There is a grieving process that you'll go through as you try to accept the fact that he is gone. In fact, one of the steps in this process is called denial—sort of what you've been feeling when you expect him to be there when you get home from school. That's a normal feeling, which should go away soon, as you move closer to total acceptance.

You should realize that you don't have to go through this process alone. Your parents are going through this, too. Talk to them about your feelings when you miss your brother. Also, when things seem really tough for you, you might want to talk to a therapist about your feelings. Your guidance counselor at school is probably trained to talk about death, or he or she can refer you to someone who is an expert at grief therapy.

school days

Bells ringing, lockers sticking, teachers picking, grades slipping—it's enough to make even the most well-adjusted person want to run screaming to the nearest mall for a little comfort and sanity. School is all consuming—it is what you do for a living until, well, you *do* something for a living. It is where you spend five days a week, seven hours a day for most of the first eighteen years of your life. In fact, you probably spend more waking hours at school than you spend at home. That's a lot of time you're clocking, smarty-pants. It's no wonder you have mixed feelings about the place. Sometimes it is the scene of your greatest triumphs; sometimes it is the scene of your greatest defeats—academically *and* socially! Who could blame you for pondering why school is so complicated? There should be a class on it alone. Ah, but that's why you have me, silly! Since school's a fact of life, I'll help you find a way to make the best of it.

Academics

demanding dad

Dear Sari,

When my dad was a kid, he got straight As, and he expects me to do the same. His rule is that if I don't get a B average, I'm grounded for two whole months. No friends, no phone, no nothing. I have been getting a C+ average ever since middle school. Last year, I was grounded my whole freshman year of high school! He doesn't understand that grounding me won't make me any smarter. How do I deal with his stubbornness?

Sari Says:

If your dad's been this way for years, then it will not be easy to get him to change. Talk to him about a compromise, such as: if you get an A in at least one class each term and nothing below a C in your other classes, he will not ground you. Maybe you could also help the situation by explaining your problem to one of your favorite teachers. Ask the teacher to help you figure out a way that you could start earning As or Bs. For example, you might ask your teacher if you should get a tutor for extra help, or if you should be placed in easier classes. Then ask your teacher to call your dad in for a parent-teacher-student meeting. This way, the teacher can explain to your dad (with you in the room) that you work very hard in class, and while your grades do not indicate a serious problem, you have come up with a way that you can raise them because you don't want to be grounded anymore. Hopefully, you, your dad, and your teacher will be able to work something out together—and your dad will see that grounding is not the answer.

homework help

Dear Sari,

My best friend always asks me to do his homework for him. I do it, because I have already done mine and it is easy to let him copy it. I feel like he is using me, but I don't want him to stop being friends with me if I stop doing it.

Sari Says:

How much do you think your friend is learning when he copies your homework? Do you think he is really getting the gist of the Pythagorean Theorum, or understanding the pluperfect verb tense in Spanish class? The answer is obviously no. By doing his homework, you are not allowing him to learn on his own. So while it may seem like you are helping him, you could be hurting him. How will he be able to pass a test on the material if he did not learn how to do it?

Besides, what is he doing for you that is so amazing that you would even consider doing his homework all the time? Unless he's doing something equally rewarding for you, your friendship could be in trouble. Your relationship is very unbalanced because he is sponging off you and giving nothing back. Using a friend does not make for a good friendship.

You must stop doing his homework. However, there's another way you can help him: form a study buddy system. Explain to your friend that you're really uncomfortable with him always copying your hard work, and that you're really worried that he's not going to learn anything. Offer to get together one or two nights a week (or more if you want to) and do the work together. That way, you'll be helping him learn—which will make your friendship (as well as your brains!) stronger. If he is angry with you and doesn't accept the proposal, then you might have to face facts that he isn't as good a friend as you thought. You've been doing him a favor, and he should not be mad at you for putting a halt to it if it makes you uncomfortable. It's the right thing to do.

bored with school

Dear Sari,
I love reading and learning new things, but at school it is like the teachers teach for the dumbest student, and us smart kids just sit there waiting for the bell to ring. I've tried bringing a book to read during class, but my science teacher saw me reading, and told me not to. Ugh! How can I keep from getting bored in class?

Sari Says:
Some schools have special gifted classes or advanced placement classes that are aimed at students just like you. Talk with your guidance counselor or principal to see if your school has classes like these. Also,

talk with your individual teachers. Tell each one that you are bored, and ask if there is any way that you can have extra study assignments that go along with the lessons that are being taught, or if you can take your assignments to the school library to work at your own pace, then read when you are done. If you're uncomfortable doing this, talk to your folks. They might want to speak with your teacher about this at the next parent-teacher conference.

Finally, even though this upsets you, please be considerate to the other kids in your class. They are not "dumb" because they learn at a slower pace than you do, so don't let them get wind of your attitude.

stay in school

Dear Sari,
My best friend wants to quit school. I have tried to talk to him about it, but he has his mind set on it. I don't know what to do. I don't want him to ruin his life. Please help.

Sari Says:
Try to have an intervention. Get together with your mutual friends and come up with all of the reasons why he should stay in school. Then go to his house as a group and talk to him about how important it is that he hang in there. Tell him that you really want him to be around at school. Remind him how much a diploma will improve the rest of his life, and tell him that if he stays in school, you will all help him in any way you can.

If you and his other friends cannot convince him to stay in school, ask a teacher or school counselor to talk to him. They might be able to develop an alternative school program for him, in which he works at a regular job to get credit toward high school. That way he can still get his diploma and graduate with his class.

Dear Sari,

I'm new at my school and I can't seem to make friends. I was very popular at my old school, but now I just don't seem to be connecting with anybody in my classes. Help! I'm not very good on my own.

Sari Says:

Making friends isn't like making instant Kool-Aid—one, two, three, voila: friends! It doesn't work that way. Finding people to be your buddies for life takes time. You are still the great, outgoing, friend magnet you were at your old school. It's just that your reputation hasn't preceded you and you're starting from scratch. Also, maybe the students at your school are already so into their own cliques that they find it tough to welcome a newcomer. If so, you may have to go out of your way to get to know them.

Get really involved in an activity or two at school. After-school activities bring people with similar interests together. If you start writing for the school paper, or join the science club, school play, or pep club, chances are you will find lots in common with your fellow club members and, before you know, will be getting together outside of the club to hang. If you try that and you still aren't successful at making friends, you may want to look beyond your school. For instance, you could join a community youth group, or get involved with local volunteer work or a part-time job.

in love with teacher

Dear Sari,

Is it okay if you give one of your very, very, very hot English teachers a Valentine's Day card and some candy? I mean, he's very cute and nice and he's only eleven years older than I am! I am 17 and he is 28, and he knows that I like him a lot! He's soooooo damn fine!

Sari Says:

Fine or funky, you can't do anything about your feelings for him. No cards, no candy, no nothing. First of all, and most importantly, he is not allowed to have anything romantic to do with you, or any student. If he did, he could lose his job or worse. If you really care about him, you certainly wouldn't want to see his life ruined that way, would you? Secondly (and this might be a bitter pill to swallow), he more than likely isn't interested in you as anything more than a bright student with lots of potential. You might make him uncomfortable if you shower him with romantic gifts, especially because of reason number one above. It could still put him in some hot water with the principal of your school, even though he doesn't return your affections. Thirdly, you might not think so right now, but eleven years is a really big difference between you and someone you might date. There's nothing wrong with a dating a guy a couple of years older than you at this point, like a senior, if you're a junior. However, after you get past how cute your teacher is (or someone else in his age group), you'd be surprised at how little you have in common at this point. Try to find a guy closer to your age who you like, and as hard as it will be, try to get over your teacher. On Valentine's Day, put your energy into giving cards to your friends and the other people in your life who like you as much as you like them.

touch me in the hallway

Dear Sari,

My school has pretty strict PDA (Public Display of Affection) rules, and I hate them! My boyfriend and I are pretty touchy-feely. We like to hold hands, put our arms around each other, and hug. But because of the PDA rules, we can't! We hardly see each other outside of school because we are both so busy. What can we do?

Sari Says:

Nothing can replace hugs, holding hands, and the touch of someone you love. However, just because you're not allowed to touch as often as you'd like, that doesn't mean that you can't find other ways to show your affection. You and your guy could invent some way of touching that won't break the rules, but still makes you feel connected. You could stand with your feet touching each other's feet. Or you could stand shoulder to shoulder. Also, you could try to find private moments at school. If no one else is around, then it's not a "public" display of affection, right? Scout out a quiet corner of the library or find a secluded hallway. Don't get in trouble for sneaking around in the basement of the school, and don't get locked in the janitor's closet; but if you can steal some moments away from the crowd, enjoy them.

PU to PE

Dear Sari,

I hate every thing about gym: the way we pick teams, how much they make us run, showering after, and just about anything else you can think of. I don't know why they force us to do any of it! How can I get out of gym for good?

Sari Says,

No matter what different schools call it—Phys Ed, PE, or Gym—it's something that all schools have in common. Because it is a requirement, it's tough to get out of without a legitimate excuse from a doctor or parent. The reason why it's required is because schools have some responsibility for making your body fit, not just your mind. All that running might seem horrible while you're doing it, but if you didn't do it, you'd be sitting on your butt all day in school, and that's just not healthy.

Phys Ed actually helps you learn good fitness habits that can help you for your whole life. When I was in high school, I hated gym, too. But once I got into my twenties and I had to join my local gym to keep in shape, I realized that working out is not just something that teens are forced to do in school. It actually should become a way of life once you are an adult. If you can try to get into fitness in high school, then you can prepare yourself for a lifetime of good health habits.

I agree that choosing teams can be annoying, but it helps you learn the lesson that no matter what group you're stuck in you can make the best of it. As far as showering, there's nothing pretty about thirty people in a communal shower together, but the fact is that you don't want to go back to class stinkin'. If you can take advantage of gym by trying to see it as a nice break from class, instead of some method of cruel torture, then you'll be able to get through it.

Teasing, Bullies, Violence, and Suspension

teased a lot

Dear Sari,

I am not popular, because I like writing. I do not like rah-rah stuff like football, which is all anyone seems to talk about in our school. I do not really have a group of friends, just one best friend. The problem is that I get teased a lot. I am a junior, and I thought that at this point kids would grow up, but they are cruel. How should I deal with it when people make fun of me in school?

Sari Says:
You may not be able to entirely change the attitudes of the superjocks you're saddled with; however, there might be something you can do to use your writing talent to improve your situation. If your high school has a newspaper, maybe you can join, and you can write a feature article about one of the star football players. This would show the jocks that you have a lot more to offer than being the butt of their jokes. Maybe they'd even start to respect you, since with your article, you'd be influencing what other people think about them for a change.

If this option isn't available to you, or if you just absolutely don't want to get involved with the paper, then all I can tell you is bide your time until graduation with the one friend that you *do* have. One good, true friend is worth twenty hang-out buddies.

After high school, things really do change. If you plan on going to college, you'll find more people who have similar interests. In fact, if you're not doing it already, get catalogues from colleges with great writing programs so you can start getting excited about your future. Then, the next time some lug head gives you a hard time, just smile and think (but don't say out loud), "I won't be seeing *you* in my creative writing classes at the university!"

threats

Dear Sari,
I was friends with this girl in school. Now for some reason she has been bothering me for weeks. She tells people that she hates me and wants to beat me up, but I just ignore her. Finally, I got so scared of her that I

told the guidance counselor, and she talked to her, but she doesn't know if anything got solved. What should I do?

Sari Says:
You should talk to a teacher or guidance counselor again if this girl keeps threatening you. Also, talk to your parents so they know what's going on. As far as what you can do in school, try to keep ignoring this girl. If she says things to you, do not even try to respond or make a "comeback." Just walk away from her. Try to hang out with a friend or two at school all the time, so you are not alone. If she ever touches you, don't do anything back. Just walk away and immediately go get a teacher. Bullies like this girl usually get bored if you ignore them, and they usually stop. But if she keeps bothering you and threatening to fight, you must find a teacher who takes you seriously and can keep her away from you.

gun fears

Dear Sari,
One of my best guy friends and my ex-boyfriend were in an argument the other day, and my ex threatened to bring a gun into school and shoot us both, and then, "shoot up the whole school." Then when we were walking home from school, he followed us and took what looked like a gun out of his jacket and told us that's what he was going to use. Should I tell someone? I asked my friend if I should tell and she said, "Definitely, yes! What if the Columbine thing happens here, too? It'll be your fault because you never told anyone about it." My Social Studies teacher once told our class that you must report guns, and the police will get involved, but I am afraid of that. What should I do?

Sari Says:

Because of the horrible tragedy at Columbine High School in 1999, and several other high schools across the country over the last few years, this issue is on a lot of people's minds. It's very scary that we have to deal with this sort of violence, but you are in a position to help right now, and that's good. Your friend is right when she told you that you could do something to prevent the possibility of another tragedy. And I agree with your teacher—you need to come forward. It was illegal, dangerous, and sick for that guy to show you a gun and threaten to kill you and others. What if the gun had accidentally gone off? Even if he had not gone that far, he still should be reported just for making the threat. Guns do not belong near schools, loaded or unloaded. Period.

Tell an adult you trust. Ask the adult to keep your name out of it when he or she goes to the school or the authorities with the information. Perhaps you could talk to your parents, and they can help you figure out what you want to say about this and who else needs to know. Your parents might want to go to the principal or directly to the police. Don't be scared by this—you're doing it to keep your school safe. If you don't want to talk to your parents about it, then talk to that Social Studies teacher. He or she will probably be understanding and know what to do next.

Stress Relief

Grades, teachers, bullies, cliques, college choices all cause lots of stress in your life. Here are some ways to help you deal with the stress when you get home every day.

- Take a bath with candles all around.
- Read a non-school-related book.
- Listen to music and sing along.
- Go for a long walk, run, or bike ride.
- Surf the Net for info on your favorite hobbies.
- Call your best friend and talk about anything but school.
- Treat yourself to something that makes you feel good: a piece of chocolate cake or a new shirt.
- Write in a journal about your stress and also about your hopes and dreams.

Dear Sari,

My friends and I protested against school uniforms by wearing cool clothes that we are not allowed to wear in school. The principal suspended us for three days and also said that now we can't go to the prom, and I really wanted to go to the prom! What should I do?

Sari Says:

You and your friends (and maybe your parents, too) could meet with your principal to try to reach a compromise. You will have to tell him or her that you accept your punishment because you understand that what you did was wrong. Say that you will not challenge the suspension, but that you want to request that he or she change the other part of the punishment slightly, so that you can go to the prom. Then offer your principal some ideas for alternative "punishments" that would actually benefit the school—maybe tutoring the younger kids or cleaning up litter around the school grounds. If your principal is not willing to compromise, then you'll just have to deal with it. You and your friends could have your own party on prom night and have fun getting all dressed up in whatever you want to wear!

College Choices

SAT anxiety

Dear Sari,

I suck at multiple-choice tests! I get okay grades (Bs and Cs), but I never do well on stuff like standardized tests. But I am scared now, because I have to take the PSAT and the SAT, and I know those have a big impact on colleges. Help!

Sari Says:

You'd think that only having four choices (a, b, c, and d) would make your life easier, yet that's not the case. Multiple choice can be tricky for lots of people, but do not fear. There are ways to improve your test-taking ability on standardized tests. Your guidance counselor can direct you to an SAT prep course, which will help you understand the format of the SAT to make it easier. Also, in these courses, you get to take a ton of practice tests, to make the real thing easier. You can also learn how you can improve your chances of doing well on the SAT on your own by reading prep books about it and taking the practice tests those books offer, such as Barron's *How to Prepare for the SAT*, or *Cracking the SAT and PSAT*.

Remember that you can take the SAT more than once, and most people's grades improve each time. Also, colleges know that some people can be very bright and still not do well on these tests; that's why they also look at your grades, extracurriculars, and your admission essay. Create a good total package, and a not-so-high SAT score should not hurt your chances of getting into a good college.

prepping for college

Dear Sari,

I am going into my junior year, and I want to go to college when I graduate, but I don't know if my record will look good enough. I have mostly As and Bs, but I have not done any extracurriculars, and I hear that you need that. I hate sports, and the other stuff at school, like yearbook, is too clique-y. Help!

Sari Says:

Yes, colleges like to see that you are a well-rounded student. If the choice were between you and another student with equally good grades but who had lots of extracurriculars, the other student has a good chance of beating you out. However, you are not limited to the activities offered in your school. You can join a youth organization or get involved with volunteer work in your community. Contact your local Chamber of Commerce or read the local paper to find out what your town offers. You could also get an after-school job, which colleges like to see, if you don't have extracurriculars. Get creative and see what interests you. It won't just help your record for college; it may also inspire your life.

Choosing a College

When you're looking for a college that's right for you, consider the following:

Do you want a large college, or a small one? Do you want to be close to home, or far away? Do you want a college that offers a diverse catalogue of courses, or that specializes in only one area? Does the college offer extracurriculars that you want to get involved with? Have you visited the school to see if you fit in with the students and the environment? Are your high school grades and SAT scores close to the requirements for admission to the college?

college guides

Dear Sari,

How can I find a college that I would like to go to? I am at a loss for what to do. My mom and dad went to a community college, but I am sure I want to go away to college, which they say I can do, but they don't know anything about it, so they said to talk to my guidance counselor. The guidance counselor in my school is totally lame. I tried and he just told me to go to the library and look in some books. *Ugh!* You went to college, so tell me what to do.

Sari Says,

Don't think of choosing a college as a dilemma at all; rather, it's an exciting choice.

Your guidance counselor doesn't sound lame to me, because books really will help, and there are many available. Check out *Barron's Profiles of American Colleges*, and the Princeton Review's *Complete Book of Colleges*, or *The Insider's Guide to Colleges* by the *Yale Daily News*. These books will tell you, everything you need to know, including what admissions looks for in applicants, available financial aid, student facilities, extracurriculars, quotes from present students, and tons more. Once you check out a book or two on colleges to start narrowing down your choices, check out the web site for those schools. Most colleges maintain sites with information, course listings, and a virtual campus tour. You might even want to get a group of your friends together who have similar interests and compile your efforts, having each of you look for schools offering certain key things that you are looking for, and then report back to each other with the results. That way, it becomes more of a fun project and you don't feel so overwhelmed by all the choices. Maybe one of your parents will even take a few of you for a road trip to visit the schools. Most of all, have fun with your college search. This is an exciting decision to make—stop fretting and start getting psyched about the great future ahead of you!

college vs. girlfriend

Dear Sari,

I really need your help. There's this girl I'm seeing who I am totally crazy about, but we haven't been going out that long. We are both applying to colleges. I think I want to go to "College A"; she says she is probably going to go to "College B." Now, I've been thinking of going to "College B," even though I know it's not the right place for me. I wish I could convince her to go to "College A," but I feel bad about manipulating her like that. I just think that it would be nice to start college with her as my girlfriend so I don't have to try to meet new girls.

Sari Says:

You both need to make your college choices on your own. Don't try influencing her in any way and don't switch your choice to follow her. You two just started going out. Your relationship should not take precedence over your choosing the best schools for yourselves. Besides, you never know how going to the same school will affect your relationship—it might not even work out once you both get to college!

College choices should not be based on whether or not your girlfriend goes there. You need to really look at the course catalogues to choose a school that has the classes that you want to take, and visit the campuses to look for a school with the environment that you like. If you pick the right school for you, then without even trying you will meet a ton of new women when you get there. Or if you really want to make it work with the one who you just started going out with, then you and she may be able to have a long-distance relationship. Whatever happens between the two of you, the most important thing right now is that you focus on yourself and your future.

friends forever

Remember when you were a little kid and friendships seemed so uncomplicated? All you needed was to have the littlest thing in common, and, bam, you were best friends. The biggest rift you and your buds ever got in was over who would be the shoe and who would be the car in Monopoly. Now, it's not always so easy. As soon as you say good-bye to grade school, life gets a lot more complicated. Social pressures, crushes, dating, clothes, alcohol, smoking, drugs, grades, teachers, parties. It all adds up to a heck of a lot on your mind. And sometimes, much as you wish it to be true, you and your friends just don't see eye to eye on all these issues.

It's great to have close friends who can laugh with you, share special moments, listen to you complain about your life, and whom you equally support when they're down. But friends can be totally annoying, too. Butting into your life, copying everything you do, even flirting with your crush! In this chapter, you're going to hear about the real-life dilemmas of real-life teens, just like you—and you'll learn how to resolve those issues so you can get better at making and keeping great friends. Let's get down to some serious buddy business.

Friends Who Drink, Smoke, and Do Drugs

drinking friends

Dear Sari,

Ever since we became seniors, all my friends want to do is drink, drink,

drink. I *hate* it! They think it's fun; I think it's disgusting. Should I let them know that it is bothering me? If they're true friends, they will see where I'm coming from, right?

Sari Says:

You have every right to express your discomfort with their chug-a-lugging. For one, it's illegal to drink under age, and you can get yourself in some trouble doing so. Second, if your friends are getting in cars and driving around while they're under the influence, they are putting your life—and the lives of others—in grave danger.

Begin by telling them that you're not into drinking, and when you spend time with them, it's boring for you if that's all they do. I bet that at least one member of the group agrees with you. One of them might just have felt pressured into drinking to seem "cool" and may really benefit from your ability to set things straight with the group.

If you really don't want to have this talk with them, you can simply avoid being around these friends in situations when you think they'll be drinking. For example, do they drink even when they go to the movies? If not, maybe you could hang out at a movie, but avoid going out to parties with them. That way, you can still have some good times with them—and let them have their drinking times without involving you. You might also want to find some new friends who share more things in common with you.

Getting Over Alcohol or Drugs

If you often get drunk or use drugs, then you need help getting over this problem. Seek help for yourself by calling one of the hotlines listed in the back of this book. If you suspect a friend might be dependent on alcohol or drugs, you could gently suggest that he or she call one of the hotlines. Or you could call to get more information about how you can help your friend.

pukin' his guts out

Dear Sari,
I threw up from drinking. It was gross and everybody made fun of me. How can I learn to get drunk without throwing up?

Sari Says:
Sure I tell people that I can try to help them with any problem, but I don't think your parents would appreciate it if I gave you instructions about how to drink just enough that you get drunk, but not so much that you throw up. In the long run, you wouldn't appreciate it either, because drinking that much is very bad for your body (and mind). The reason why people throw up from drinking is because their bodies literally cannot handle all that alcohol. Your body was protecting you. In some tragic cases, a person's body shuts down before it vomits, and the person dies from alcohol poisoning! That is why you should never try to drink too much. When you are legal to drink, you can learn to drink responsibly, which means that you would have one or two drinks, and you'll know that will have to be your limit so that you do not get drunk. If you drink to get drunk, that is a sign that you could have a drinking problem.

drunk driving

Dear Sari,
My mom once told me that if a friend of mine is ever drunk and is going to drive, I should call her so she can pick me up instead. I have had to deal with that before, but the thing is, I can never call my mom to get a ride. If I did not go with my friends, they would think I was a freak! I know it is dangerous to let them drive drunk, but the peer pressure is too much. It is like we are all laughing and then we just get into the car. I

could not put a buzz kill on it by being like, "Duh, I have to call my mom." But I know drunk driving is wrong.

Sari Says:

Drunk driving is not just wrong—it is deadly! Thousands of teens die every year just because they were too embarrassed to say "no" to getting in a car with a drunk driver. You must start asking your mom to pick you up. It does not matter what the other kids say. If you need to make up some excuse, then think of something—think of anything—just so you do not get in the car with them. You could say that your mom has to get you because you are going to stop off somewhere on the way home. Or better yet, you could be really strong, and talk to your friends about their drunk driving. Do you realize that by not stopping your friends from getting behind the wheel drunk you are allowing them to potentially kill themselves, and others? You seriously need to intervene here, if you care about your friends at all.

Friends do drugs

One of my best friends has become addicted to LSD. Ive tried telling her how bad it is for her and shes not listening. Im really scared because I used to do drugs and I never listened when people told me not to, and I ended up getting hurt. How can I save her from making the same mistake? — Scared 4 her

Sari Says:

As you know, when someone has his or her mind made up about something, it is extremely tough to change it. You can try talking to her again, telling her the side effects of LSD and the risks it can have on her life: it can cause high blood pressure, loss of judgment, and depression. There is also the chance of having a "bad trip," in which the person panics and may do something life threatening (the classic example: jumping out of a window to get away from imagined monsters).

Also, in addition to periodic minilectures, spend more time with her and help her hang out with people who don't do drugs. Getting her involved in activities that take her away from drug use can really help. You and she could even join a school group together, or get part-time jobs together.

You said that she's addicted to LSD, but the fact is that the drug itself is not physically addictive. It can cause psychological addiction, meaning that the person might enjoy the hallucinations that they have while on the drug so much that he or she wants to take the drug to feel that way all the time. One way to get her over that addiction is to introduce her to new and more exciting things in a drug-free life. If nothing works, try to convince her to seek help from a drug abuse hotline. You can find phone numbers for these in the appendix in the back of this book.

Experimenting with Drugs and Alcohol

It's only natural to want to experiment, especially when all your friends are doing it and nothing bad seems to happen to them. But drugs and alcohol have serious risks. Before you succumb to peer pressure, make a list of the pros and cons of whatever you are thinking about doing, and give real thought to the effect it can have on you. Adolescent psychologists have found that teens "don't understand the consequences of their actions." But I believe that you're smart enough to figure out that some things can hurt and are worth avoiding—no matter what your friends are doing!

Dear Sari,

My best friend started smoking. I told her I don't like when she does it, and many of my friends have told her that if she keeps smoking they won't be friends with her. I don't know what else to do or tell her.

Sari Says:

When a friend gets into smoking it can be a real drag. Smoking is an addictive habit that, unfortunately, is very hard for most people to stop. However, your other friends aren't reacting in a way that's going to have a positive effect on the smoker in question. Threats generally don't work—and, if you're really her friend, you'll stick by her and try to help her kick the habit.

You already told her that you wanted her to stop smoking. What did she say? If she really wants to stop, then tell her that you will support her. For instance, when she gets cravings for cigarettes, you can be there—to offer her a snack, or just to lend an ear so she can complain about how tough it is to stop. Maybe you can take up a healthy after-school activity together, like biking or running. However, if she told you that she does not want to quit smoking, then there is nothing you can do.

If you feel so strongly that smoking is a disgusting and dangerous habit, then ending the friendship is a choice you might consider making. However, I would caution you to think very carefully before you do so. If roles were reversed, and you were doing something that wasn't good for you, wouldn't you hope that your friends would try to help you through it? If you want to maintain your friendship with her and, no matter what you say, she wants to keep smoking, then you'll just have to accept her habit.

Dear Sari,

Lately I've been thinking that maybe the person I am isn't who I should be. I wish I were like my friends who drink, smoke pot, and fool around with guys. I feel like I am lagging behind all my friends, since I'm 15 years old and I've only had alcohol a couple of times, and I've never done anything else. Please let me know if I need to change and come out of my shy shell, or should I just be proud of the fact that I can beat peer pressure?

Sari Says:

The person who you are is exactly the person you should be! Be very proud of yourself for being yourself—and for resisting peer pressure. It's normal that you may have an "identity crisis" from time to time, wondering if you should conform to be more like your friends. To get through this feeling, think hard about your personal values. If you think that drinking, smoking, and fooling around are not for you, then stick to that. Stay true to yourself.

Of course, this can get confusing, because you may change and evolve. If you ever want to explore something new, think it through first to make sure that it's within your value system. You could even come up with a self-test—a few questions to ask yourself if you are considering trying something new. Here's what I mean:

1. Is this something I think is good and healthy?
2. Is it something I really want to do to be happy?
3. Could it bring pain and problems into my life, and if so, will I be able to handle that?
4. Would I be happier with myself if I avoided it?

If you do something that really goes against your personal values, you could have serious regrets afterward. In order to feel good about the things you do, don't doubt your beliefs. If you think hard, I bet you'll discover that you really do know who you are, what you like and don't like, and what makes you feel good or bad. If you want to, make a list of the things that you enjoy in life. Focus more time and energy on doing the things that make you feel great about yourself. Also, find a few new friends who like the things you like, who are not always drinking and smoking and fooling around. Getting involved in more positive activities will help you stay strong!

Party Matters

party list

Dear Sari,
I'm having a party next weekend and I don't know who to invite. Should I invite all the people on the "A" list only, or should I invite everybody? Help!

Sari Says:
Hey, party girl! These are some of the things to think about:

1. How many people can you have, total? Figure that out based on how rowdy a party you want, and how much space, food, and drinks you have on hand. Smaller parties tend to be mellow, large ones can be fun, but sometimes get out of hand.
2. If you are having a small party, only invite your tightest friends. If you are having a huge bash, then you can invite more people: your so-called "A list" . . . and then a B and C list, too.
3. Try to invite people who really like you *and* who get along with each other. In other words, if a guy just broke up with a girl and she just started going out with a different guy, then you probably should not invite all three of them.

4. Make sure that when you invite people, you tell them whether or not they can bring friends. If they do bring other friends, will there be too many people at the party? Also, if you don't know their friends, do you want strangers at your party? And, if you do know their friends, are they people who you like and want at your party? It is perfectly fine to say to people who you are inviting, "Please don't bring anyone, because I already have all the guests I can handle." *Or*, "Please only bring one person, and let me know who it will be."

5. Invite people who are generally fun for *you* to be around. If you don't like someone that much, you probably don't want that person at your party . . . even if that person is popular with everyone else.

6. If there is someone who you really want to get to know a lot better, then maybe you could invite that person to the party, too.

7. If someone always invites you to his or her parties, then you should invite that person to your party.

Now I have a question for you: Do your parents know that you are having a party?

not invited

Dear Sari,
I have always thought of this girl as a friend of mine. But she had a party with all of our friends and didn't invite me. Should I ask another friend of mine to ask her why I wasn't invited?

Sari Says:
If you want to find out what happened, talk to your friend who threw the party. Asking another person who attended the party might not fully answer your question, and it may cause a lot of nasty gossip. There are ways to talk to your friend without having a fight with her about this. Ask her if you and she can go out to a movie or to the mall or something.

Then when you are having fun hanging out, casually tell her that you really value her friendship and you are not mad at her because she didn't invite you to her party, but that you did feel a little confused and slighted by the snub. It's best to bring it up when you're alone and *definitely* better to talk about it as calmly as possible. Don't make accusations because you haven't heard her side of the story yet. She may have been hurt by something *you* did recently, or maybe she was in a situation where she had to invite someone who she knew you didn't like. There is no way of knowing until you ask her. Find out if she had a good reason for not inviting you. Once you have all the facts from her, then you can decide if you can forgive her or if it's time to rethink your friendship with her.

poo-pooing the prom

Dear Sari,
All my friends are going to our junior prom and I'm not. It doesn't really appeal to me, but they will not stop bugging me about it. What can I do to get them off my back?

Sari says:
Oh, the calamities of being popular! Before I start giving you advice on how to get out of attending, I want you to take a step back a second and think about how lucky you are. You have good friends who can't bear to be without you on a day they consider important and fun—this, my friend, is a good thing. Bask in that for a second.

Okay, now on to the nitty gritty—there are many ways that you could handle this situation:

1. You could talk to them honestly, explaining that different people enjoy different things and the prom is simply not something that you think you'd enjoy. Tell them you respect the fact that they think it'll be a cool event. Then ask them to respect your decision. They

shouldn't paint a big "L" on your forehead if you forego the festivities. Tell them they must drop the topic.

2. You could compromise by skipping the prom, but arrange to meet your friends afterward to hang out with them. That way, you'll still be adding to your stockpile of great memories with your pals, but you won't have to deal with the prom if you really don't want to.

3. You could avoid the prom—without having to explain and without having to compromise—by making plans to do something else that night. Then you'd be able to tell them, "I'm so sorry that I am missing the prom, but I have to visit my grandparents that weekend" (or whatever you end up doing). This gives you an easy way out, and they can't bug you anymore.

4. You could go to the prom. I'm not suggesting that you do something you really don't want to do; however, there's a chance that you could really have fun with your friends. It sounds like they certainly want you there, and they probably think you'd add to the good time. Once you're there, you'll see that it's just a party like any other—music, dancing, talking, standing around—people just make a big deal about it beforehand.

5. Tell them that you'll skip this year, but you'll promise to go to the senior prom. During my junior year of high school, I wasn't into going to prom at all, so I skipped it. But by my senior year of high school (when I had my first real boyfriend), we were both really into going, and we had an amazing time. If this year is your junior prom and you really, truly just aren't into it, you can go to prom next year as a senior. Tell your friends "maybe next year."

jewish at a christmas party

Dear Sari,
I am Jewish and this year my new best friend, who is Catholic, invited me to her family's Christmas party. I feel funny about this because I have

never really been to a Christmas party, except ones at school. Are there religious things that go on? I am afraid to ask my friend what goes on at the party; she might think that it's weird that I have not been to a Christmas party. But I am more afraid that I will do something wrong, or that people will know I am Jewish and treat me differently.

Sari Says:

Christmas parties are generally not religious events. The religious aspects of the holiday most often take place during a church service, such as midnight mass on Christmas Eve. At most Christmas parties, people hang around drinking eggnog, eating Christmas cookies, and talking about, well, nothing special. In fact, it will probably be a lot like the Christmas parties that you've been to at school.

Your friend's house will more than likely be decorated for Christmas, with a Christmas tree, lights, and some other stuff. There might also be some religious decorations, like a nativity scene—small statues arranged to represent the story of Jesus' birth. If there is a sit-down dinner at the party, they may or may not say a prayer before they eat, but you will not be asked to say or do anything religious. Basically, you won't have to know anything special about Christmas to be there. No one will know that you are Jewish, unless it comes up in conversation, but you also shouldn't feel like you have to hide your religious background. There really is nothing to worry about.

If you want to know more about what the party is going to be like, it's perfectly fine to ask your friend. You don't even have to tell her that you've never been to a Christmas party before. Just ask her, "What's the party going to be like? Will there be a lot of people? Will other people from school be there? Should I bring anything?" Ask her whatever will make you feel more comfortable. She won't react badly—she'll probably be excited to talk about the party and share parts of her background with you, just as you would be psyched to tell her about your own traditions. Most importantly, just have fun!

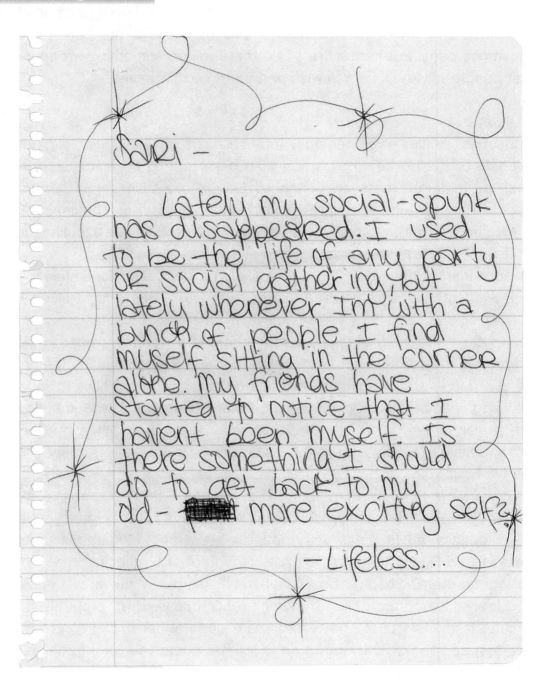

Sari –

Lately my social-spunk has disappeared. I used to be the life of any party or social gathering, but lately whenever I'm with a bunch of people I find myself sitting in the corner alone. My friends have started to notice that I haven't been myself. Is there something I should do to get back to my old-~~████~~ more exciting self?

–Lifeless...

Sari Says:

Since you are aware of the changes in yourself, you can work on them; if you want to, that is. First consider why you may have changed. Are you depressed about anything in your life? Have you gone through any major changes at home or in school? Sometimes, people have a problem that they have not entirely dealt with, so it shows up in some weird way, until they deal with the actual cause. If you come up blank when you try to determine what might be behind this, then consider that you are just changing. Maybe always being the life of the party was starting to drain you, and you are preserving your energy for close friends. As long as you still have fun, then don't worry so much about it. However, if you seem to get more depressed, then you should try to find a therapist to talk to by asking your parents or a counselor at school for a referral. Remember, you do not have to be the life of the party, but you should be able to enjoy the party—and enjoy your life.

Making and Breaking Friendships

Friends are enemies

Dear Sari,

I have two cliques of friends. One group is popular and one is unpopular. They hate each other. All I hear from my popular friends is, "Oh, they are such losers, how could you hang out with them?" and from my unpopular friends, "They are such preps, how could you hang out with them?" This is driving me *crazy*! I have tried everything from getting them together to talk about it (which turned into an argument), to just talking about it among ourselves to see if I could do anything, but nothing is working! Can you help me?

Sari Says:

Since you've tried your best to help them get along, and they still can't do it, it seems to me that you'll have to just accept that they don't like each other. Keep them apart; there is no reason why they need to hang out together. Avoid talking to each group about the other group—especially about what a great time you had with the other. Also, ask them to stop bad-mouthing each other to you. Explain that part of being a good friend includes respecting the fact that you may have other friends whom they don't like. Tell them that you *know* that they don't like each other, so they don't need to keep telling you that! Ask them to "agree to disagree"—and then get over it.

will you be my friends?

Dear Sari,
There is this group of really great people I know, and I want to become the kind of friend who they call on the weekend and ask if I want to do anything. They are all skaters and I'm into skateboarding, too, but I worry that if I tried to hang out with them more, they might think of me as a poser or something. How should I become *good* friends with them?

Sari Says:

It's tough to become part of a clique, because the people in it are already so close that you have to catch up to the level of friendship they've already established. You can try a couple of things. First, tell one of them that you like to skateboard and you would love to hang out with him or her sometime because you haven't found a good place to skate. That way, you aren't just saying that you want to hang with them because they're cool; you'd be approaching one of them on an individual basis and showing them that you have something in common and you want to do that activity with them. (It's also less intimidating to approach one than ten!) Next, when you hang around them, don't be too clingy. You want to get them to like you gradually. They'll need to adjust to having someone new in their group, so it might take time. Finally, understand that you cannot always control who your friends become. If they do not accept you for whatever reason, just realize that it was not meant to be. Don't take it personally; just try to find another group. If they're that exclusive, maybe you didn't really want to hang out with people like that anyway.

shy guy

Dear Sari,

I'm a nice guy, and I just want to make friends, but I can't. Every time I go up to someone, I can feel butterflies flying inside me. When I speak, I get nervous and forget what I have been saying. I've felt this way since I went to high school, and now this is my third year. I have no friends because of this problem. Is something wrong with me? What can I do to be less shy?

Sari Says:

There are a few things you can do to feel less shy when you talk to people. First, talk a lot to the people you trust and feel comfortable with, like your siblings or parents. Pay attention to how relaxed your body feels—how you're able to laugh or gesture without even thinking about it. In your mind, mentally label these relaxed feelings as: "Easy Talking." Once you can recognize these feelings, try to feel them at times when you are not talking. When you're just walking around school, or when you are sitting in class, think to yourself: "If my best friend were here, I would feel calm enough to have some Easy Talking with him." (Sure, it might sound stupid or corny, but nobody else will know what you're thinking— so who cares?) If you can recognize that calm feeling, it means you can tap into it when you talk to other people.

Next, make several efforts to try to talk at times when you would normally feel tense, shy, or scared. Notice when you feel the butterflies start. Notice whatever else is going on with your body—such as a lump in your throat, or a tendency to fidget, or your shoulders getting tense. Then take a few deep breaths. Say to yourself, "I felt calm a minute ago. I can feel that way again. I can make this into Easy Talking if I just calm down." Breathe, relax, and let your body take on the feeling of Easy Talking that you know it can have. Then start talking, all the while telling your body to chill out. Focus on getting your body to feel like you are just talking to your best friend (or your mom, or whomever you find it easiest to talk to). Then your muscles will start to relax, and the butterflies will go away. You'll be talking away very easily! Just keep trying.

Many people have trouble talking to others, and they learn to get over it naturally. But if you're still having trouble talking to people after a while, and you think something more serious is wrong, tell your parents, or maybe even a counselor or a doctor. It could be that this is something that needs professional treatment, such as panic attacks or depression.

getting popular

Dear Sari,
I never quite feel like I fit in at school. I would like to make lots of friends and be popular now that I am in high school. Do you have any advice?

Sari Says:
The key is being yourself and getting involved with the things that you like. For example, if you love acting, join your school drama club. If you love art, work on the photos for the yearbook. Or join a sport, or any type of club. Then once you get involved, be nice to all the other people in that group, and they will probably like you, since you will have things in common, too.

You can become popular in that group, and that is a start. I also think that a key to being popular in school is not dissing other kids, or other cliques. The most popular people are the ones who are well liked all around. The people who "hate jocks" or "hate brains," or whatever, are less popular, because they close themselves off to a whole bunch of people. Similarly, the ones who dress to conform to one clique shut out the possibility of fitting in elsewhere. Bottom line: get involved, be yourself, be nice.

cheer fear

Dear Sari,
I want to try out for cheerleading, because I love dancing, football, and I have school spirit. I think it could be great for me, but I feel like a hypocrite, because last year, my friends and I all used to make fun of the cheerleaders. Also, my friends think I'm going to become stuck up and ditch them if I get into cheerleading. What should I do?

Sari Says:
Instead of thinking about what your friends would think, focus on whether this is something you want for yourself. From what you said, it sounds like you could be really good at cheerleading. If you become a cheerleader, and you want to be friends with some other cheerleaders, then you should also take care to stay close to your old friends. As long as you don't neglect them, I'm sure they'll adjust to your new activity.

As far as feeling as if you are a hypocrite: It's no big deal to change the way you feel about something. Maybe last year you thought cheerleading was uncool, but this year you think cheerleading is awesome. So what? Nobody is keeping score, so just live in the present. Besides, the fact that you used to make fun of cheerleaders will be good for you if you get on the squad, because you will know not to take it personally if people make fun of you!

Dear Sari,

My best friend and I are huge Backstreet Boys fans. They are having a concert that we both really, really want to go to, but we couldn't get tickets. Yesterday my mom told me her friend from work has one extra ticket, and I could go! I thought my friend would be really happy for me, but she ended up getting all mad at me; she was like, "If I were in that situation, I wouldn't go without you." She made it sound like she'll stop being friends over this! I feel guilty, I don't want to be selfish, and it is not worth going if she's gonna hate me for it. But this concert is like the one thing that would make me the happiest I can possibly be. Should I go or not?

Sari Says:

You should go. Don't worry about being selfish, and don't feel guilty. It was an unpredictable situation that resulted in your getting a ticket. Your mom's friend was very generous to invite you, and you should accept. Giving the ticket to your friend is not really an option; it's from *your* mom's friend. What would you do if the tables were turned? It sounds like you'd be bummed that you didn't get to go, but that you'd be genuinely happy that at least your friend would have the experience.

Before you go to the concert, you should have a longer talk with your friend about this. Let her know that you wish the two of you could go together. Tell her that you are feeling guilty about accepting the ticket when she can't go, but explain again why you had to accept it: Since there is one extra ticket, and since it's your mom's friend, you kind of have to go. Ask her not to be mad or jealous. Tell her how much you care about her, and that you would never want to upset her. Say that even though you're psyched to go, it really isn't going to be half as much fun as it would be if she were going, too. You can even try to give her a new perspective on this matter, by telling her that the BSBs wouldn't want her to be mad at you about this either, if you believe the kinds of things that they sing about. In their songs they sing a lot about unconditional love (like: "I don't care who you are, Where you're from, What you did, As long as you love me."). Since you and she are really best friends, then your going to the concert shouldn't hurt your love for each other! Finally, offer to get her anything she wants at the concert: a T-shirt, program, or other souvenirs. Tell her you'll blow a kiss to Nick for her. Let her know that you will really miss her, and you promise that the next time BSBs are in town, you'll both try extra hard to get two tickets so the both of you can go together.

dumped by friend

Dear Sari,
My friend told me last night that I have changed too much these last couple of months and that she doesn't think she wants to be friends anymore. I told her that she couldn't just bail like that, but she said, "Oh well." What can I do?

Sari Says:
I'm sorry to say this, but there is not much you can do. Friends sometimes just grow apart. If your friend needs to move on for whatever reason, then she must. All you can do is tell her that you hope in the future you two can be friends again. Then move on, yourself! Go out there and make new, better friends who you can trust to stick by you. If after a month or two you want to see if your ex-friend would want to try again, ask her to go to the mall, or a movie, or whatever you like to do together. She may say yes and be into it, and everything will be fine again. On the other hand, sometimes friendships really break up for good. If this is what's happening, then unfortunately you'll have to let her go.

The End of a Friendship

It can be scary to think that friendships can end, but when they do, you can find a way to move on. Keep yourself busy with lots of activities. Find a new hobby. Join a new club. Make every effort to meet new people, and soon, you'll have tons of new friends. Also, do not take it personally when a friendship ends. People change. Let this transition change you for the better.

witchy woman

Dear Sari,

My best friend got all weird this year. She started hanging out with the skanks, and saying she's a witch, into "Wicca," and all this wild stuff. We still talk, but I don't like going out with her anymore, because her friends are all odd, and they dress all in black. Should I just stop being friends with her altogether?

Sari Says:

Sounds like your friend has watched too many episodes of *Charmed*. However, she is still your friend and diversity comes in all shapes and sizes—if what she's doing isn't harmful to you, herself, or anyone else, then just chill out. It's not like she's asking you to eat eye-of-newt stew! She's found something new that interests her—just because it's not your bag doesn't mean that it's bad news. Ask her to tell you a little more about it. Maybe if you understand it better, it won't seem so weird.

On the other hand, if you find that she and her new cauldron of friends are doing destructive things, though, you don't have to put up with that. Express your concern. Tell her you really value her friendship and that you feel like you know her well enough to say that this new interest of hers is more wicked than Wicca. She might not react well, but it'll give her food for thought. Voicing your opinion might save her from heading down a bad path. But be prepared for her not to listen—if she doesn't and she thinks you're a big drag, then it might be best to break the broomstick and find a new friend.

So-Called Friends

hacker is no friend

Dear Sari,
One friend of mine hacked into my computer screen name, then wrote me this mean letter saying how she could hurt me with everything she learned from the stuff she read on my email. I have other friends who dis me and sell me out, too. I've told them that I don't want to be friends, but then I keep going back to them, because I don't have any other friends. What should I do and how can I get over them?

Sari Says:
Listen and listen good: These friends sound horrible! You deserve to be with people who treat you well. Not threatening, conniving, bad-news troublemakers. To get over them, first you need to stop talking to them—entirely. Go cold turkey. You can say hey in the hallways at school (no need to stoop to their level of meanness!), but as far as hanging out goes, ditch 'em, and fast. There's a sure-fire way that you can find new friends: Join a club, take up a sport or other activity that you're interested in. By doing this, you're surrounding yourself with people who have similar interests and enthusiasms. If you are equally outgoing, you're bound to strike up at least a friendship or two. And that will lead to more. It will take effort; you'll have to go out of your way to talk to lots of new people and make friends, but it will be worth it in the end. Once you start making new friends, it will be easier to get over those awful old friends. Honestly, by brushing off those so-called friends who have been tormenting you,

you aren't losing a thing—but you are gaining your dignity. Remember, it's very simple: Friends should make you feel good about yourself. If your friends hurt you, then they are not your friends.

likes girls, but not that way

Dear Sari,
There are two girls who go to my school who are a year older than I am, and I look up to them. Because I say great things about them my friends called me a lesbian. Of course, I'm not! It makes me so angry when they say that. (Even though I know that there is nothing wrong with being a lesbian, and one of my closest friend's mom is a lesbian.) How do I let my friends know I really don't appreciate being called a lesbian?

Sari Says:
Your so-called friends are trying to upset you. That's all. Unfortunately, they are using the word "lesbian" because they think of it as an insult. I doubt that they really think you're a lesbian; they're just trying to be cruel. As you said, there is nothing wrong with being a lesbian—that's why it is sad and stupid that the word should seem like an insult. If a woman is attracted to women, that's just the way she is, and that's fine. Lesbians and gays are still discriminated against by people who don't understand that there's nothing wrong with homosexuality.

No matter what they call you, their goal is to upset you and make you defensive. Don't let them. When they start with their ridiculous name-calling, act nonchalant as if it doesn't bother you. If you show that this "insult" gets to you, they will keep using it. Also, although you clearly have a good head on your shoulders and a good heart, if you react badly to this accusation, you're helping to perpetuate the discrimination that your "friends" are spewing. If they don't act nicer to you, try hanging out with a different crowd altogether.

76

more than friends?

Dear Sari,

I asked one of my really good friends to the annual Valentine's Day dance at our school. He accepted with an ear-to-ear smile on his face. How do I know whether or not we are going as friends, or if it will be more than that?

Sari Says:

Looks like you may have inadvertently borrowed Cupid's arrow and shot it dead center in your pal's heart. He may well think that you want more than just a friendship since you asked him out for Valentine's Day. This situation is a little tricky, but you can finesse it without either of you getting hurt. Although you may mean it sincerely, having an "I want to be just friends" conversation might hurt and embarrass him. Before the dance, you might want to try saying something to him over lunch in the caf, like, "I'm so glad you said yes—it's so much cooler to go to a dance like this with a friend. There's too much pressure to go with a date-date." This way, he'll learn your intentions and be able to save face, too.

However, just in case you may want more than just friendship, I suggest not talking to him about this before the dance. Wait to see how it goes while you're grooving out on the dance floor. See if he asks you to slow dance and, if he does, how he dances with you. In other words, pay attention to the signals he sends. If it is obvious that he likes you as more than just a friend, and you feel good about that, then you are all set. If it is not quite obvious, find a quiet moment after the dance to tell him that you want him to be more than just your friend . . . you want him to be your Valentine.

talking trash behind her

Dear Sari,

I'm a guy and my best friend is a girl. (We have no feelings for each other besides friendship . . . really.) The new guy she's dating is a complete jerk. Only two weeks ago, he was telling everyone in gym about how "easy" she was and how he was going to, "do her in front of the entire basketball team." I'm afraid that she'll get upset with me if I say anything to her. On the other hand, I don't want her to get hurt. What should I do?

Sari Says:

If you just blurt out Dr. Evil's locker-room talk, it might have the opposite reaction than you'd hope. For one, she might be so hurt that she doesn't want to believe you and she'd take his side. Secondly, she might, in her anger, ask you why you didn't stop him (which, by the way, is a question you might want to ask yourself).

The best thing to do is talk to your friend about her feelings for this guy, rather than telling her that her boyfriend is talking trash behind her back. You might find out that she is not really all that into this guy, and they might break up soon anyway. If that is the case, you don't need to say anything. If she asks your opinion about him, you can certainly tell her what you think. I bet that once you and she start talking openly about how she feels about him, she will be interested in hearing your perspective.

she cheats

Dear Sari,

My best friend in the whole world cheats on all of her boyfriends and tells me about it. Now, she's dating and cheating on a guy I am friends with. I don't want him to get hurt, but I know she would want me to shut up.

Sari Says:

Your friend is wrong to put you in the middle of a tough situation. Do you stay loyal to your best friend no matter what, or do you give her present beau a ticket out of chumpland? Since she's your best friend *in the whole world*, you should not betray her trust. Instead, talk openly with her. Tell her that you don't approve of her two-timing.

Also, tell her that she should not mention it to you when she cheats. Yes, friends should be able to tell each other their deepest, darkest secrets, but this kind of secret is way too uncomfortable since you are friendly with this guy. If she cares about you, she'll stop telling you the gory details. If she cares about her boyfriend, she'll stop cheating altogether. If some time goes by and she does not stop cheating, and keeps telling you, then give her an ultimatum: for example, in five days, you are going to tell him that she cheats on him, unless she stops cheating, or tells him first.

boyfriend cheated with best friend

Dear Sari,

My boyfriend cheated on me with my best friend. She knew we were going out—should I be mad at her for it?

Sari Says:

Are you kidding me? If I were you, I'd be mad at her. Really mad. She broke one of the biggest Friend Commandments: Thou Shalt Not Scam on Your Friend's Significant Other. She's a rotten best friend to do that to you. But then again, it takes two to tango, if you know what I mean. This is his fault, too. He's no great catch if he would do something that low. Best friends usually last longer than boyfriends, though, so if you do decide to forgive her, and dump him, you'd be better off in the long run. You need to let her know that you're hurt, though, and see if she's very sorry for her actions. If she's not, then dump them both.

The Friendship Code

Develop an honor code with your friends when it comes to dating. Here are some things to start you off, then work on it more with your friends:

- You will not date each other's crushes.
- You will not date each other's ex's.
- You will not date each other's siblings.
- You will still be attentive to each other even when one or both of you gets in a relationship.
- You will respect that some things are private between couples, and friends can't know everything.
- You will try to fix each other up, if you ever have the chance.

pushed aside for her boy

Dear Sari,

My friend and this guy are going out, but ever since they became a couple, she hasn't been spending as much time with me. Now that it's summer I never see her around. I go out and hang with other friends, but I miss our friendship. It's like, he's her life and that's all she ever talks about. I don't know how to get her to see me, and I don't want to have to wait until school starts again until I see her around. I want us to be friends this summer, even though she has a boyfriend.

Sari Says:

If you had a new boyfriend, you'd probably want to spend most of your time with him, too. Usually, friends know to sort of back off to give each other time with a new relationship. Then, if the relationship mellows out or ends, a good friend is right there to hang out with all the time again. But, of course, it makes sense that you miss your friend. That's why you should still call her and try to get together with her once a week. (Even though at this point she might only want to talk about her boyfriend.)

Encouragingly remind her that it's fun to hang out with friends, and that her boyfriend will not leave her if she spends a few hours a week with you!

makeout madness

Dear Sari:
I was at a party, and this girl who I think likes me was there. Now this guy friend of mine *really* likes the girl, too. We were both flirting with her, and she pushed him away, but told me to join her on the couch. The girl and I made out on the sofa, and he saw us. Now he's mad at the girl and me for making out because he said that we knew how he felt about her, and that I should not have touched her. I liked this friend; was I in the wrong? What should I do? I really like the girl, and I'm not sure of her feelings yet; all I know is she doesn't like him. Help!

Sari Says:
Dude, that *was* kind of uncool. Think about if you had been in his shoes and your friend flaunted in your face how he got the girl and you didn't. You should have had more control over yourself and not made out with her right at the party. Explain to him that you are sorry that you kissed her in front of him, but you lost your head because you really like her. Then ask him if it is okay with him if you go out with her. If your friendship with this guy is important to you, you should not mess it up over a girl. If he's okay with you going out with her, the next thing you need to do is talk to her. Be honest with her. Tell her that you like her and you want to know how she feels about you. Then if she says she likes you, you can ask her out. In the future, if your guy friend is around, wait to make out with her . . . get a room.

juicy tell-all

Dear Sari,
My best friend wants to know everything when I go out with my boyfriend on dates. I can't stand it any longer. What should I do? Help!

Sari Says:
Just because she's your best bud, doesn't mean that you need to kiss and tell. You aren't obligated in any way to reveal what goes on between you and your boyfriend. Try to glean a little insight as to why she's so eager for the juicy deets. My guess is she's pretty inexperienced with guys and is trying to live vicariously through you. That's understandable, but it doesn't mean you have an obligation to dish. Tell her whatever you feel comfortable telling her.

If she begs, "Tell me more! You're my best friend; you should tell me everything," then you need to talk about your boundaries. Explain that you will tell her almost everything, but sometimes there will be things that have to stay just between you and your boyfriend. Remind her that you don't tell other people the things she asks you not to tell—and this is basically the same thing. While you and she are best friends, you are still allowed to have your private lives. Reassure her that you always tell her the things that are important for her to know.

You may want to suggest that she hang out with you and your boyfriend sometime. Maybe you can set up a double date. That way, she can get an idea of what you two are like together, and she won't feel as if she is missing out on something.

Dear Sari,

My boyfriend and I are having sex. I told this secret to two of my friends, because I thought I could trust them. I told both of them not to tell anyone. One of my friends kept her mouth shut, which I am thankful for, but the other friend told someone. I don't mind that she told only one other person, but that person told nine others! It feels like the whole world knows about my private life now—I can't stand it! I'm really mad! Help me—I don't know how to handle it. I just want to punch her!

Sari Says:

Unclench that fist! Don't punch her. Don't even yell at her. No matter what you say to her, she can't take back what she did. Some people can keep secrets; others can't. Now you know this girl is someone who can't. Just make sure that you *never* tell this girl any secrets of yours ever again. You don't need to tell her any of this; all you need to do is make it a personal policy. If you can calmly talk to this friend, you could tell her you were disappointed that she spread your secret. But I don't think you should start a fight with her. Move on and ignore the fact that people know your secret. Remember: Some people might think that what this girl said is not true anyway, so unless you tell people yourself, they will never know the real story. Please, try not to worry about this so much—your concern about who knows will pass very soon. Just be more careful about telling your secrets in the future!

blabbermouth

Dear Sari,

My problem is that I have a big mouth. I tell everyone everything they're not supposed to know. I've lost so many friends because of that. People actually call *me* to find out what so-and-so says about them, and the worst part is, I tell them! I can't help it! It just seems like everything I say comes out whether I want it to or not! *Help*!

Sari Says:

My dear Big Mouth, you *can* help it. You need to learn how to keep a secret and fast. If you can't keep a secret, there'll be something else you can't keep: a friend! Sometimes it makes someone feel important if he or she is the one who knows everything. Maybe the reason why you tell everybody everything is because you like to be the one with all the dirt.

You say that you can't help it, and everything just comes out whether you want it to or not, but I think that you're just getting a little too addicted to the power of being the one in the know. You need self-control; trust and privacy are very important if you want to keep friend-ships.

Tell yourself "stop" anytime you want to say something that you're not supposed to. The next time someone calls to ask you what you heard about something, just say "I don't know, but if I did know I wouldn't be able to tell, because I can keep a secret." It might feel fake at first, but eventually it'll become your new code of honor. You'll feel so proud of yourself for doing this, that it will be much better than "knowing it all." Also, you'll have closer friends, as people will learn that you are really good at keeping things private.

pants on fire

Dear Sari,

My friend always lies. For example, she lied by saying she was going out with a senior—so not true! She lies about her family being rich, and all kinds of other stuff. What do I do?

Sari Says:

First thing you need to do is ask yourself why you think she's living in the land of make-believe. What's going on with her that might be causing her to lie? Sometimes people lie to get attention and to feel important. Other times people lie because they feel ashamed or embarrassed about their real lives. Try to figure out why she's wading in the murky waters of the untruth. It could be for one or all of these reasons.

Have a talk with her and try to get to the root of the problem. Tell her all the reasons why you like being her friend, and that because she's all these great things already, there's no reason for her to fib. Tell her that life is not always exciting and that just because there's a lull in the action, that's no reason to make up stories. Explain to her that you like her a lot, just the way she is, and all this phony bologna hides the good stuff. Hopefully, she will start to see she's putting your friend-ship in trouble if she keeps telling lies, and that it's much cooler to be herself.

not a slut

Dear Sari,

My best friend thinks I'm a slut because I'm a big flirt, and I mess around with guys. The reason I like to be all over guys is because the first person

I was ever in love with broke up with me after one year by writing me a note saying he didn't care about me. That made me feel like a piece of trash. Don't you think instead of calling me names my friend should stand by my side?

Sari Says:
Usually, I would say that you need to tell your friend to stop calling you names, mind her own business, and accept you for who you are—but you've got more to deal with here than just a friend with a bad attitude. True, your friend shouldn't be calling you a slut—that's just not cool, ever. But, your bigger problem is that your flirty behavior is a negative, self-destructive way to dull the pain of losing your guy. Love can really bite you in the butt sometimes, but the worst thing you can do in reaction to it is become the Queen of the Backseat. If you stay on this path, you might actually start believing the cruddy things your ex and your friend have said to you, and that would be a shame.

I bet that your friend is actually concerned and she's trying to help you; it's just that she doesn't know the best way to talk to you about this. Tell her about what she can do to help you get over your ex in a healthier way. Instead of asking her to just stop calling you a slut, suggest that she gently and subtly remind you to stop flirting so much when she sees you doing it. (Maybe you and she could have a code word that she'd say in front of you and the guy when you're flirting.) Also, spend more time with her and your other friends. It will only build up your self-esteem and show you that you *are* a valuable, wonderful person with lots to offer (beyond the backseat).

Dear Sari,

My best friend is really a great person. She's pretty, nice, funny, and out-going. But the only thing is, she's very overweight. And I don't really care about that, it's just that I'm kind of worried about her. Sometimes, she just has really low self-esteem, and she tells me that she cries at night when she thinks about all the people who make fun of her. When she says that, I don't know what to tell her. All I can say is, "Just don't listen to those jerks." Is she gonna go through life like this? Is she always going to feel so bad about herself? Is she ever going to have a boyfriend? I really want her to lose that weight and gain that confidence she used to have before she got so big. She used to be an average weight, but I don't know what happened. I don't want to sound mean; I am just really concerned about her. I want her to enjoy life just like anyone else, without her feeling like a loser. Is there any way I can help her out? Because I love this chick a lot and she's just a pleasure to have around; I just want her to be happy.

Sari Says:

It's great that you are such a good friend, and that you are willing to help no matter what it takes. You have already noticed that her weight seems to affect her moods and make her sad. So talk with her about this some more—ask her what she thinks she could do about her unhappiness. Your friend has two choices. Either she can accept her weight and ignore what other people say, or she can try to lose weight.

It *is* possible for your friend to regain her confidence without having to lose weight. If she thinks she'll have trouble losing weight, then she should disregard other people's opinions about her. To live a happy life, she needs to do what is best for her. She needs to learn to be comfort-able with herself. She can rely on your continued support to help her feel good, and to ignore other people. Her confidence could grow over time, and that will make her feel stronger. If she takes this route, then as long as she is happy and confident, you do not need to worry about her. She can live happily even if she is overweight. By the way, whether she is fat, thin, short or tall, every girl can get a boyfriend someday.

If your friend tells you that she does want to lose weight, then she can choose to start dieting and exercising. You can support her there, too. Go with her to the school nurse and ask for advice for both of you on choosing a healthy eating plan and exercise program. Obviously, the nurse will give you two separate plans—*your* eating plan will not be a diet just to lose weight; it will just be a commitment to eating balanced meals and avoiding junk food. But if you are trying to eat better, too, that can help encourage your friend to stick to her diet. Also, exercise with her every day. Being exercise partners will motivate her and benefit both of you. If you and she stick to a good program, soon you will notice that she's losing weight, with your support.

Friend with HIV

Dear Sari,
My best friend told me she has HIV. I am so confused; I know what it is, but I don't know how to react. It seems like she is so strong and now she is not. I could use some help.

Sari Says:
You should react with love, understanding, and support. Ask your friend if there is anything you can do for her. Talk to her about her feelings, and be there to listen to her.

Also, you should realize that your friendship with her does not need to change. People who have HIV can still live long, happy lives. HIV is the virus that damages a person's immune system and then leads to a group of diseases, which are collectively referred to as AIDS. However, when people have the HIV virus they may not seem sick, and it may not turn into AIDS for ten years or more. Even though your friend has this virus in her system, she is the same person, and you should treat her the same way you always have. Remember, you can*not* get HIV from hugging her, kissing her, touching her, sharing food with her, or any casual contact like that. Therefore, this does not need to affect the way you interact with her. You may want to learn more about HIV and AIDS so you understand what she may be going through. You can get information and advice from the AIDS hotline number listed in the appendix in the back of this book.

suicide threat

Dear Sari,
My friend says she is going to kill herself. I don't know what to do!

Sari Says:
Tell your friend how much you care about her and that you do not want her to commit suicide. Talk about all the things that you want to do with her, and try to get her talking about things that she still wants to do in her life. There is so much of life still to be lived, so try to get her to see that! She may feel desperate right now, but she must not make an irreversible choice such as suicide. Tell her you are always here for her, but also tell her to get more help than you can offer her. She must start seeing a therapist. Bring her to the school counselor if she won't go alone. Tell her to call a suicide prevention hotline. If she won't do any of those things, and she keeps talking that way, please tell your mother and her mother to help. With your support on her side, if she sees a doctor, therapist, or counselor, they can help her get over these suicidal thoughts and start living a happier life.

Helping a Suicidal Friend

If you or a friend need to talk about suicide, call the national hotline at 1-800-SUICIDE (784-2433) to get connected to a crisis center near you for therapy and support. If it is an emergency, and you or a friend is about to try suicide, or have just caused a self-inflicted injury, call 911. If you have a friend who often talks about suicide, then do not try to be the only source of support your friend has. He or she must get professional therapy.

you've got style

You know how there's that one person in your school who always seems to look perfect? It's the trend-setting girl who wears the latest and the greatest before anyone else, or the guy who effortlessly strikes that perfect balance between looking really good and looking like he couldn't care less about his appearance. These people are so cool that they even look good after gym class. How do they *do* it?

Here's a little secret about style: It is one part fashion, two parts personality. "Oh great," you say, "Tell me where I can buy a personality!" You don't need to buy it. You're more ahead in this game than you know. Everyone has his or her own unique style—you just might need a little help bringing it out.

The secret to fashion isn't hidden behind the secret door of a secret club that has a secret knock just to get in. It is merely a means of expressing your opinions, your thoughts, and your *style*.

In this chapter, I'm going to help you uncover the style in you. Along the way, I'll help you with the palate of options to help you express it: makeup, clothes, shoes, hairstyles, tattoos, you name it. *Vogue*'s got nothing on you!

What to Wear

date-dressing distress

Dear Sari,
How should I dress on a date?

Sari Says:

The key to dressing for a date is to wear something that makes you feel comfortable. Whatever you do, don't overdress to impress. I once bought an expensive maroon-colored fuzzy short-sleeved sweater, because I thought it would really make a new guy sit up and take notice. The first time I wore it was on our date, so I didn't find out till that night that the sweater shed little maroon fluff balls. It got even worse, as I was a little nervous about our date and started sweating. The sweat made those little maroon balls of fluff stick to my arms in a way that was beyond gross! I didn't want the guy to see, so whenever he'd look away for a second I would try to brush the fluff off of my arms. Then the fluff was stuck to my hands! Finally, I excused myself to go to the ladies room. When I looked in the mirror, I saw the maroon fluff all over my face. I guess I'd touched my face with my fluff-covered hands. I was a pathetic mess.

The moral is: I had a rotten date, just because I tried to wear something totally new. You should wear something that you have worn before, a tried-and-true comfortable and attractive favorite. You do not have to dress up. Wear something just a touch nicer than what you'd wear to school, but generally, since you will probably be doing something casual, such as going to a movie or a meal, then you should dress casually. Most importantly don't let your clothes interfere with the enjoyment of your date, the way that horrid sweater ruined mine.

chesty hefty

Dear Sari,

My friend is big chested and hefty. She wears these tiny shorts that her butt hangs out of and tight tops that her breasts pop out of. She looks like trash. I've tried talking to her about "covering up," but she thinks that she looks good. What should I do?!

Sari Says:

Everyone has her own style of dressing, and it's tough to get someone to change her style. Your friend would probably look better if she dressed to flatter her figure, not flaunt it in an inappropriate way. You can try to help her understand the fine line between looking sexy and looking sleazy. The first thing you could try is to tear out some magazine pictures of girls who have big chests and still dress tastefully. When you talk to her, mention how some cool actresses look sexy without letting it all hang out. Some good examples are Mary J. Blige, Queen Latifah, Drew Barrymore, or Tiffany Amber Theissen. They have large breasts, and always look good, but never look slutty.

You could try to show your friend what you mean if she'll let you do a makeover on her. Say to her, "Hey, I saw a talk show where they had friends making each other over. It seemed like a lot of fun. Let's do that: You make me over, and I'll make you over." Then one weekend, go through your closets and dress each other up. It should be fun, and if you make her look good, but not slutty, maybe she will like it and dress your way every once in a while.

high hopes

Dear Sari,

I want to wear high heels to the junior prom, but I have never done it before. Most of the other girls have, and I feel stupid about asking my friends about this. But how do I walk in them without teetering? I can just see it: Me falling flat on my ass at the prom!

Sari Says:

The first step in wearing high heels is being able to visualize yourself walking tall and with confidence. Stop visualizing yourself falling! Next, probably the most important thing is to pick a shoe that is comfortable and not too tough to walk in. Try on lots of pairs in the store. Tell them it is your first pair of high heels; walk around in the store as much as you need to test the shoe. For your first pair of high heels, pick shoes that have:

- A thicker heel, rather than a really thin heel. Thick heels give more support. Chunky heels are generally the most comfortable.
- A good hold on your foot. Do not pick a strappy sandal. Choose a closed shoe, like a pump, for your first time in heels.
- A good fit. Do not get a shoe that pinches you, would cause a blister, or that your foot falls out of. You will have to wear them all night.

Also, you should choose a shoe that you can wear panty hose with, like a closed toe pump. If you go barefoot in the shoe, it may become more uncomfortable as your feet start to sweat over the course of the night. Another tip, before you wear them the first time, to keep the soles from being slippery on the ground, scuff the bottoms of them with sandpaper or by scraping the shoes on pavement. Finally, once you choose a good pair of shoes, wear them around your house for a couple of hours for a test run, er, I mean, test walk.

the dreaded bathing suit

Dear Sari,
I have to go to a pool party, but I cannot find a bathing suit that fits me. I mean they fit, like a size 10 or 12 suit, but they look horrible. The worst part is my fat thighs. I want to just cancel the party, unless I can figure out what to wear!

Sari Says:
Almost all girls have a tough time finding a bathing suit that looks great. But you can find one that is good enough. Here are some tips for buying a one-piece bathing suit if you are not-so-thin:

94

- Find a solid-color suit. Black or navy blue may be best.
- Get a plain-shaped suit. Avoid suits that have cut-out sections. Get one that is a simple "tank" shape.
- If you have medium or large breasts, get underwire built into the suit. That will raise up your breasts so they look better.
- Find a suit that has leg holes that are near your hip. If you choose a suit that has lower leg holes, they might emphasize your thighs more.
- Make sure your butt is fully covered by the suit. You don't want your cheeks to be hanging out the bottom.

Also, if you are going nuts about how your thighs look, then at the pool party, wear shorts or a short skirt, or a sexy sarong. You can take it off when you get in the pool. Remember, once you are in the pool, your body is not really noticeable. Finally, have fun! If you are smiling and chatting with friends, they won't be thinking about your body, and neither should you.

Love Your Weight!

Don't worry so much about your weight. If you are really overweight, then ask your doctor or the school nurse to put you on an exercise and healthy eating program. Otherwise, you can learn to love your body! Keep these things in mind: Models twenty years ago weighed 8 percent less than the average woman. Today they weigh 23 percent less. Beauty and sexiness come in all sizes.

the baggy jeans cover-up

Dear Sari,

I like to wear baggy jeans 'cause I don't really like having my legs show. But my mom is mad since it's almost summer, she wants me to start wearing my shorts again. I told her I'd rather wear jeans, but she says I can't because all my clothes will go to waste!

Sari Says:

It sounds to me like you are embarrassed about your legs. I don't think you have anything to be embarrassed about. Sometimes people get embarrassed about body parts for no good reason, except self-consciousness. If you wear shorts once in a while, you'll find that the self-consciousness will die down. You'll realize that not only do your legs look fine, you feel fine wearing shorts. If you are worried about fashion, there are lots of good-looking shorts that you can wear—even baggy types—so you won't be stuck in something ugly or geeky. Try to vary what you wear: sometimes shorts, sometimes baggy jeans. That will make both you and your mom happy. Eventually, you will get over your self-consciousness about your legs, and you'll just wear whatever makes you feel cool, both fashion-wise and temperature-wise.

nerd to beauty

I am known as the nerd of my school. I wear glasses, pull my hair back, and get good grades. I'm thinking of going all-out for the prom because I know I look kinda pretty when I put on makeup and let my hair down. Should I?

Sari Says:

Absolutely! You should make yourself look as beautiful and glamorous as you want to. Your friends will enjoy seeing you look different from the way you usually do . . . not that there is anything wrong with what you usually look like! So shock them, and have a great time.

itty-bitty tittie

Dear Sari,

Okay, here's my deal. I am having trouble finding a prom dress, because I have a relatively small chest—"itty-bitty tittie committee"—a small A, to be exact. What kind of dress would look good on me?

Sari Says:

There are many different styles that look fabulous on small-busted girls. Think of Gwyneth Paltrow's pink dress at the 1998 Oscars, or Cameron Diaz in the black dress she wore to the Oscars in 2000. See if a local store has photos or a catalog of girls modeling different dresses, and pay special attention to what the smaller-chested girls are wearing. Once you start to notice styles that you think might look good on you, go shopping to try on similar styles. Also, try dresses with and without a bra and see which looks best. (Someone working in the underwear department should be able to help you find the right padded bra if you want to go that route.) Choose a dress that makes you look good all over, not just in the chest.

The most important thing: If you are confident, then you will look great! When you put on a dress that looks amazing, stop thinking about your chest. When you walk into the prom, do not pull at your top, don't try to hide yourself, don't even mention to your girlfriends that you feel self-conscious. I'm sure you will look great if you put effort into finding a dress that looks nice on you—and you will find one. Be confident. Your attitude matters; your breast size doesn't.

Bra Measurements

Bra sizes consist of a number (called the bra band measurement) and a letter (called the cup measurement). You can find the band measurement by wrapping a tape measure around your rib cage directly under your bust. (If it is an odd number, then round up to the next even number.) The most common measurements are 32" or 34" or 36". To find your cup measurement, measure with a tape measure around the fullest part of your breast, the mid-line of your breasts near your nipples. If this bust measurement is 1" greater than your band measurement, then you are an A cup. Two inches over, you're a B cup. Three inches over, a C cup. Four inches over, a D cup. Five inches over, a DD. If you are not sure about your measurements, then have someone in a bra store measure you, and try on several bras to be sure.

guy's Fashion

Dear Sari,

I am a guy who never cared about how I dress, but now there is a girl I like, and I want her to notice me. She usually goes for preppy types. How do I figure out how to dress in something other than concert T-shirts and jeans?

Sari Says:

For a more clean-cut look, try wearing khaki pants instead of jeans, and solid-colored T-shirts or button-down shirts. Also, try lighter colors, like a beige or white cotton button-down with khakis. For more ideas, you can ask a salesperson to help you at a store like The Gap or Banana Republic, J. Crew, or L.L. Bean. Maybe your mom or a woman friend would even go shopping with you to help. Also, take notice of how some preppy TV characters dress, like Dawson on *Dawson's Creek*. Finally, while I am all for your idea of developing a new style of dressing, make sure that this is something that you want to do for yourself—not just for the girl you like. You could always decide to keep dressing the way you do now, and try to find a girl who goes for guys who wear concert T-shirts and jeans.

Face Forward

makeup lesson

Dear Sari,

I don't have a clue when it comes to wearing makeup. How can I do it without looking overdone? My parents say that it's okay if I wear it, as long as I don't look like a clown. Please help me learn what to do.

Sari Says:

The key to great makeup is using just enough to bring out your natural beauty. A great way to learn details about how to apply makeup, and what colors to choose, is to go to a makeup counter at a department store. They will make you up for free, and you do not even need to buy products from them. It's much less expensive to buy makeup from a drugstore. So learn at a department store counter, but buy a similar product at a drugstore.

I've had tons of makeup counter makeup sessions and I've learned a few things about makeup. Here're some of the makeup tips that I've learned over the years.

Foundation and Concealer: Foundation is used to even out your skin tone and cover blemishes. If you have dark circles under your eyes, or lots of pimples, you may want to put a concealer over them before you put on foundation. When applying either, you should use it lightly. Dot a tiny bit of concealer over the things you want to hide, then blend it in with a patting motion. With foundation, put a small amount on your fingertip or on a makeup sponge, then blend it (in an upward motion) all over your face. Blend it very well (especially at your jawline), so people cannot even tell that you have it on. You need to find a foundation that matches your skin tone, so your face looks the same color as your neck and body. Also, choose an oil-free foundation that is noncomedogenic, which means that it will not clog your pores, thus will not cause acne.

If you want to set the foundation and concealer so they last longer on your skin, then you can put powder on top. Use either a pressed powder that matches your foundation, or a translucent loose power that you put on with a big brush. But be careful with how much or how often you use powder, since it can clog your pores. Also, while powder can sometimes give your skin that "flawless" look, other times, especially if you have a lot of pimples, it can make you look dry and bumpy, actually accentuating the pimples.

Blush: To make your cheeks look healthy, apply a little blush with a large fluffy brush. You can wear a color that is a brownish hue, or a pinkish hue. Get blush on the brush, then tap it so the excess falls off. Brush it on, starting at the apples of your cheeks, and moving in one motion upward toward the space between your eyes and ears. Only use a couple of strokes.

Eye Makeup: You can use eyeliner, eye shadow, and mascara. Or you can just use mascara if you want a more natural look. For most people, black mascara looks best. If you have light blond hair, try a brownish-black mascara.

If you want to wear eye shadow, try earth-tone shades, such as brown, smoky green, or gray. Cover your lid lightly with the soft neutral tones. If you want to experiment, you can try putting one color on the lower part of the lid and a slightly darker color in the crease, and a slightly lighter shade on the upper part of the lid. In fact, you can buy eye shadows that come with contour shades like this, and the instructions on where to apply each.

If you want to use eyeliner, you can try black for emphasis on your eyes, or a more natural color for a subtle line. You can line the top lid just above your lashes to make your eyes look slightly larger, then blend it in a little with an eye shadow applicator. Or you can put it on the inside of your lower lid if you want the eyes to stand out, but look a bit smaller.

Lipstick: For day-to-day use, use a lipstick color that is neutral, such as beige, brown, or a rosy-colored lip stain that is just a shade deeper than your natural lip color. Or you can even just wear lip gloss. Try flavored gloss for extra tasty fun; my fave is Hot Fudge Sundaze Liplix by Bonne Bell. For special occasions, you may like a bright red or deep plum-colored lipstick. You can apply lipstick directly from the tube, filling in your natural lip line. You don't need a lip liner, since it tends to have too harsh of a line. Remember, the key is to look natural!

brace yourself

Dear Sari,
I wear braces, and I was wondering if wearing lipstick will make them look more—or less—noticeable. I would love to find a way to hide my braces.

Sari Says:
If you choose a neutral-colored lipstick, or if you just use lip gloss, then it should not draw attention to your braces. Also, make up your eyes a little with mascara to draw attention to your eyes. Things to avoid: Red lipstick when you aren't wearing any eye makeup will make people notice your braces more.

No matter what you do, you cannot make your braces disappear. You can try to think of them as something kind of cool. Silver braces add a sparkle to your face that can be attractive—like jewlery. If you don't agree, then there may be some alternatives for you. Many dentists offer plastic braces, which are much less visible, or colored braces, which can be a fun fashion statement. Talk with your parents and your orthodontist about these choices if you want to try to reduce the impact that braces will have on your style.

pale face

Dear Sari,
I am very pale, and I want to be tan. When I go out in the sun, I burn. I tried self-tanners, but it looked streaky. What can I do?

Sari Says:
If you really want a tan, you can ask someone else to apply a self-tanner to your skin. Or if you have the money, some salons offer self-tanning

application, where a professional can do it for you. If self-tanners really don't work for you, then you can try a makeup that has a bronzer. However, maybe your best bet is learning to love your pale look. Think of all the celebrities who embrace their pale skin: Winona Rider, Gwyneth Paltrow, Drew Barrymore. They know that there is something really cool about being yourself and not faking a tan.

hair cut

Dear Sari,
How can I get a haircut that I like? I am always afraid that the hairstyles will not do what I want, so I am avoiding getting a haircut.

Sari Says:
Before you go to a hair salon, flip through magazine to look at hairstyles that you might like and rip out the pages. Look for people whose faces are close to the same shape as yours, and whose hair type (curly or straight, thin or thick) and hair color looks like yours. Next, go through old pictures of yourself and see if you looked great in any of your old hairstyles. Then when you go in for your haircut appointment, before they wash your hair, talk with the hair stylist about what you have in mind. Show him or her the pictures. Discuss it, and if the hairstylist does not think that it will work to cut your hair the way you want, then listen to his or her suggestions. But remember, it is your hair. If you feel at all uncomfortable, you do not have to get your hair cut by this person. Also, if you have long hair, and you do not want it too short, before the stylist makes the first cut, have him or her show exactly where he or she is thinking of cutting your hair. Once the first cut is made, it's too late. So make it all very clear before the scissors are in hand.

Sari,

I always see these really cool fashion trends on models, like snakeprint fake leather pants, and I buy them to look cool and fit in. Then I wear them once, and then I never wear them again. It costs me too much, and I have a closet full of expired trends. Here are some things I bought beside the snakeprint pants: a silver sequin tube top, a Hawaiian shirt, a floor length purple skirt, and the worst of all a $200 jacket made of feathers, which I had to have because I saw it in a magazine, and now I don't know what I was thinking. I know, I need help. How can I learn what trends to buy what to ignore? Help, please, Sari!

Sari Says:

The key to buying trendy items is only spend a little on them, and to buy the trend in an accessory, instead of in a major article of clothing. For example, if animal prints are in, then get a cheap scarf with the print you like, rather than a pair of pants or a shirt. Besides just saving your money, you'll save space, since a small scarf takes up less storage space than a pair of pants. And you'll want to hold on to it. Trends usually don't last for long, but they do come back. Having a great animal print accessory will come in handy in a few years when the trend is in again. Also, remember, rather than get hung up on trying to fit in with the latest trend, focus more on buying what you like and creating your own look.

model heights

Dear Sari,

I am very pretty and can very easily pass as a model, but am told that I am too short. Why do all models have to be tall?

Sari Says:

A model's job is to sell clothes. When a fashion designer decides that he or she wants to design an outfit, instead of making thousands of copies of the outfit, first the designer makes one or two samples of the outfit. When the designer makes those first samples, they are always made to fit tall, thin models. The sample sizes are usually about a size 6, and made for a woman who is at least 5'7". In fact, many models are about six feet tall. The designers think that a tall woman walking down a runway shows off the outfit best. Those samples are worn by models for fashion shows. After the fashion show, if the outfit is well liked, then the designer makes thousands of copies of the outfit in all different sizes to send it out to stores to be sold.

The other reason why models are tall and thin is because our society puts a crazy emphasis on some phony ideal look. Real women do not look like models. The only women who look like supermodels are the supermodels. If you want celebrities as role models who are short, then check out Jennifer Love Hewitt or Christina Ricci. For celebrity role models who are not stick thin, look at Ricki Lake or Kate Winslet.

More importantly, think about what is beautiful about yourself. People are beautiful whether they are tall, short, fat, thin, or whatever. Beauty is about confidence, not about height. The fact that you think you are as beautiful as a model is great. It's your confidence that will attract people to you. So enjoy yourself, and others will, too.

dressing sexy to attract guys

Dear Sari,
I'm sick of seeing girls my age walk around half-naked to get guys! It's so dumb! If they're out there flashing everything they have to get a guy, they need a self-confidence boost! They don't need to wear these tiny tube tops and booty shorts. I'm not saying they can't dress cute if that's their style, but please dress tastefully, at least.

Sari Says:
You're right . . . to some extent. When a girl dresses sexy every day to try to attract guys, that could mean that she has a problem feeling good enough about herself.

She might be copying the images that she sees of pop stars on MTV who dress in really skimpy clothes. But she should remember that Britney Spears *is* a pop star, that's why she dresses that way. Dressing sexy will not make someone a star.

Wearing sexy clothes does not mean that you become sexy and attractive to guys. The best way to be sexy is to look confident and relaxed. If a girl walks into a room and she is standing up straight with a smile on her face, then guys will look at her and see that she feels good about herself. That's attractive. Most people want to hang around others who feel good about themselves. Of course, dressing in a way that looks crisp, fashionable, and put together does help. But if you hold your head high and have confidence, you can look sexier in jeans and a T-shirt than you would ever look in a tiny tube top and booty shorts.

mixed-up styles

Dear Sari,

My best friend tries to mix styles. Like a few days ago, she was wearing Adidas pants with Nike sneakers, which is cool . . . but then she was wearing a spaghetti-string tank top and a black sweater over that. I mean if you want to be sporty, then dress like it! You *cannot* mix hooch, sporty, and preppy—it just doesn't work. How do I tell her that what she wears is just bad to look at?!

Sari Says:

Talk to your friend about fashion and style. Ask her how she decides what to wear, and how she defines her style. Maybe she'll tell you that she loves to mix styles. If so, then back off and let her dress however she wants. She might be trying to express her individuality . . . and that is totally cool! If she likes the mix of styles, then it really doesn't matter whether or not you like it. If you are a good friend, you should let her be herself without imposing your ideas about fashion on her.

On the other hand, if she tells you that she does not have a clue about fashion and she usually just ends up throwing stuff together, then you can suggest some changes. Tell her what the trends are now, and let her know what you think would look good on her. Show her some fashion pages from teen magazines. Be nice to her, and be positive: Tell her some of the things that you like about her style, then try to help her find ideas for new outfits.

tattoo fashion statement

Dear Sari,

I am not sure, but I might want to get a tattoo to make a fashion statement. Is there any harm in it? How can I decide if I should do it?

Sari Says:

Do your research about exactly what you want to have done. You'll have to talk with people who have tattoos, as well as call a few tattoo parlors, to find answers to lots of questions, such as:

- Where can you go to get a good tattoo from an experienced tattoo artist who uses sterile instruments?
- How much will it cost?
- How do you take care of it right after you have it done so that it does not cause infection?

Then there are the questions you will have to answer for yourself:

- What design do you want?
- What size?
- Where on your body?

Make a long list of all of the reasons why you are sure that you will want to have this tattoo on you for the rest of your life! You will need much better reasons than "it will look cool" or "all my friends have them."

Remember, a tattoo lasts forever, so you are making the same fashion statement over and over. Yes, some tattoos can be removed by a doctor, but with difficult laser treatments. That's why, while you are considering if you want a tattoo, you might as well also call a dermatologist to ask how much laser removal costs and what kind of scar it would leave.

After you have gathered all this information, then try to decide. You could always decide that instead of a real tattoo, to make different fashion statements with different outfits, temporary tattoos might be the best way to go!

Tattoo Safety

If you are going to get a tattoo, you must be really careful to choose a place that is safe and clean. HIV, the virus that causes AIDS, as well as the hepatitis C virus, can be transmitted from sharing needles, such as the needles that are used to give a tattoo. Therefore, you must make sure that the tattoo artist uses all new needles on you. Tell him that you want to see him open the packages so you know that they are new.

you're no body till you love your body

Ask yourself: Do you love your body? If you immediately answered, "No way," then you're not alone. In fact, most teens have some issues with their bodies that keep them from really loving them. Your body has been changing so much on you lately, and it just might not be exactly what you had hoped for. Media images certainly don't help. TV shows aimed at teens show all gorgeous teen actors and actresses, with perfect skin, model physiques, and fabulous clothes. Well, that's just television and those are just actors. When they leave the studio and aren't being filmed by flattering camera lenses and don't have the use of makeup artists or wardrobe specialists, they probably go home and look in the mirror just like you do and say, "Ugh! Who is this ugly duckling looking back at me?"

Maybe you think you're too thin, or too fat, or too short, or too tall. Maybe puberty is doing wacked-out things to your physique, like making you bulge in certain places. Maybe you've suddenly sprouted a whole lot of new hair . . . down there. Or maybe your face has erupted into a volcanic acne factory. Or maybe everyone around you is going through changes and you have the same body you had in the fourth grade. Whatever your dilemma, in this chapter I'll help you get through a lot of those negative, insecure thoughts about these changes, so you can figure out the truth about your body, and get to the bottom of all your concerns about what is or isn't going on with it. You can learn to love—and understand—your body!

too skinny?

Dear Sari,
Everybody always tells me that I'm so skinny and it's really hurting me. Do you know how I could gain weight, or is there anything I could say to people?

Sari Says:
Being skinny can be tough, but we don't hear as much about it because more girls worry that they're overweight. Girls who are skinny either hear, "I wish I were thin like you!" constantly, or they are hassled about being so thin and have to defend what is natural for them.

No matter what you weigh, you should love your body! If your body is just naturally thin, try not to be upset about it or by what people say. Instead, try to think of all of the positive things about your body, like the fact that you can fit into a lot of great "skinny" clothes.

If you want to gain weight, you should talk to your school nurse or doctor about an eating and exercise plan that will help you put on some weight. Keep in mind that gaining weight is not always possible; at this moment in your life, your body might just want to stay at the weight it is now. If people bother you about it, you can nicely say, "This is just the way I am. Please don't hassle me about it." You can tell them that you are not anorexic and that you are very healthy, just thin. By the way, your body may change as you get older. After puberty, many girls gain some weight; during their twenties, women tend to gain weight again. So enjoy being thin now; your body may change on its own, later.

Dear Sari,

I'm a 16-year-old girl who is chubby. I weigh in at 170 pounds and I'm 5'2". People don't really tease me much anymore 'cause they say I am so likable to be around, which is a good thing, I suppose. But I still want to lose weight—not for other people, but for myself! I want to look in the mirror and just smile. Well, everyone says I'm pretty, but that's really not enough for me! Do you have any diet and exercise tips? I'd really appreciate it.

Sari Says:

I love that you wrote that you are so likable that people don't bug you about your weight—that is a great attitude. You know that what matters most is inside! But in terms of weight loss advice, I suggest that you talk to your doctor or school nurse. A medical specialist is the best person to put you on a diet and exercise program. Also, talk to your parents, because they should know what you want to do. Most girls and women struggle with food and weight issues for their whole lives. I advise anyone under age 18 not to diet on her own. (Sometimes when girls make up their own diet plans, they wind up overdoing it—like girls who starve themselves or throw up. That can seriously damage your physical and mental health for your whole life!)

You can eat healthier by eating more fresh vegetables and less junk food, such as candy bars, French fries, chips, and doughnuts. Beyond that, have a doctor, nurse, or at least a parent supervise you.

In terms of exercise, any physical activity is great. You could join a team sport, or club, to have the chance to get fit while having fun. Otherwise, ride a bike, or go for long walks, or swim, or whatever you like. The most important thing is that you feel good about yourself, no matter what you weigh. You should be able to look in the mirror and smile every day!

weight worries

Dear Sari,

I'm 15 years old and I wear a size 10. I have a little bit of fat on my stomach but not enough to hang out at all. I was just wondering if I'm overweight.

Sari Says:

Size ten is perfectly great. Women can be beautiful whether they're a size 4, 10, or 16. All that really matters is that you feel good about yourself. So stand up straight. Be proud that you look great—no matter what size or shape you are. By the way, even at age 15, your body will probably change a zillion times before you are a fully grown woman. So don't stress out about it. We all have to accept the joys and challenges of our bodies.

anorexia?

Dear Sari,

My best friend doesn't eat for days just to look good. She always says that she is fat and she is like way too skinny. She lost ten pounds in one week. My friends and I talk to her about it, but she doesn't listen. I am really worried. What should I do?

Sari Says:

Usually when a girl has an eating disorder, it is very hard to get her to get help. But your friend needs help. Take a look in the appendix of this book for the number for an eating disorder hotline. Encourage her to call to talk to someone who understands. Also, make sure that she knows that you love her, and you are always there for her, no matter what. Hang out with her a lot, to try to keep her happy and feeling accepted. Tell her that she is really beautiful, inside and out, and that she should not be hurting herself by starving. Also, give the same hotline numbers to her parents, and tell them that you think they should help her. If she still won't get help, talk to your school nurse or counselor.

General Signs of Anorexia Are:

- Losing a lot of weight quickly, such as 20 percent of the person's body weight (that would be like going from 120 pounds to 96 pounds in a couple of months).
- Menstrual periods stop altogether.
- Personality changes, such as aloofness, or a lack of interest in socializing.

too tall?

Dear Sari,
Does it matter to girls if a boy is a lot taller than the girl is?

Sari Says:
It does not matter to most girls if a guy is a lot taller. In other words, some girls will be attracted to you, and some will not—but this goes for any guy, whether he's tall or short. Just because you're tall doesn't mean that your experiences with girls will be different than any other guy's . . . as long as you feel confident and proud of your body and your height.

Face Matters

picking pimples

Dear Sari,
I guess I have what they call "pizza face." I have tons of zits, and I am obsessed with picking my pimples. Help!

Sari Says,

You need to treat your acne and stop picking at it. For treatment, first try stuff you can buy in any drugstore. Go to the section of the drugstore that has all kinds of acne treatments. You should get three things: 1) a soap that is intended for people prone to acne; 2) cleansing face pads with salicylic acid (like Stridex pads); 3) and cream with Benzoil Peroxide (like Oxy cream, but the vanishing kind, not the color-tinted kind). Follow the directions on the boxes of these products and use them as directed. At the same time, force yourself to stop picking your pimples. If you have to find a new behavior to do instead, then find something to do with your hands, such as writing, drawing, typing, even knitting, just whatever you can do to stop yourself from picking. Picking your pimples makes your acne look worse than it has to, and it may cause permanent scars. If you cannot stop picking, then you may need to see a therapist to teach you how to change this behavior. The desire to pick pimples could be related to anxiety that you need to try to resolve with professional help. Also, if your acne does not clear up with the drugstore treatments, or if your acne seems to have cysts that develop under the skin, instead of just pimples, then you must immediately see a dermatologist for professional treatment. Acne is treatable, if you take the steps needed to take care of it, or see a doctor to get specially prescribed products or medication.

what is accutane?

Dear Sari,

I have very bad acne, and to clear it up my doctor wants me to take pills called Accutane. My parents seem to think that I should not take it. How can I know who is right?

Sari Says:

Accutane can be a great medication for some people, because sometimes it can entirely clear up very severe acne for good if the person takes it for a period of about four to six months, as the doctor prescribes. However, Accutane is also a very strong medication, and can have side effects, including some or all of the following: painful skin dryness, mouth dryness, nose dryness, irritation of the eyes, joint and muscle pains, temporary hair thinning, headaches, decreased night vision, and it is even suspected to cause severe depression and thoughts of suicide in some cases. Also, it could affect a person's liver, so when on Accutane, people need to have their blood tested monthly. The most serious side effect of all is that if a woman gets pregnant while she is taking Accutane, the child would most likely have extremely severe birth defects, so doctors who prescribe Accutane also ask that women who are sexually active take birth control pills and use a second method of birth control. Some doctors ask that, before they prescribe the drug, the woman sign a statement agreeing that if she got pregnant while on the medication, she would have an abortion.

Because this is such a strong medication, your parents are right to be unsure if you should take it. Ask your parents if they would go to the dermatologist for a second time to discuss your medical options, or if they would see a new dermatologist with you for a second opinion. If a second doctor also thinks that Accutane is for you, then your parents may agree that you should take it. If they do not want you taking Accutane, there are other pills, such as antibiotics, that can be very useful to treat acne, and many creams and lotions that the doctor can prescribe to treat it as well.

nose job

Dear Sari,
I'm 17 and I hate my nose more than words can say. It is a gigantic honker. Do you think that it is a good idea for me to have a nose job?

Sari Says:

Teen plastic surgery is a touchy issue. On the one hand, if you know that you hate something about your body, then why not change it as soon as you can? But on the other hand, you are so young that what if in a couple of years you start to love that you have a unique nose? It can be ultra cool (and sexy) to have a large nose. I know many people who love seeing big noses, and who are attracted to people who have them.

While this decision should really be based on how *you* feel about your nose, not how others feel, it can be helpful to talk with people about it. To help you make your decision, talk with people who can give you an objective opinion: an adult family friend, relative, or counselor. Maybe someone else will help you see that your nose is really fine, and you just need to boost your self-esteem and love yourself exactly as you are.

If this is an issue of self-esteem, then try to get your mind off of your nose. Don't waste your time, or your mind, obsessing about one body part. When you walk into a room, your nose does not jump out at people. They just see you as a total person. Try to work on loving yourself and your body. Delay any thought about a nose job for at least a year, or even two years.

If after, say, two years, your self-esteem feels higher, but you still think that changing your nose is really the right thing for you, try to get as much information as you can about nose jobs: cost, the procedure, the success of the results, complications. If you still think that this is the best way for you to go, then talk with your parents about going to the doctors with you for a consultation. Take your time choosing a doctor; ask if you can meet some former patients. Also, see a therapist for at least a few sessions just to make sure that you are really making the right choice. Too many teens want to change things about their bodies, because they feel the normal self-consciousness that almost all teens feel. Surgery is not the remedy to insecurity.

Hair Down There

Dear Sari,

Are girls supposed to get rid of the pubic hair down there somehow? Before I have sex for the first time, should I get rid of the hair, or do the guys just kinda know it's there and not care? I wonder because I have not been naked with a guy yet, and I have a lot of hair.

Sari Says:

Everyone has pubic hair. (To be precise, everyone has pubic hair after puberty.) Some people have a lot, some only have a little bit. The fact is, it doesn't matter how much pubic hair a girl has—a guy should expect that she will have pubic hair and he should not care about it.

Pubic hair does not get in the way of sex play. Some women choose to trim their pubic hair for "personal hygiene" reasons: for example, when women have a lot of pubic hair, some of it might show around the edge of the bathing suit, so many of these women trim it. Also, hair often grows on the inside of the thighs or the "bikini area," as it is called, and some women shave (or wax, or use hair remover) on their thighs, so it won't show when they're at the beach or the pool. (If you want to do this, you might want to ask your mom or a close friend for advice and help—it can be tricky.) Beyond the issue of whether it's visible when you're wearing a bathing suit, you don't need to worry about your pubic hair. It's perfectly normal and natural. If you want to trim it, you can, but you don't need to.

Dear Sari,

Whenever I shave my bikini area, the next day, I get all these disgusting white bumps that get reddish, then go away. I feel trapped between having hair there and having those bumps. How can I shave there without getting bumps?

Sari Says:

Those bumps are usually caused by irritation to the hair follicles or by ingrown hairs. Most women who have thick or dark hair get these after they shave. There are a few tricks that you may want to try when you shave to reduce them.

First, before you shave, make sure the area is warm and moist by taking a warm shower and preparing the area to be shaven by applying shaving cream or shaving gel (not soap). Shave while you are still in the shower (just turn away from the water). Use a new razor blade that you have not even used once before. Shave in the direction that the hair grows, not against it. Do not overshave; remove the hair with one or two razor strokes. After you are done, rinse with warm water in the shower. Then when you get out of the shower and are toweling off, apply some corn starch powder (not talcum, not perfumed powder) to the area. The day you shaved, avoid wearing jeans, panty hose, tights, or anything that would rub against the area to irritate it. If redness or bumps start to appear, then twice a day apply a lotion that is supposed to help, like Bikini Zone, or any cortisone cream. Also, the next time you shower, gently exfoliate the area with a loufah. If these steps do not help, then ask a dermatologist for more tips.

Dear Sari,

I have had my period for two years, and I have only used pads. They are like wearing a diaper, and they are so inconvenient, because I can't do stuff like swim. But I hear that tampons are hard to use. Please help me figure out how I can use tampons.

Sari Says,

Tampons are actually easy to use, once you learn how. They can make your period so much easier. I highly recommend that you learn how to use them! Here are some tips that will help you:

- Use the smallest size tampon you can buy, such as Tampax brand's "Slender Regular," which are thinner than the "Regular," or try the Tampax "Lites," which are also smaller than "Regular."
- Read the directions from the box. They're very good, and if you read them over a few times it should help.
- Before you attempt to put the tampon inside you, take a close look at it so you know exactly what will be going inside you. Push the tampon through the applicator when you're holding it, just to get an idea of how the applicator works and what the actual tampon looks like. After you're done checking it out, throw it away—don't try to reuse it!
- Take a look at your vagina in a mirror, so you have a sense of where you'll need to insert the tampon.
- For first-time tampon inserters, some positions work better than others. Try standing with one foot on the floor and the other foot on the edge of something like the bathtub or toilet, so that one leg is bent and you are squatting a little. It might be easier to reach the entrance to your vagina if you tilt your pelvis up just slightly, too.

- Hold the tampon applicator at the entrance to your vagina, so that it is positioned as if you are going to push it into your vagina. It should be at a slight angle—as if you are aiming slightly up toward your middle back. Don't worry so much about getting it in just the right position. The main idea is just to find a way to get it in.
- From there, try sliding it in. As the tip of the applicator goes inside you, push the bottom of the applicator up to insert the tampon.
- Some women find it easier to insert a tampon into the vagina if they wet the entrance to their vagina a bit. Just a few drops—you do not want to get the tampon itself damp. Also, you need to keep your hands dry to be able to push the tampon through the applicator.
- Once the tampon is inside, you should not feel it. If it feels awkward, or if it hurts a little at the entrance to your vagina, that means the tampon is not in far enough. Take it out and try again with a new tampon. Practice makes perfect. After a few times, it will get easier.

One final note: Change your tampon at least every four to six hours, and at night, insert a new tampon before you go to bed and then remove it when you wake up. Also, I mentioned that when you start learning how to use tampons, you should use the smallest ones. However, once you get the knack of how to use them, then you should always use the absorbency of tampon that is right for your type of flow. If you have light flow, use a "regular" or a "lite" or "slender." If you have heavy flow, use a "regular" or "super." For more info read that package insert again.

period pain

Dear Sari,

When I get my period, I have so much pain, aches, and cramping that I don't want to do anything! It is really bad pain. Is there a way to make this better?

Sari Says:

I'm not a doctor, but I do know that one of the most common complaints gynecologists hear from girls and women is painful menstruation. Medically speaking, it's called "dysmenorrhea." Sometimes pain during your period is caused by muscle contractions in your uterus, and it feels like bad cramps. Other times, painful periods have more to do with the fact that there is a lot of blood in your pelvic area at that time, causing inflammation or congestion that can make you feel achy or swollen.

There are several ways to treat your problem. First of all, you should see a gynecologist. The doctor will examine you to make sure that your pain is only related to your period, and you are not having any other problems. If the doctor finds out that yes, in fact, this is dysmenorrhea, the doctor might prescribe medication for you. Sometimes the doctor will put a woman on birth control pills so that her periods are lighter. Or, the doctor may just prescribe anti-inflammatory pills to relax your muscles during your period, or suggest that you take over-the-counter medication such as Tylenol, Midol, or Motrin.

One thing that the doctor probably won't tell you: It is a scientifically proven fact that another way to relieve some of the pressure or pain a woman may feel during her period is masturbation! I know it sounds funny, but having an orgasm helps the uterus contract and relieve some of the congestion of blood. However, I am not suggesting that this is a substitute for medical treatment. You still need to see a doctor.

no period

Dear Sari,
I have never had a period in my whole life. I am 17. Is this normal?

Sari Says:
If you have never had a period, you should see a gynecologist. Sometimes

it is completely normal when a girl does not get her period until she is in her late teens, like you are. But other times it could mean that something is wrong. You should see a doctor to get checked out, just in case.

irregular periods

Dear Sari,
One month I didn't have my period, then the next month it was fine. But every now and then I seem to skip a period. I have never had sex, not even close. Is this a normal thing that happens to girls?

Sari Says:
It's normal for a girl to have irregular periods during the first few years. It sometimes takes a year, or two, or three for a girl's periods to occur regularly every month. Even after your period is regular, it's still not always a big deal if you miss one once in a while. Illness, diet, and stress are all factors that may affect whether or not you have your period on time.

However, once a woman is sexually active, she should see a doctor after missing one period. And whether you are sexually active or not, you must see a doctor if you ever miss more than three periods in a row.

It may help you to note in a calendar when you have your period each time; that way you can keep track of them and begin to predict when you will have your next one. For more information, talk to your doctor.

Breasts and Stuff

boob teasing

Dear Sari,

I like this guy and he's always saying what big boobs I have. My friend asked him if he likes me and he said yes, but I don't know if it's because of my boobs or not. I really don't know what to do about it, but I like him. Can you help me out at all?

Sari Says:
When a guy makes comments about a girl's breasts, it sometimes means that he doesn't see her as a person—just a body. (In fact, many people consider it harassment when a man makes unwelcome comments about a woman's body.)

If you do not know this guy very well, and you've never really talked to him about yourself, then he doesn't have any real basis for liking you except what he sees. That means he might only like you for the way you look. If you want to find out if there could be something between you two, try talking to him (but not about your body!). However, I wonder if you should be liking this guy at all. You'd be better off trying to find a guy who likes what's inside!

saggy breasts

Dear Sari,
I started getting my boobs when I was in fifth grade, and now I'm in high school and they're sagging. Is that not normal, and should I be worried about what my boyfriend will say if he sees them?

Sari Says:
It's perfectly normal for breasts to sag. In fact, it's beautiful! Everyone's breasts are different. Usually, small breasts are perky, and large breasts sag. But regardless of whether they're saggy or perky, small or big, they're all beautiful. Love yours, because they are a beautiful part of you! Someday when a guy sees them, he should love them as much as you love them.

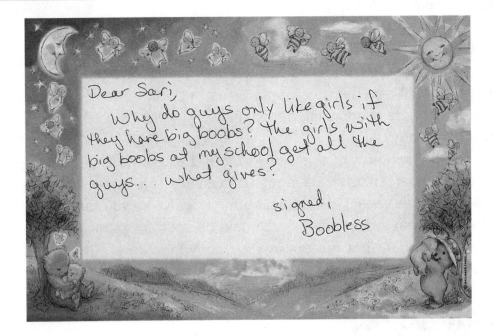

Dear Sari,

Why do guys only like girls if they have big boobs? The girls with big boobs at my school get all the guys.... what gives?

signed,
Boobless

Sari Says:

Not all guys only like girls with big breasts. Sometimes it seems that way, because in our society, there's an emphasis on big breasts as opposed to smaller ones. That's why so many Hollywood actresses get breast implants, and that's why there's a restaurant chain called "Hooters" but no restaurant chain called "Flat Chests." In middle school and high school, some guys like to brag about the girls they date, and so they might like dating a large-breasted girl to show off to their friends. However, that will change. As guys get older, they develop individual preferences: some go for large breasts, some for small. Most importantly, most men will tell you that they are not looking for a girlfriend "who has big breasts." Rather, they want to find someone who is simply confident, smart, fun, and pretty. Breast size does not matter. So feel good about yourself. Guys love confidence more than breasts.

new boobs

Dear Sari,
I'm an average 14-year-old girl. How big will my boobs get?

Sari Says:
There is no way for me to tell how big your breasts will get, even if I were looking right at you. Your breast size is determined by your genes: what your mom's breasts, your grandmother's breasts, and even your great-grandmother's breasts looked like. If all of the women in your family's history had a particular size of breasts, then you will probably have the same size as theirs. But then again, genes are tricky. Even if you study old family pictures, you still might be surprised. Really the only way to tell is to wait until you are fully developed. For some girls, this can be when they are as old as eighteen. So be patient. Enjoy all the changes that your body is going through. And remember, big or small, pointy or saggy, all breasts are wonderful!

breast cancer?

Dear Sari,
I'm not really sure, but I think there is something wrong with my breast. Near my nipple on the aureole is a white bump that is prominent. I can't stop worrying that it's cancer. I know breast cancer is rare in teenage girls, but it does happen. Can you please tell me how to do a self-examination?

Sari Says:
As you said, the chance that a teenage girl has breast cancer is rare, but possible. Most of the time breast cancer feels like a small hard lump under the skin of the breast. Your lump might just be the way the area around your nipple looks; it could be a harmless bump, since the aureole

125

can, in fact, be bumpy. However, I am not a doctor. I cannot determine what your bump is. You must go to see a gynecologist to have your breast examined.

Besides a yearly visit to a doctor who can check your breasts, it is recommended that all women also do a breast self exam once a month. Do this at the same time every month, preferably the week after your period ends, so your breasts are not swollen or tender. Here is how you do a breast self exam:

Lie on your back with a pillow under your right shoulder, and your right arm behind your head. For your right breast, use the three middle fingers of your left hand and press firmly to feel for any lumps. You should be pressing with the flat top third of your fingers, not poking with the tips. Start at the top, outer edge of your breast, then move in toward the nipple. Repeat, moving around the entire breast. Move your fingers using small circular motions, searching for lumps under the skin within the breast tissue. You will feel some glands inside your breast; you should be able to feel the same glands symmetrically in the two breasts. Cover all areas including the breast tissue leading to the underarm area. Repeat this with your left breast, by switching the pillow and arm position to your left side. Finally, gently squeeze each nipple to check that there is not any discharge. If you notice any problems, tell your parents and go to a doctor. If you feel a lump, it might not be cancer; it could be a harmless cyst or fibrous lump, yet you should still see a doctor to make this determination.

different sizes

Dear Sari,
Why is one of my breasts bigger than the other? Is this normal? Sometimes in clothes I can barely tell, other times, it looks terrible. What can I do?

Sari Says:

In many girls, one breast is slightly bigger than the other. This may balance out as your breasts fully develop, or they may stay different sizes for your whole life. In some women, one breast is actually a whole cup size different. Don't worry about it. It is just the way you are. You are probably best not doing anything to change the way it looks, because if you try you might make it more noticeable. However, if you feel very self-conscious about the way it looks when you wear tight clothes, like fitted T-shirts, then you can get a pad to put in the bra of the smaller side. Ask in any department store bra section for help with this.

inverted nipples

Dear Sari,

My nipples on both my breasts go in, instead of sticking out. *I hate it.* What is wrong with me? I can't stand having "innies."

Sari Says:

Inverted nipples are totally normal (about 10 percent of girls have them). They will come out when they are stimulated, like if your body feels cold or if you touch them, or (when you are sexually involved with someone) if the person sucks on them or rubs them. Also, someday when you have a baby, you will be able to breast feed.

The only thing that seems to bother some people who have inverted nipples is if they feel self-conscious about the way they look, especially when they are naked around someone. There is a surgical procedure that a plastic surgeon can do that may make your nipples come out for good. But the surgery does not guarantee that they will definitely stay out— some people have had this surgery and then the nipples go back in. Also, if you have the surgery, then you will never be able to breast feed. Since it would be expensive, may not work, and would prevent you from feeding your baby someday, it is probably best for you to just enjoy that you are different, rather than trying to change it. Think of it this way: Your nipples do more than some other girls', so there is more to play with! Try to learn to love them.

boy's boobs?

Dear Sari,

I am a 15-year-old male, 6'2", and I weigh 174 pounds. I am not fat; the problem is that most of the fat in my body is in my chest. I know it is strange, but it is true. I have been teased a lot by the guys and girls (I am called names like "titty boy," or I am asked what bra size I wear). This makes my dating possibilities with girls pretty slim. My mom and I have talked about surgery as a possibility, but it is expensive. I just want to know if there is any other way to get girls to notice me without noticing what other people say about me. Also, is there a way to get rid of this fat?

Sari Says:

First of all, when you meet a girl who doesn't join in on the teasing, and who likes you for who you are, then you have met a great girl. The guys and girls who tease you are jerks; they would probably find something to tease you about even if you didn't have a biggish chest. Do not get carried away by what other people tease you about. You need to focus more on feeling confident, rather than worrying about what you think other people think of your chest. Confidence is more attractive than anything anybody could possibly look like.

Often teens tease the person who will let them. You do not need to stand for the way they treat you. You are 6'2" tall! Next time they make a joke about your body, just look down on them, glare, then walk away feeling "above" them, rather than feeling hurt. Feel good about your other features: your height, your looks, your personality, whatever you like about yourself.

Regarding your build: Your body is going through so many changes right now because of puberty. Be patient with your body. Since you seem very worried about this, talk to a doctor or school nurse to see if they think it would be a good idea for you to get on an exercise program. I do not think that cosmetic surgery should be something that you are considering at this point; yet as you get older, maybe in five years, after your body changes, after you increase your self-esteem, then if it still bothers you, you can revisit that idea. For now, try to find friends who care about you, not your body.

Penis Concerns

making it bigger

Dear Sari,
I heard that it is really important to girls for guys to have a big penis. I am not sure if my penis is fully grown, but if it is, are there ways that I can make my penis bigger?

Sari Says,
After puberty, when you reach sexual maturity, the size of your penis is the size it will always be for life. Of course, a penis gets a bit bigger when it is erect (hard), and it may seem smaller when it is not erect, and especially smaller when you are cold or after you go swimming. But in terms of the general size, there is no way to change your penis. If you ever hear about lotions, pumps, or pills that are said to increase penis size, do not believe it! They do not work. Instead of worrying about the size of your penis, please learn to love it no matter how big or small it is. Penises of all sizes are great. Women don't really care about penis size. They care more that the penis is attached to a great guy!

cut or uncut

Dear Sari,
Hey, I was wondering how can I tell if my guy is circumcised. Help! I want to know this.

Sari Says:
Circumcision is the surgical removal of a boy's foreskin, which is a small loose piece of skin that extends over the head of the penis. It is removed when a baby is only a few days old. Once it is removed, the head of the penis is visible all the time. If a guy does not get circumcised, when his penis is not erect, the head is covered with this piece of skin. When an uncircumcised penis becomes erect, the foreskin rolls down past the head, so it looks about the same as a circumcised penis.

To give you a better idea of what the difference in appearance is between a circumcised and uncircumcised penis, consider this image. Of course, it is not exactly what it looks like, but you should get the idea: A circumcised penis looks kind of like a person wearing a turtleneck shirt, whereas an uncircumcised penis looks like the person rolled the turtleneck up over his head.

In America, circumcision is considered a standard practice in hospitals. Therefore, most guys born in this country have been circumcised. (In other countries, it is not as common as it is here.) Also, in the Jewish religion, it is required that boys be circumcised.

are blue balls for real?

Dear Sari,
When my girlfriend and I fool around (we do not have sex), afterwards, my balls really hurt. I have heard people call it "blue balls," but then I have heard other people say that "blue balls" doesn't really exist, and it is just a way that guys pressure their girlfriends. Which is it?

130

Sari Says:

Blue balls really does exist. When a person gets sexually aroused, more blood flows into the genitals. This rush of blood cannot quickly flow back to where it came from, so it causes a feeling of pressure, achiness, congestion, and general discomfort when it remains in the penis or testicles (balls) for a few hours. It will subside on its own, but if you want to relieve it quickly, the best way is for the man to have an orgasm.

Some guys do try to use this as a way to pressure a girl into having intercourse, oral sex, or giving him manual stimulation, but the fact is that a guy does not need sex to get rid of blue balls: he can masturbate when he is alone instead! By the way, when girls get sexually aroused and do not have an orgasm, they too can feel pressure and an achiness in their genitals because the situation with the blood flow is similar. Maybe we should call this "pink pelvis."

wet dreams

Dear Sari,
I am a 16-year-old guy, and I still have wet dreams. Is it normal that I still get them, and is there any way I can stop them?

Sari Says:

There is no need to lose sleep over wet dreams, especially at your age. Wet dreams (technically called "nocturnal emissions") are a way for your body to get rid of semen, since your body naturally produces too much of it to store it all in the testicles. As you get older, your body will adapt and you will not have wet dreams as often or at all. Although occasionally some guys have them when they are in their twenties or thirties. Guys usually find that if they masturbate, then they do not have wet dreams, because they are helping their body get rid of the semen. Plus, masturbating can be rather fun. So if the wet dreams are getting you down, then try masturbation.

testicular self-exam

Dear Sari,

Is it true that guys can get cancer in their balls? Should I worry about this?

Sari Says:

Testicular cancer is one of the most common types of cancer found in guys ages 15 to 34. You do not need to "worry" about it, but once you are about 15 years old, you should start giving yourself a self-exam once a month.

The best time to do the exam is when the scrotal skin (the skin on your balls) is most relaxed, such as after a shower. To do the exam, simply place the index and middle fingers of each hand under your testicles and your thumbs on top. Roll each testicle between your thumb and fingers, feel its weight and texture. Keep in mind that the testes are not the only thing inside the scrotum. There is a structure called the epididymis which is set at the back of the testes and will feel lumpy when you rub your testicles. Aside from the epididymis, your testicles should feel smooth. If you feel a hard lump, it's time to make an appointment with your doctor.

Girls' Sexual Health

vaginal discharge

Dear Sari,

I am a 15-year-old virgin, but I get this stuff in the bottom of my underwear. It's like creamy stuff; it looks like snot. It's gross. I always get this stuff; some times more than others. Is it normal? What is it?

Sari Says,

Girls have natural vaginal secretions that are normal, and may end up dried on their underwear, as you described. The amount, consistency, color, and odor of the discharge varies with the time of month; this is normal, too. This is just part of having a healthy vagina. The discharge is usually clear and colorless; but a heavier, or whiteish, discharge is normal, too.

Abnormal vaginal discharge, on the other hand, usually has a bad, fishy odor and an unusual color or texture (it could have the texture of cottage cheese, and be tinted yellowish or greenish). It may cause itching. This type of discharge may be the result of one of many types of vaginal infections—which can occur even if you are a virgin. If you have this kind of abnormal discharge, then you need to go see a doctor for treatment.

urge to pee

Dear Sari,

I've been having to pee sooo much more than usual lately. I feel like I had to go about a hundred times today. Do you have any idea what could be wrong with me?

Sari Says:

It's impossible for me to tell if there is anything wrong with you because I am not a doctor, and also, all I have to go by is your letter. I can tell you that the frequent urge to urinate sometimes means that someone has one of three things: either a sexually transmitted disease (STD), or a bladder infection or a urinary tract infection. If you have never been sexually active, you would not have a sexually transmitted disease. More likely, the problem could be an infection of your urinary tract, or an infection in your bladder. The good news is that most infections like these are very easily treated by medication that a doctor can give you. Of course, as I said, I cannot diagnose you. You could have something more serious than what I mentioned . . . or on the other hand, you may have nothing at all. Hey, it could just be that you've been drinking more water than usual! The bottom line: You should see a doctor about this as soon as possible.

First visit with a gynecologist

Dear Sari,

My mom is making me go to the gynecologist! It's my first time. What are they gonna do? And will they tell my mom I'm having sex? Or can they tell?

Sari Says:

Yay for your mom! Every girl should go to a gynecologist once a year—as soon as she starts having sex, or if she is over age 16 (whichever happens first). Unfortunately, not all moms tell their daughters that they have to go to a gynecologist, and not all girls feel comfortable asking their moms to take them . . . so they end up going on their own, or not going at all. It's great that your mom is doing this.

Seeing a gynecologist is really nothing to worry about. The exam itself only takes a couple of minutes and it's painless. Here's what happens.

When you go into the exam room, you are asked to take off all your clothes, and put on an exam gown. Then the doctor will examine your body in general—he or she will listen to your heart and take your blood pressure, for instance. Next the doctor will ask you to open the gown a little bit. He or she will take a look at your breasts and feel them to make sure they do not have any abnormalities. This only takes a minute; it's not embarrassing—it's very clinical and it's just part of the procedure.

After that, the doctor has you lie down on your back on an examination table, bend your knees up and put your feet in "stirrups," which are really just foot holders that help you keep your legs spread apart. You can cover your chest with the exam gown, but you'll be naked from the waist down so the doctor can examine your vagina. He or she will insert a gloved, lubricated finger inside your vagina to feel for any abnormalities. He or she will also gently push on your abdomen from the outside, to feel your uterus and ovaries. Then the doctor will take out his or her fingers and insert a "speculum" into your vagina. The speculum is a narrow metal instrument that holds the vagina open. It does not hurt, since there are few nerve endings deep inside the vagina. It can be used even if you are a virgin. By using the speculum, the doctor can examine your cervix (at the back of your vagina) to make sure there are no cervical infections. He or she also takes a Pap smear, which is a sample of cells to be tested for cancer. That whole vaginal part of the exam only takes one or two minutes. It is very simple and fast.

Then you can talk to the doctor about your health, your body, sex, birth control, pregnancy, AIDS, STDs—ask every question you may have. The doctor cannot really tell just by examining you whether you have had sex; however, I recommend that you tell the doctor that you're sexually active. That way, the doctor will know to talk to you about birth control and test you for STDs, if necessary.

Make sure that you tell the doctor that it's very, very important to you that everything you say stays confidential just between you and the doctor. If the doctor must make notes in the medical file that they keep about you, the doctor should keep that in a confidential area. The doctor should agree to that and shouldn't tell your mother.

say what?

Dear Sari,
I've heard that the gyno talks to you first and then does the exam. What do they ask you, and are your parents in the room?

Sari Says:

The basic questions that almost all gynecologists ask are:

- What was the first day of your last period?
- Have you noticed any unusual changes in the way your breasts look?
- Have you noticed any unusual pain or discharge in your vaginal area?
- Are you currently sexually active, or have you ever been sexually active?
- What method of birth control do you use?

These questions may vary a bit, but you get the idea. The doctor is not there to find out all the juicy details about your sex life. The doctor will talk to you in order to find out if you are in good general health, and to find out if you have any complaints or questions about your sex organs or your sexuality. That could include talking about some specifics of sex—if it is relevant to your health (such as if you are having vaginal or anal sex without using a condom, because that can put you at risk for STDs and AIDS).

Do not be afraid to talk to your doctor. Instead, take advantage of the fact that you can talk to your doctor! You are completely allowed to ask your parents to leave the room when the doctor examines you and talks to you. Also, your doctor should keep everything private, just between the two of you. But just in case, ask your doctor not to tell your parents what you talk about. Then ask your doctor *anything* about pregnancy, birth control, sexually transmitted diseases, even advice on how to decide if you are ready to have sex if you are a virgin. A good doctor will want to answer all of your questions.

Girls, Gynos, and Your Mom

All girls who are having sex at any age, or all girls who are 16 or older even if they are virgins, should see a gynecologist once a year. Because going to a gynecologist does not necessarily mean that you are having sex, you should be able to feel comfortable asking your mom if she can take you to her doctor for your first exam. An easy way to bring up the subject is by asking your mom when she had her first visit and suggesting that it may be time for yours.

Drugs and Your Body

effects of marijuana

Dear Sari,

I think it would be fun to get high on pot, but I'm scared. I would want to do it with some friends then spend the night at one of their houses so my mom wouldn't know. I think it will be a blast, but could I get addicted by trying it once? What are the risks?

Sari Says:

There are many reasons why you shouldn't smoke pot. One of the reasons is apparent just from what you wrote to me: You'd have to lie to your mom and sneak around just to try it. Doing drugs leads to lies—and right now you're already starting to create a web of lies. That's dangerous, and you might get caught.

As far as your questions about the risks, smoking pot one time could lead to an addiction, but it will not cause an addiction in the most literal sense of the word. What I mean is, if you smoke once, you won't wake up the next morning feeling an uncontrollable urge that you must smoke again, immediately. However, if you smoke once, you might feel like you want to smoke it the next time you are around these friends, and then the next time, and the next time . . . and soon you'll be addicted. Once you smoke around these friends, it might be tough to be around them later on and say "no" when they want to smoke.

Even after smoking it once, marijuana blocks the messages going to your brain and alters your perceptions and emotions, vision, hearing, and coordination. Chemicals in the drug (especially a substance called THC) flow into your brain and attach to places on certain nerve cells. This causes those areas of your brain to go through changes, and sometimes the changes can be permanent. The area that the THC affects the most is the area that controls memory. Smoking marijuana can mess up your short-term memory and your capacity to remember new things.

As you can see from the sidebar, pot has a ton of negative effects. Also remember that it's illegal. Just because your friends smoke it doesn't mean you have to. Make the decision for yourself.

Effects of Marijuana

Here is more information about the effects of marijuana, according to the National Clearinghouse on Drugs and Alcohol:

Short-term effects of Using Marijuana

Sleepiness; difficulty in keeping track of time and remembering things; reduced ability to perform tasks requiring concentration and coordination, such as driving a car; increased heart rate; bloodshot eyes; dry mouth and throat; decreased social inhibitions; paranoia; hallucinations.

Long-term Effects of Using Marijuana

Enhanced cancer risk; decrease in testosterone levels for men; also, lower sperm counts and difficulty having children; increase in testosterone levels for women (the "male" hormone); also increased risk of infertility; diminished or extinguished sexual pleasure or sexual performance; psychological dependence and addiction requiring more of the drug to get the same effect; impaired or reduced short-term memory.

ecstasy experience

Dear Sari,

I want to try the drug Ecstasy. Don't try to talk me out of it, because I know what I am doing. Well, once you answer this, that is: What effect does Ecstasy have on the brain?

Sari Says:

I would rather talk you out of it, and here's why: The effect that Ecstasy has on the brain and body can be serious and life threatening. (Drugs like this are illegal for good reasons!)

First let me explain the general effect it would have on you. Ecstasy affects the levels of a brain chemical called serotonin, so that you feel happy and high for about four hours when you are on the drug. But Ecstasy uses up serotonin, and it takes time for the levels to get back to normal, so for a day or two after you'd feel tired, depressed, irritable, or moody. Also, while on the drug, Ecstasy causes elevated blood pressure, and it causes your body temperature to rise. Some of the tragic accidents that people have had while on the drug were caused because they were dancing vigorously while on Ecstasy and drinking alcohol, so they became dehydrated, overheated, passed out and injured themselves, or they actually put themselves into a coma. While it is not known if Ecstasy is physically addictive, tolerance builds up to the positive effects of the drug, while negative effects increase with increased use, so the more people use it, the more they need, and the more dangerous it becomes. Long-term effects of the drug may include constant paranoia, liver damage, and heart attacks, and it has produced brain damage in scientific research on rats and monkeys. If you are sure that you are going to take this risk, then no one can stop you, but whatever you do, be careful. If you insist on trying any drug, you must be in a safe environment with people you know well and trust, including some people who are stone-cold sober. Also, you must fully acknowledge beforehand the serious risks, and the illegality.

Other Serious Body Issues

Fear of touching

Dear Sari,
I like guys and I am a 16-year-old girl. I get uncomfortable and won't let anyone touch me though. I have no self-esteem at all and I am so afraid they are always going to like think I am a bad kisser, or they will see how fat I really am. I was never abused or anything, so it has nothing to do with that. I am almost 17 and it is really driving me crazy. I am afraid I am always going to be like this and never be able to have a boyfriend.

Sari Says:
I am so glad that you are writing to me, because this is something that you need to work on. You are capable of having someone touch you and love you. You just need to learn how to let someone. You see, when someone touches you or kisses you, he will not be thinking about your weight, or the way you kiss. He *will* be thinking that he is very excited and privileged to get to touch you! You have to start realizing that.

In order to work on your self-esteem, say out loud to yourself, "I am a good person. I am worthy of good things in my life. I deserve to get love and affection." Repeat this until you start believing it.

Being able to be loved and touched is something that you learn. Most people learn it from the affection that their parents give them when they are kids. Kids who did not get a lot of hugs (or who were abused) often have issues with receiving affection. You can try to get affection now from your friends to help you get used to it. Ask a friend for a hug, just to feel it every once in a while. Also, if you don't have a pet, consider getting one. If you really like animals, and your parents would allow you to have a cat or a dog, that would be perfect. Otherwise, ask if you can at least get a small animal—such as a hamster or guinea pig. A pet needs you to touch it. By petting an animal, it becomes easier to think of touch as something that is a necessity to give and receive. Pets often help people get over this sort of block against giving affection. You have more work to do beyond that, however. To work on your body image issues and insecurity, you might benefit from seeing a therapist. Ask the guidance counselor at school to refer you to someone who might be able to help. You can overcome this, and someday you will have a boyfriend!

Friend cuts herself

Dear Sari,
I have a really good friend who cuts herself on her arms when she is depressed. What should I do?

Sari Says:
Your friend needs help. Cutting, sometimes called self-mutilation or self-injury, is a serious disorder—it involves a depressed or unbalanced person cutting, scratching, or burning himself or herself (most often on the arms or legs). It usually causes wounds deep enough that they bleed and scar, and it can leave permanent damage. The illness can be related to other disorders such as anorexia, bulimia, obsessive-compulsive disorder, and suicidal tendencies.

People who cut themselves may not understand exactly why they do it. Often it is related to their inability to express their feelings, or a depression so deep that they say they can't feel anything emotionally, so they want to hurt themselves physically. Or the person may have been abused and feel guilty about it, so he or she cuts as a means of self-punishment.

Cutting not only causes serious physical harm, it also makes psychological problems worse.

Your friend desperately needs help. Her parents need to know what she is doing, and she needs to see a medical doctor, as well as a psychiatrist. If she does not believe you when you tell her that she needs help, then you need to talk to her parents. For more information and a hotline number, look in the appendix in the back of this book.

totally crushing

You are walking down the hallway at school on the way to your locker. Suddenly, your head feels light and your heart begins to pound out an unnamed rhythm that echoes between your ears and drowns out the chatter of your friends walking beside you. Beads of sweat trickle down your forehead as your body begins to feel like a furnace, while simultaneously your hands become clammy and tundra cold. Your breath catches in your throat and you have the sensation of tiny, little needles being pricked into your skin all over your body. What *is* this? Too much caffeine? The flu? Bora-Bora disease? Well, not exactly. You are demonstrating classic symptoms of *chrushus amorus*. In other words, Cupid's arrow has taken aim at your poor, unsuspecting heart and you've got it bad, my friend.

But why is it called that? Crush. It doesn't sound too positive, does it? Let's do a little word association—what does crush make you think of? Smashed. Mashed. Trod upon. Broken into a million itty-bitty pieces. It certainly doesn't sound like it's going to end well. But that's the thing about crushes: They come as quickly as they go. (Or at least they should!) Sometimes they leave you with a broken heart—but other times they make you feel better than you ever imagined possible. The bad news is the outcome is a gamble—but the good news is I'm here to help you!

crush vs. love

Dear Sari,

I just wanted to know, is two weeks too early to tell if you really love someone?

Sari Says:

When you feel like you love someone after only knowing him or her for two weeks, that usually isn't love. That's more like a crush, or puppy love, or lust. A crush feels like an amazing sugar rush. All you can think about is this person, and everything about him or her seems perfect.

But a crush can also make you feel insecure, jealous, and afraid that the person does not like you as much. Real love is not like that.

Love evolves after months, or even years, of getting to know someone deeply. It is a calm feeling. When you are in love, you feel happy, and the feeling adds joy to your life, rather than turning it upside down.

After two weeks, you can't really know what kind of a person this one is—all you know is how the person acts at the beginning of the relationship, and that's sure to change! If you want, you can tell yourself that you have a big crush, but don't fool yourself into thinking that it's real love until you have been in a relationship with this person for a few months or longer. By the way, many couples first say "I love you" after about three to six months of going out, but some couples wait even longer.

crush on best friend

Dear Sari,

I have a crush on my best friend. How do I tell him?

Sari Says:

Well, are you sure you should tell him? If you tell him, and he says he does not feel the same way, then you might be putting the friendship in jeopardy. I think you should give it more time—maybe another month or two—to see if you really want to tell him. If you do decide to tell him, try to be kind of casual about it, like: "You know, I like you so much. Do you think we could ever be more than just friends?" That way you won't freak him out with a major declaration of your *love*.

star crush

Dear Sari,
I am so in love with Matthew Perry from *Friends* that I can't think about anything else. I have pictures of him all over my room. Thinking of him makes me so happy, but then I get sad and cry and cry. Is something wrong with me?

Sari Says:
No, there is nothing wrong with you. You just have a major crush on good ol' Chandler. It is totally normal. How can any girl resist those big brown eyes and that goofy smirk? But since your crush has gotten so severe that it makes you feel sad, then it is time to snap out of it!

Give yourself a reality check. You do not really know Matthew Perry. You just see a character that he plays on TV. Matthew is a good actor who has great writers writing awesome one-liners for him on *Friends*. Chandler does not really exist. If you start obsessing about Chandler, just remember those silly-looking sweater vests that he wore in the first few seasons of *Friends* . . . yuck. Or if you start obsessing about Matthew, remember that you will be much better off finding a guy who is your age who you can really get to know. I promise that you will be much happier if you start to like a guy who you can actually talk to, rather than one who is just taped to your wall. Good luck mellowing out the crush.

Struggling with a Mad Crush

I'm 18 years old and have a really mad crush on this guy in my high school. He's really smart, on the football team, and is majorally popular. I haven't been in a lot of his classes because he is so smart. I was in his Art and Math class and used to follow him ~~to him~~ to the bathroom just so I could look at him walk down the hall. He sometimes looks at me when he's not with his friends but don't think ~~to~~ it means anything. I'm really shy in school, and don't want to make a fool of myself. What should I do?

Sari Says:

I just went to my high school reunion, and there I ran into a guy I'd had a big crush on in high school. I told him that all those years ago, I used to like him, and he told me that he had liked me, too! Then he said, "If you had told me that you liked me when we were in high school, maybe we could have dated back then!" Based on that experience, I give you the following advice: Find a way to talk to this guy and try to ask him out. This would mean that, first of all, you need to stop following him around. Talk to him the way you would talk to anybody. Get over your obsession with him by acting normal around him. Then you will see if you can ask him out.

sister's boyfriend

Dear Sari,

I have a crush on my sister's boyfriend. They've been going out for two years and he likes me. What do I do, Sari?

Sari Says:

It totally makes sense that you would like your sister's boyfriend, because you and your sister probably have more than a few things in common. But the unspoken "sister rule" is that you should keep your hands off of her man. Try not to spend time around them. Go out with your friends when your sister and her boyfriend are hanging around the house together. Get over your crush so you can meet a guy of your own!

liking your friend's crush

Dear Sari,

My best friend has a crush on a guy, and I think they look so cute together. But her crush likes me, and I don't like him. We're all good friends so she knows that he likes me more. I don't want to hurt his feelings or anything but I feel weird now. What can I do?

Sari Says:

The next time you are alone with the guy, tell him you think he's a great friend, but you don't like him more than as a friend. That should clear things up.

Also, to help this love triangle resolve itself, let your best friend and this guy spend time together without you. For example, if the three of you are planning on hanging out, tell them you don't feel like hanging out—right before you're supposed to meet them. Encourage them to go ahead and hang out without you. Maybe that time alone together could help a romance blossom.

crush overheard

Dear Sari,

My problem might sound funny, but the guy I have a crush on overheard me talking to my friend about my "Aunt Flo," and now he makes fun of me. Before this, I was sure that he liked me, because he told one of my friends that he liked me. What should I do?

Sari Says:

For anyone wondering who the heck Aunt Flo is: Aunt Flo is slang for getting your period—your menstrual flow, get it? That's what is meant by "getting a visit from Aunt Flo." When this guy overheard you talking about your period, he probably felt embarrassed—that's probably why he's teasing you about it. It made him feel uncomfortable, so then he tried to make you feel uncomfortable in return. However, I don't think he will keep this up forever—in a week or two, he will move on to something else. If you want to get him to cut it out now, though, try talking to him about other things. Maybe then he'll realize that he should stop making fun of you and that he can just be cool with you and have a normal conversation.

Don't worry about this affecting whether or not he likes you. I am sure that he still likes you—if he didn't, he wouldn't have bothered to tease you in the first place. Teasing is a way of flirting, so this "Aunt Flo" incident might actually be a good sign.

footsie with crush

Dear Sari,
My crush flirts with me, but when I asked him out he said no. He even played footsie with me. Please help!

Sari Says:
Sometimes a flirt is just a flirt. This guy obviously likes flirting with you, but does not want to date you. Maybe he just isn't ready to start dating you and he'll come around in a few weeks or months. Maybe he just likes having you to goof around with at school and that's it. Whatever the deal is, if you like flirting with him, then keep it up. As long as it's fun for you, then enjoy it. Ask him out again in a month to see if he says "yes." If he keeps saying "no," then see how you feel. Eventually, there may be some good reasons to stop flirting with him: 1) if he gets on your nerves, 2) if you start obsessing all the time about why he won't go out with you, or 3) if you meet someone else you like. If any of those things happen, then tell him to leave you alone and end your flirtation.

the devil made me do it

Dear Sari,

I have a huge crush on this guy, but I don't know if he likes me, because he calls me "devil woman." Is this a sign of flirtation? Should I ask out my crush, or does he think I'm a loser?

Sari Says:

If a guy goes to the trouble of making up a nickname for you, he probably likes you. Of course, it's tough for me to tell. If he's calling you "devil woman" in a cute, sexy, teasing kind of way, as in "you're devilishly delightful," then that's flirting. But if he's calling you "devil woman" as in, "stay away from me," then you should take the hint and find someone else. If you sense that he's flirting with you (he smiles nicely when he calls you this, makes it a point to touch you when he's around you, etc.), you should definitely ask him out!

How to Stop Obsessing

If you can't think of anything besides your crush, then you need to get over it. Every time you think of your crush, tell yourself to stop, then think of something else. Do anything to get your mind off of your crush. Hang with friends, join a club, go to a movie, whatever you can think of to get over it!

will he call?

Dear Sari,

My friend gave my number to my crush and told him to call me. Well, now it's one month later, and he still hasn't called. Do you think he will ever call? A friend of mine said I should call him, but he never gave me his number. I can get it from his friend—but if I call him, I don't want him to get mad at me. What should I do?

Sari Says:

If a guy has your number for a month and he still hasn't called, chances are he's not going to call. It's not a good idea to use a go-between (your friend), anyway. In the future, you should go up to the guy yourself! Then after you talk for a few minutes, ask him if you can "exchange numbers." That means you'll have his number and he'll have yours—so you can call him if he doesn't call you after about a week. As far as what to do next about your crush: Forget about him for now, until you run into him again. Then when you see him again—if you still think you like him—talk to him yourself and exchange numbers.

crutch crush

Dear Sari,
I met this guy in eighth grade, and we're now both in tenth. I've liked him for so long, and he knows it. I know that liking him only hurts and disappoints me, but I just can't seem to ignore or get rid of the feelings I have for him. I don't know if I should continue to pursue a romantic relationship with him, or if I should forget it?

Sari Says:
You've admitted that having a major crush on this guy for the past two years hurts you, so what do *you* think you should do? You should get over the crush! Do whatever you can to stop thinking about this guy. Of course this will not be easy, because you have become so used to having the thought of him in your mind. Your crush has become a "crutch"—that is, a way for you to occupy the part of your mind that wants to feel romance but has not yet found a real relationship. Now is the time to let the crutch go. You have to force yourself to stop thinking about him. Every time you think about him, tell yourself "*stop*." Also, make a big effort to meet new guys. The only way you will open yourself up to meet someone new—someone who may actually like you as much as you like him—is to clear your mind of your old crush. In fact, I bet that over time you'll meet a new guy, and you'll realize that you like him way more than you ever liked this crush.

crush on teacher

Dear Sari,

I have a huge crush on my teacher. He seems to flirt with me. I thought it was in my imagination, but now I know it is not! Three times this week he has asked me to hang out in his room to talk with him alone about personal stuff during my lunch period. Is this bad?

Sari Says:

Yes, the fact that he encourages you to spend time alone with him talking about personal things is wrong.

If you have a harmless crush on a teacher, that's not such a big deal. Lots of people like their teachers, and even daydream about them, but they would never dream of really flirting. Since you have taken this to the level of flirting, this is not good. More importantly, since your teacher is flirting with you and inviting you to hang out with him alone, he is crossing a boundary. You need to stop being alone with him, and if he doesn't stop flirting, then please talk with your parents or your guidance counselor about it immediately.

the dating game

You have the ticket in your hand. You have been standing on line for this roller coaster ride for what seems like forever and a day. You see the entrance getting closer and closer as you inch forward. You stand there, watching everyone else having what looks like a great time. Finally, it's your turn. You are escorted to your seat, locked in, and *whoosh!* You're off! You are hurtled up and down, round and round, and you scream and feel sick and excited all at once. You've never experienced anything like it in the world, and as soon as the ride pulls to a stop, you want to do it all over again, even though you're shaking and dizzy and think you're going to puke.

This, my friends, describes dating to a tee. Just like a roller-coaster ride, dating can be the most fun in the world . . . or it can be totally traumatic. It's one part bravery, one part self-esteem, and a pinch of throwing caution to the wind. Are you afraid to ask anyone out? At a total loss about what to do when you go on a date? Well, you're not alone. But look, dating does not have to be so tough. Remember, just like a roller-coaster ride, the best part about dating is having fun. And, if you're really lucky, falling in love.

Dear Sari,

I'm 16 and I have never had a boyfriend in my life. My friends think that girls are nerds if they don't have boyfriends. None of them know about me yet, but they will figure it out. That's one problem, but the bigger problem is I can talk to guy friends, but if it's a guy I really like, I won't go near him.

PLEASE HELP ME!

Sari Says:

Don't worry—you haven't had a boyfriend yet simply because you haven't met the right guy. It *will* happen. It just takes time. No matter what your friends say, the truth is that there are lots of people who never dated or had boyfriends in high school. Then once they got to college, or just got a little older, they have tons of guys chasin' 'em down. Even I didn't have a real boyfriend until my senior year of high school. I promise you that you won't always be a solo act.

If you need help talking to guys, then this tip may help: When you see a guy you like, try to trick yourself into treating him just like you'd treat a guy who you don't like as much. Walk up to him, and say over and over in your head (not out loud!), "this guy is not any different from any other guy, I just want to say 'hi' to him the same way that I talk to my guy friends." Psych yourself into thinking that this is not a big deal. Developing a relationship with a guy is not all that different from developing a friendship with a guy, and since you have guy friends, that should be no problem.

Finally, do not worry about what your friends think. You'll date when it is your time. If they say anything to you, just tell them that you are picky and you do not want to go out with anybody who is not really terrific. In the meantime, don't worry so much about dating. Have fun with those guy friends of yours, instead. Who knows—maybe you will even start liking one of *them*.

First date locales

Dear Sari,

Where is a good place for a first date? I am looking for somewhere that isn't uncomfortable and doesn't require much talking.

Sari Says:

The best place for a first date actually *is* a place where you will be talking! On a first date, you should try to get to know each other a little bit.

Yet if you're not a big talker, then you may want to go somewhere where you don't have to try too hard to come up with conversation. A restaurant would be a tough place for you for your first date, because all you'll have to talk about is yourself and your life, and maybe a little about the food. However, if you go bowling, or shopping, or ice skating, or to an amusement park, then you can talk about what you are doing, or people watch, and talk about everyone else. More ideas: You could go to a cool interactive science museum that has lots of activities for you to do together. Go to see a sports event, so then you could talk about the game. You could go to the zoo and talk about the animals. Of course, there's always the old standby—the movies, then dinner! The great thing about a movie–dinner date is that it helps ease you into being together without too much initial talking, and then afterward, you have a sure-fire piece of conversation: the flick! What ever you choose, pick something that you feel comfortable doing; places where you know what to expect. It will be easier to talk when you feel relaxed.

almost ready to date

Dear Sari,
My mother just told me that she thinks I am old enough to date. I have been waiting for this almost all my life, but now I am nervous. Could you give me advice on how to make a first date work out?

Sari Says:
Congrats on being allowed to date! However, keep in mind that just because you have permission, that doesn't mean you have to date anyone yet. All this means is that if someone asks you out, you now have the option of saying "yes," or if you like someone, you can ask him out. So don't put so much pressure on yourself to start dating. Just let it happen.

As far as making your first date work, it's mostly about being yourself and *relaxing*. All you should try to do on a date is have fun. If you get really stressed out because it is a d-a-t-e, your nervousness will show, and could make things awkward. If you get nervous, tell yourself, "I'm just hanging out with someone, that's all. No big deal." Repeat that in your head until you mellow out.

Also, to help the date go smoothly, plan what you want to do ahead of time. Before you go out, talk with your date about what you'd like to do together. That way you won't spend the whole date saying, "What do you want to do?" "I don't care . . . what do you want to do?"

What to Talk About on a Date

When you're on a date, talk about things you and your date have in common, and ask each other what you want to know about each other's lives. Such as: what kind of music, TV shows, and web sites you like; what books you've read; your favorite hobbies or sports; after-school jobs or activities; how many people are in your family; school; movies; stuff like that.

Asking Someone Out

conversation starter

Dear Sari,
I like this guy. It seems like he likes me, but I'm not sure. I need to find out! I need a good conversation opener. I really want to tell him I like him, and maybe ask him out. Please tell me what to say to him.

Sari Says:
There are some great opening lines that you can use to start a conversation with a guy you like. Sometimes the best thing to say is something really natural, like: "Hi, my name is _____. What's your name?" You could try to be chatty about something that you and he might have in

common. For example, you can go up to him and say, "Hi. We're in the same grade, right? I noticed you in my English Literature class. What do you think of the teacher?" Or you could try this one: "Hey, I was wondering if you could give me a guy's opinion on something. All my friends think that (say the name of a band) is a cool band. What do you think of them?" Whatever you do, don't start the conversation by telling him how much you like him. Even if he has noticed you too, that might be too forward and scare him off since you don't know each other yet. Just be nice, say some friendly things to him, and he will figure out that you like him. Once you get a conversation going, you can ask him if he wants to go out to the movies, or even just hang out after school one day. If he likes you, he'll let you know by saying "yes" to your offer to hang out. Be brave. It will be worth it.

ask again?

Dear Sari,
I know this girl and I asked her out, she said she does not want to go out with me now. Should I ask her out again, or would I seem desperate?

Sari Says:
Well, that depends. Does she have a boyfriend? She may have said no because at the time she was seeing someone. Is she allowed to date? Maybe she said no because she's not allowed to go out with guys alone yet. Before asking her again, you might want to see if you can sleuth around and find out the answers to these questions. Also, if you just asked her recently (within the last month, let's say), you might want to wait a bit. You could seem like you're coming on too strong if you are relentless. But it is flattering when a guy tries to get the girl he wants. If you ask her a second time, you will just seem really into her, not desperate. So ask her again. If she says "no" again, then get over her. Twice is okay;

even if she doesn't think you're desperate, three times will make you feel like you are.

picture perfect

Dear Sari,

There is this girl I really like at my school, but I think she'll never go for me because, frankly, she is perfect. I mean, this girl is a model and actress who has been on TV and in magazines. She has always been really nice to me and I was thinking of asking her out, but I am afraid she will say no because she can do better. What should I do?

Sari Says:

You should definitely ask her out! Since she seems to like you, she might say "yes." But if she says "no," you can handle it . . . it's not such a big deal. You have to at least give it a shot. As far as your thinking that she can "do better," that's nonsense. No girl is too good for you, and no girl is perfect. Just because she models and acts doesn't mean she should only date a movie star! All she probably wants is a nice guy who will treat her well. Don't miss out. Ask her out.

serious about second date

Dear Sari,

I went on a date last night and it was really fun. I want to go for a second date, but I don't know when I should I call. The night after the first date or the week after? It would help if you could also tell me what to say.

Sari Says:

Some people have hard and fast rules on this particular dilemma. "No calling for at least three days, or six days, or one week!" That's just silly.

Call the person whenever you are thinking about him or her. The day after is fine, if you just want to say that you had a great time. If you have lots of other things going on in your life right now, you can wait a few days. Don't wait more than a week, or your date might think you lost interest.

As far as what to say, you've got an easier opening for a second date than for the first—you can say you had a great time on the first date and want to know if he or she would like to go to (the movies, skating, the park, a dance, or wherever you pick) next weekend. For the rest of the conversation, here are a few things to talk about: something funny you saw that made you think of him or her; follow up on some topic that you talked about on the date; what has been going on in your life since the date. Make the conversation natural, like you're talking with a friend, and you should be able to get that second date.

Who Pays on a Date?

Even at this point in time, there is *still* confusion over who should be flipping out the bills when it comes to paying the check on a date. The best rule of thumb to follow is if you asked, you should expect to pay. However, if you are the askee, it's always polite to offer to throw down some cash and not make assumptions. You can also make "deals" with each other. If your date refuses to take your money, you can offer to pay for something else later. Say something like, "Okay, but I'm getting the popcorn and soda at the movie!" If you are splitting the bill at a restaurant, remember to factor in the tip: Gratuity is at least 15 percent of your check.

playing hard to get

Dear Sari,
There is a guy I like more than I've ever liked anyone. I know he is going to ask me out, but I don't know if I should say "yes" because I want him to really, really want me for a relationship. Should I play hard-to-get games?

Sari Says:

If you don't take a chance on this guy, you'll never know if he wants to be in a relationship with you. Playing games definitely won't help you find out that information, either. If you play hard-to-get, you might not get him. And also remember that relationships take time to form. If he asks you out and you say "yes," try to be cool. You can't predict the future, and you shouldn't try to force it on him either. That's a sure-fire way of making him *not* want to form a deeper relationship with you. Say "yes" if he asks you out. The only way to start a relationship is based on mutual interest and honesty—not on game playing. You like him, so act naturally; don't jerk him around.

now what?

Dear Sari:

I recently met this girl, and we flirted and we found out that we have things in common. I know that she's interested in me and I am definitely interested in her, but I am afraid to ask her out. I'm always interested in long-term relationships, and I worry that if she's not then I will get hurt. How can I keep her as a steady girlfriend?

Sari Says:

There's no magic love potion to guarantee your future with this girl. You have to work with what you know: She likes you and she is giving you all the signals that she wants you to go out with her. So, ask her out. Do not worry about what will happen if you get into a relationship. Just decide what you want to do on your first date with her. Take this one step at a time. Any time your mind jumps ahead, pull yourself back to today and to reality. The only way to make a relationship last is to allow it to develop gradually. Just be decent, kind, and above all, your wonderful self. If it doesn't work out, she wasn't the girl for you.

What a Disaster!

It goes like this: I know this guy, Mr. All-that, and he and I dated for a while. I really liked everything about him, from his personality to his body. After a while of calling me non-stopped, he never called again. At first, I thought that Mr. All-that must be busy and he would called later, but he didn't.

A couple of weeks later, a group of my friends and I decided to go out and who did we run into, none other than Mr. All-that. As the night progressed, Mr. All-that was all over my BESTFRIEND! I was devastated! However, I knew my bestfriend didn't like him, because she likes Mr. Grunge, but Mr. Grunge has been calling me and asking me out, lately. I know that he, Mr. Grunge, likes me, but sadly I am hung on Mr. All-that. No matter how hard I try I can't get Mr. All-that out of my head even when I am with Mr. Grunge, but most of all I do not want to hurt my bestfriend! Yiks! What should I do

— Confused Love

Sari Says:

You should always go with the guy who likes you as much as you like him. It sounds to me like neither Mr. All-that nor Mr. Grunge fit that description. One likes you, and you aren't interested in him, and the other you like, but he's over you. Therefore, try to forget about both of them! Tell this to your friend, too, because she's in the same boat. Try to find a new Mr. who likes you back.

dating on the job

Dear Sari,

I started working at a retail store. One of the store managers recently caught my eye. He is not the manager of the department I work in (I work in juniors, he manages home life). I have never talked to him, basically because I don't think he will get involved with an employee. He's not much older than I am (my mom would approve), and I think he may be single. So should I give it a shot and try and talk to the guy, or just keep things easy and back off?

Sari Says:

Many people meet their significant others at work. If the manager is single, not more than a couple years older than you, and not in your department, and if your store does not have a policy against it, then he's fair game. (If any of those conditions were not true, it would probably be a mistake.)

Try to get to know him better, but take it slowly. See what it feels like to talk to him at work. Stay friends for a while. If it feels good, then maybe you can do things together outside of work. Start with something small, like going for a walk after work. If it seems okay after a month or so, then it might be all right to take it to the next step and really date him. Make sure that you keep it quiet, though. If everyone at work knows, it could get messy. Also, be careful that your feeling for him doesn't get too intense—imagine how bad it would be to date him, then break up. You'd still have to deal with him at work every day. Don't let messing around at work mess up your job.

hanson heartache

Dear Sari,

I totally loved the band Hanson, until I met a guy at school—and boy did we hit it off! He is very cute, but doesn't look anything like Taylor (the cute one in Hanson). I still like Hanson, but not nearly as much as I used to. I want to go on a date with the guy from school, but I don't know if I should, because I feel bad about Hanson! What do I do?

Sari Says:

Just because you like Hanson doesn't mean that you can only like guys who have long blond hair and say, "Mmmm," a lot. It's fun and exciting to have a crush on a celebrity; however, it's much more important for you to go on a date with a real guy. Taylor Hanson would not be good enough for you, since he would not be available for you to date. Your guy from school sounds great!

Don't feel bad if you start to like Hanson less; crushes usually fade when you start dating someone. As long as you still like Hanson, listen to their music, and keep their posters on your wall. When you stop liking them, simply take down the posters and don't feel guilty. Someday, you might have a picture of a real boyfriend to put up there instead. Celebrities are exciting, but a real guy really rocks!

best friend's crush

Dear Sari,

My best friend likes this guy who is going to ask me out. What should I do? I really like this guy but I love my friend and don't want to hurt her.

Sari Says:
You should talk to your friend right now. Tell her yourself that this guy likes you, so she doesn't hear it from someone else. Before you go out with him, ask her if she will be okay with it. Tell her that your friendship is more important to you, and you don't want to upset her. Try to be mellow when you talk about it—downplay the whole thing—but be honest. Make sure she understands you are not doing this to hurt her, you are just curious to see what it's like to hang with this guy. If she's really hurt and upset, you might want to back off. She may come around when she has a little time to realize that your happiness makes her happy, too.

short and sweet

Dear Sari,

I'm going out with this one guy. He's really cute, sweet, and everything, but he's shorter than I am by like four inches. I really like him a lot, and I don't want people to tease us, even though I already know they will (we started dating like a week ago). Should I just ignore the other people? Is there anything wrong with going out with a guy who's shorter than you?

Sari Says:
Of course there is nothing wrong with dating a guy who is shorter than you! If you feel comfortable with him, then ignore people who make a big deal about your height difference. The only time a girl should not date a

guy who is shorter is if she is just not interested in him, and the same is true with a taller guy. If you like him, enjoy your little man! Have fun.

dating on the rebound

Dear Sari,

My boyfriend of three months just dumped me for another girl. I like another guy already. Is it wrong for me to start dating again after I just broke up three days ago? It seems like it might be wrong, but I really like this new guy, and if my ex is gonna start dating again, he shouldn't care that I do too, right?

Sari Says:

If you want to start dating three days after the end of a three-month relationship, there is nothing wrong with that. However, if you want to start dating the new guy just to get back at the guy who dumped you for another girl, there is something wrong with that. If you are still angry at your ex, give yourself some time before you start dating. Make sure that it feels right and you are dating because you want to—not to get back at your ex. On the other hand, if you want to go out with the new guy because you genuinely like him and you feel as if you are over the other guy, that's okay.

age of consent

Dear Sari,

A guy I like in my school is almost 18 and I just turned 15. If we wanted to date, I was wondering: Do the laws of ages and dating deal with us, too? What does that restrict?

Sari Says:

Laws exist to protect young people from being coerced into having sex with an older person. Generally, they state that it is illegal for an adult to have sex with a minor (someone under the age of 16, 17 or 18). Every state has slightly different laws about the age of consent. At least 33 states have laws that say that it is illegal for someone over age 18 to have sex with someone under age 16. Remember, these laws are about having *sex*. There are no laws that apply to how old you have to be to *date* anyone of any age.

Realistically, if you and this guy feel that your dating is on an equal level, and (most importantly) if your parents think it's okay, it may be fine. Tell your parents about this guy and tell them how old he is. Get them to meet him. If they like him, and they say that it is okay for you to be dating him, there shouldn't be a problem. Then you just need to make sure no one else would complain or be suspicious that you are having sex—such as this guy's parents, or someone at school. The key here is that you would need to get your parents to say it's okay just to make sure that there won't be a problem.

online dreaming

Dear Sari,

I met this guy online. We have never seen each other, because we live far apart, but we talk online everyday. It feels like a real relationship. I was wondering if I should pursue this or if I'm dreaming. He says he loves me, and I'm beginning to think that I love him too. Please help me!

Sari Says:

You'd be better off starting a relationship, or even a friendship, with someone at your school or in your hometown. Online relationships can be fun, but you don't really know someone the way you do when you hang out together. Sometimes people have relationships online because they are afraid of trying something real, live, and in person. Writing romantic email messages can make you feel like you love someone, but that's not love! It's just words on the screen. Love is also about how someone looks at you, the little things he does for you, what it feels like to hold each other, and what it feels like to really be in someone's life.

Do you even know for sure if this guy is a nice, kind, single guy your age? I'm sure you've heard that sometimes people online pretend to be other people. Online relationships with strangers can be very dangerous. My advice: Turn off the computer and go out with friends. Stop emailing this guy online. It will be more fulfilling for you to have a real guy who calls you and takes you out and hangs out with you and your friends, rather than a guy who just gives good email.

cheating rep

Dear Sari,
Well, just today this really fine guy asked me out. I really like him, except I heard that he cheats on his girlfriend when he has one. I said yes to a date, do you think I should have?

Sari Says:
If you hear a lot of bad rumors about him, then maybe they are true. But the only way that you will know if he's faithful to you is if your relationship develops and he commits to you. Right now, you're worrying about this way too soon. You haven't even had one date yet. After your first date, you might decide that you don't like him. Or maybe he'll start dating someone else, and not want to see you again. See how the first date goes. If you keep dating, then you can decide if you trust him enough to take it further and commit to being boyfriend-girlfriend. Go one step at a time. For now, just have fun on the date! And remember, sometimes rumors are just that—made-up stories. You can't always believe everything you hear.

asking out a flirt

Dear Sari,
I am totally in love with this guy. He's sweet, cute, and we're friends. I really want to ask him to my semiformal, but I'm afraid he'll say no. He's the kind of guy who flirts with a lot of girls and has a ton of girls liking him. As far as I know, he doesn't like any of them. He flirts with me, but I'm still afraid he'll say no when I ask him. What should I do?

Sari Says:
You should definitely ask him out! If you want to date him, don't sit back and watch him flirt with those other girls who like him. Instead, you need to take action and do the one thing that they aren't doing: You must ask him out! I would bet that the reason he isn't dating anyone right now is because all of those other girls are too afraid to ask him out. If you can muster up the bravery to ask him out, then you will stand out among all of those girls as the one who was bright enough, cool enough, and strong enough to go for it.

too picky to date

Dear Sari,
Really cool guys always ask me out, but I never go out with them, because of one small aspect of either their looks or personality. I'm sooo picky. I can always find at least one bad thing about their personality. I'm 17, and I'm afraid I'm going to miss out on some great guys by being like this, so can you tell me if there is another perspective I can look at them from?

Sari Says:
If you met Matt Damon right now, and he told you that of all of the women in the world, he wanted to date you, I bet you'd turn him down, because you'd think that the end of his nose looks funny, and his hair is kind of

stringy! Or if you met Tiger Woods, you would think, "Well, he can play golf really well, but he can't play football!" You need to stop looking for imperfections in perfectly great guys. Instead of looking for their flaws, find their strong points and their best characteristics. I'm not saying that you should go out with guys you don't find attractive or interesting. But if you meet a guy who's good looking, or a guy with a great personality, and he likes you, then take time to get to know his good points. If you start to fixate on some little imperfection, make yourself stop. Instead, force yourself to come up with three things that you like about the guy. Focus on the positive and you will find more to like—and less to dislike—about the guys who ask you out.

What Do You Want?

What are the top qualities that people look for when they date?

- Personality (treats you with respect, smart, funny, and able to express feelings).
- Looks (cute, neat, and hip, but not too trendy).
- Common interests (such as sports, music, acting, writing, or the same TV shows).

Beginning Dating

making the first move

Dear Sari,

Do guys like it when girls make the first move, like asking him out or holding a guy's hand first on a date, or do they get turned off by a forward girl?

Sari Says:

Some guys like it when girls are forward; some get turned off or run away. The best thing to do if you are a girl who wants to make the first move without scaring off a guy is to be subtle and a little clever. Make a mellow move that lets him know you are ready for him to make his move. You can ask him if he wants to hang out with you and your friends, instead of asking him on a one-on-one date. Maybe that will hint to him that he can ask you out next. You can call him to ask a homework question and only stay on the phone for two minutes; that can be a hint that he can feel free to call you sometime. You can pick up his hand for a second and say, "I like your watch," rather than holding his hand—a hint that it's okay for him to hold your hand if he wants to.

goodnight kisses

Dear Sari,
I don't know when to kiss a girl on a date. Like what's the right time?

Sari Says:
The easiest time to kiss someone for the first time on a date is usually when you are saying "good night." Just lean over, and turn the "good night" into a "good night kiss"! Another optimal time to kiss someone during a date is when you are alone having an intimate or romantic moment. Maybe you hear a romantic song come on the radio, or you just happen to be telling her something that you like about her, or you're reminiscing about something fun that you did together on the last date. Those are all good moments to lean over and kiss her. It might help you get the feel for it if you start by gently stroking her hair, or gently holding her face in your hands just before you kiss her. For more ideas of how to initiate a kiss, try watching some TV shows that have lots of dating or kissing scenes (like *Popular*, *Felicity*, or *Dawson's Creek*). You might even want to watch a romantic video together to create the mood for kissing. Kissing is not always like it is in the movies, but at least it will give you some ideas.

talking on the phone

Dear Sari,
With the guy I just started dating, talking on the phone is so uncomfortable because of the silences. I usually love the phone; with a guy it is too hard. How can I stop these silences?

Sari Says:
You really only have two choices: You can keep talking, or you can hang up. If you want to keep the conversation going, one of the best things to do is to ask the guy questions. Since you two just started dating, you should be trying to get to know each other better. You could even make a list of things you want to know about your guy before you talk on the phone—what his family is like, what he likes to do on weekends, which movies he likes. Then anytime there's a pause in the phone conversation, just jump in with a question to keep him talking. If those nasty silences keep coming up, you might decide it's time to hang up. You don't need to have a long phone conversation with a guy every time you talk—sometimes just a short chat is fine. If the silences seem to indicate that it's time to wrap up the phone call, just let him know—nicely—that you're ready to hang up: "Well, I guess that's it for now. It was good talking to you; let's talk again soon." When you hang up, don't worry that he won't like you— he's probably just as relieved as you are to bring an end to the silences. Finally, I want to assure you that this won't last forever. As you and he get more used to talking on the phone, there should be fewer and fewer silences—just a little something to look forward to.

new places for dates

Dear Sari,
I'm a guy and I have been dating a great girl for a year. We have run out

of things to do for dates. We movied ourselves out. We never want to go to the mall again! We have even tried some creative things: I've taken her to a deserted island for a picnic, and we've had candlelight cuddling. Please help us with more ideas so we don't get bored!

Sari Says:
Grab a pen and paper, your local newspaper, your local phone book, a calendar, and a phone. You should each make a list of your favorite interests and hobbies. Once you have both made lists, your next step is to find activities in your town that are related to your interests. Look through the newspaper to see what's going on: sporting events, bands, festivals, etc. Choose as many events as you can, and mark down on your calendar when these will take place. If you need to buy tickets, then call to do that; if you need to ask your parents' permission, do that, too. Next, look in the Yellow Pages of the phone book to find museums or tourist attractions in your town. Choose some things that fit each of your interests and mark those down on your calendar, too. Finally, figure out what hobbies you could start together. For example, if you both like to draw, then why not set aside time when you two can get together to draw (maybe in a park or something)? By now you should have a whole bunch of things written down that you can do for dates.

When It's Just Not Right

letting him down easy

Dear Sari,
This really sweet guy keeps on asking me out. I don't know how to say no without hurting his feelings. I wanna be just friends with this guy. He keeps on telling me how great I am but I just wanna be friends. *Help!*

Sari Says:

Tell him that you also think he is great—a great friend. Tell him you like him, but only as a friend. Rejecting someone is tough. But if you do it gently, then hopefully you can keep him as a friend without hurting his feelings too badly. At first he might ignore you or act weird around you, but after a couple of weeks he'll probably go back to acting like a friend to you. Who knows, after a while maybe you could even offer to fix him up with one of your girl friends. He sounds like a nice guy.

dump the dumper

Dear Sari,

I went to the movies with a guy on a first date. He said he was going to go get some popcorn. Then he didn't come back, and I sat through the whole movie myself. The next day I saw him talking to this other girl in school, and I found a note in my locker from him saying he wanted to break up. I am popular, smart, pretty, and kind, so I don't know why he dumped me. I need to get him to want to go out with me again, or I will lose my title of "the girl everyone wants to go out with." Help!

Sari Says:

Listen, popular girl, if you try to get this guy, then you'll get this title: "the girl who is desperate to date a jerk!" The way that he treated you—leaving you at the movies—is absolutely horrible. You should not take him back after he treated you so badly! And that was only a first date! Imagine how terrible he must be as a real boyfriend? Be glad that he doesn't want to be with you, because if he did go out with you again, he would probably treat you terribly again. Do not even think about him for another second, unless you are thinking, "He's a jerk. I am so glad I am over him."

Polite things to say to turn down a date:

- "I just want to be friends."
- "I am not looking for a boyfriend/girlfriend."
- "My parents don't let me date."
- "I'm seeing someone."
- "I'm sorry; I don't think of you that way."

touchy feely

Dear Sari,

I have been going out with this guy for about a week. But when he tries to put his hands on my waist or chest, I feel uncomfortable. I want him to stop, but I don't want him to think that I don't like him, and I don't know what to tell him when he does it without hurting his feelings or something. What should I do?

Sari Says:

You are going to have to tell this guy to get his paws off of you. You could be getting uncomfortable because your body is telling you that it really isn't right for him to be touching you. Or you could be getting nervous simply because this may be the first time a guy has ever tried to get physical with you. Whatever the reason, you need to tell him to stop. You said that you don't want to tell him because you don't want to hurt his feelings. However, he is hurting *your* feelings, making you nervous and uncomfortable by touching you when you don't want him to. Talk to him. Even if it makes him feel funny, that's no worse than what he's doing to you. Next time he puts his hands on you in a way that makes you feel uncomfortable, immediately say something like, "Hey, you know I like you, but please, I don't want to get physical," or simply, "I'm not ready for that." Hopefully he will stop after you ask him once.

online danger

Dear Sari,

I've met this guy online about a month ago. We talk on the phone and on AOL, but the problem is that he wants more than just talk. He wants to play around in person. The bigger problem is that he is 25 years old and I'm 14. What should I tell him to make him slow down?

Sari Says:

You need to do more than tell him to "slow down." You need to tell him that you never want to talk to him again online or on the phone, and you will never meet him in person. This guy could be dangerous—and he's definitely a creep! It is not only wrong for an older man to try to develop an intimate relationship with a 14-year-old, it's also illegal. You need to keep away from any older man you meet online who is trying to get you to see him. You should no longer read or respond to his emails or his phone calls. If he keeps contacting you online, then change your screen name. Also, you must talk to your parents about this! They might be upset at first, but they need to know about it. There are some really messed-up people in this world who try to get close to young girls by meeting them online. This worries me, and it should worry you, too. So play it safe. Please cut off all contact with him.

waiting for the right person

Dear Sari,

I always seem to have bad luck with guys. It seems the ones whom I am interested in are flirts (like myself) or interested in someone I know. The guys I am not interested in are the ones who want to get with me. Is there something wrong with my situation, or something wrong with me?

Sari Says:

There is nothing wrong with you. Meeting the right guy takes time. The basic reason why people are single is that they have not yet found the person who likes them whom they also like. Over the years, you will meet lots of guys who think you are the brightest, hottest, coolest girl in the world—but you'll think they are total geeks. And, you will meet tons of fantastic guys who don't seem to want a relationship with you. My point is that someday you'll meet a guy who's just right for you, and the feelings will be mutual!

best guy friend syndrome

Dear Sari,

It seems every female I have tried to enter into a relationship with seems to diagnose me with best friend/big brother syndrome. They start off having some interest in me; we go out once or twice; things go well. Then the girl all of a sudden tells me everything about herself, all her problems. I never ask them to, but they do. It seems instantly that I become a best friend or big brother because within a few days they tell me, "You are the sweetest guy I know, it's just that I think of you as a good friend, and I wouldn't want to ruin our friendship," or worse, "You have become like such a brother to me, I couldn't date my brother!" I am a "nice guy," so to speak. I was raised to be old-fashioned and chivalrous: opening doors, seating the lady, paying for dinner. I am also a hopeless romantic. Maybe these things have something to do with my syndrome. I don't know what to do! Do you have a cure?

Sari Says:

Don't worry, sweetie. Usually the cure for your syndrome is age. Sometimes girls in high school are looking for the daring "bad" guy. But a few years later, they're often looking for the nice guy. So in a while, you will be getting all the girls, and the tough guys will be all alone. Yet I'm sure you would like to date now, so in the meantime, here is something you can do to help your situation. The next time a girl you like starts to tell you about personal things, to make you into a friend, tell her, "Please, tell those things to a friend, because I like you as more than just friends." It seems that now you are letting the girls talk, because you're nice. However, you do have some control over whether you play the friend role, or the boyfriend role. Tell them (interrupt if you have to!) to stop talking about those things. Let girls know you're not playing the friend role anymore.

dating a friend

Dear Sari,
This girl was a very good friend of mine. About two weeks ago we started dating. The problem is, I don't really feel any romantic attraction for her. I seem to feel the same as I did when we were friends. When I think about being with someone, it's not her. Maybe I'm just too shallow because I don't think she is all that (physically) attractive. Anyway, should I keep going out with her?

Sari Says:
Ideally, a couple should have a great friendship—plus attraction. If you don't find your friend physically attractive, and you don't feel any romantic feelings for her, then you must tell her that you want to be "just friends." You need to be very careful and compassionate when you talk to her about this. Let her know that you love her friendship and you do not want to lose it. Then tell her that you just don't feel right dating and getting into a boyfriend–girlfriend relationship with her. Don't come right out and say that you do not find her attractive! You can say that you still feel like "just friends," and that you have not been able to make the leap from friendship to romantic feelings toward her. I hope that she can

handle this and just be friends with you. If she's very upset, let her know that you will give her space until she wants to be friends again. Take a break from being friends for a few weeks or months, if she needs that. Then, as soon as she is ready to be friends again, be there for her.

just friends

Dear Sari,

I am friends with a girl who I wanted to ask out. When I tried to tell her that I like her as more than just a friend, she said that we should just stay friends, and she prefers dating men she meets as strangers. I don't get it. How could she be passing up a good dude—me—for some guy who she knows nothing about?

Sari Says:

You've forgotten something that's important to dating: attraction. She may have said that she wants to only be friends because she is not attracted to you. Some people feel more chemistry with someone who is new and, to them, exciting. Some people should consider whether they like any of their friends as more than just friends—and if they do, they should talk with that friend about the possibility of dating. It's wonderful when a friendship evolves into a great relationship. But if the relationship fails, most of the time the friendship ends, too. So if one of your friends eventually does want more than just a friendship, think it over carefully before you take it to the next level.

jealousy pangs

Dear Sari,

I'm really confused. There is this guy that I've been sort of seeing the last few weeks, but we aren't official yet. And I really hate it when he checks out other girls when I'm with him . . . is that wrong, or is it OK to be jealous?

Sari Says:
Sure it is okay to be jealous, but what I am wondering is if he really wants a relationship with you. Since he has not made it official, and since he's looking at everything in a skirt and tight baby tee, then maybe he's not the type to settle down. I don't want you to get hurt. Ask him if he wants to make it official with you. If he says "no," then forget about him and his wandering eyes. If he says "yes," then ask if he could quit checking out other girls when you're around.

stopped calling

Dear Sari,
I've gone out with this guy a bunch of times in the past month. At first he was so sweet to me. He took me out to dinner, called me whenever he got a chance . . . but now he never returns my calls! I feel like he doesn't want to talk to me at all. I just don't know what to do!

Sari Says:
Maybe he is really busy with school, or going through some stressful times with his family. It could be that he still wants to go out with you, but he may need some time to himself. On the other hand, he might not want to go out with you anymore, and he's afraid to tell you. For some people, telling someone that they do not want to date them anymore is so hard (especially if they still like the person) that they simply avoid getting together with the person and try to more or less ignore them, hoping that he or she "gets the hint." You can never be sure of what someone is "hinting" at. Therefore, you have to ask! Call him and say something like, "I was wondering if you want to get together. I loved it when we used to talk a lot, and

I am starting to miss that. Do you still want to go out?" If you ask him this calmly, without sounding upset, he may be able to tell you how he feels.

dating with child

Dear Sari,

I am a teen, living with my parents, and have a six-month-old daughter. My baby's father and I no longer speak, though he visits her regularly. I have moved on with my life and so has he. My problem now is with my current boyfriend. His father and mother dislike the fact that I have a child. His father threw a fit, cursing me over the phone. I wish his parents could understand that I'm still a teenager and I still want to have a boyfriend. My boyfriend has told me that he wants to stay with me, even though his parents are against us. I thought about talking with his parents, but I'm afraid that they won't listen. What can I do to make them understand that I'm not doing their son any harm?

Sari Says:

You could try to explain to them what your life is like, and why you are a responsible (and normal) teen, even though you have a baby. Talk to your parents about this, too. Maybe they can help. If your parents let you invite him and his parents over for dinner, that could help them understand your situation. However, if his parents won't listen, won't come over, and are still closed-minded, then you may want to consider dating other guys. I know that you want to be with this guy, but it is not the best thing for you or your baby. Look for someone whose family will treat you the way you deserve.

pucker up

Kissing is without a doubt the most fun you can have with four lips. There is nothing like that sweet moment when your lips meet another pair they've been thirsting to touch. The simple act of a kiss can alter your whole, personal universe. Just before you kiss, as your bodies move closer and you begin to breathe in sync, everything around you becomes slightly fuzzy. The air feels a little warmer and your heart speeds up. And when your lips finally meet, you are lost in that intimate moment where you are so totally connected, that you feel transported to a world that belongs only to the two of you.

On the flip side, kissing can also fill you with more self-doubt than a pop quiz. Before you have enough practice, you can be left wondering: Are you doing it right? Are you a good kisser? Is the person you're kissing feeling as good about it as you are? Are there kissing techniques you should know about? How do you French kiss? Can you make someone kiss the way you want them to? If you don't kiss "right," will the object of your affections ditch you for someone who can? Well, here's a little secret for you: Chances are if it *feels* good, you're doing just fine. If it feels awkward and a little odd, maybe you or your smoochable other just need to relax a bit, or maybe you could use a tip or two. But that's the great thing about kissing—practice makes perfect!

Who'd think that something so easy and natural could cause so many questions? But it does. So, maybe you need a little help in this department. Consider this chapter your very own kissing manual. Here you will get loads of lip tips, plus I'll answer your questions about all of the confusing or embarrassing moments that can occur because of kissing. Ready, set, pucker up!

never been kissed

Dear Sari,
I am a 17-year-old girl, and I have never kissed a guy. I was wondering if I was the only one.

Sari Says:
There are millions of girls and guys who have not kissed at age 17. In fact, there are lots of people who haven't even gone on a date until they are over 18. Frankly, sometimes the social and dating scene in high school is not so great. That's why lots of girls can't find guys to date—or kiss—until they go to college, or get out in the real world. Don't worry. And when you do meet someone who you want to kiss, don't be concerned about the fact that you're a beginner. Most people are naturals when it comes to kissing—so you'll probably be good, without even trying.

when to kiss

Dear Sari,
Should you kiss on your first date?

Sari Says:
Kissing is important and fun, but truly getting to know each other is even more important on the first date. If all you do on the first date is kiss, then you could be creating a relationship based on kissing. It is best to talk on the first date, and save the heavy kissing for later on. Most often, the perfect first date kiss is the "good-bye" kiss. Of course, if it feels really right and you want to kiss more than that, then you can—just make sure that you also do some talking.

neck kissing

Dear Sari,

When a guy is kissing your neck, what do *you* do? Do you just sit back and enjoy it, or are you supposed to be kissing him wherever you can, as well?

Sari Says:

It's perfectly fine to just sit back and enjoy it. You don't have to do a thing. But if you want to, you can run your fingers though his hair, massage his neck, or touch anywhere on his body that you can reach. When you're ready, if you want to exchange the favor and kiss his neck for a while, that's cool, too. But you should never feel like you have to kiss his neck just because he's kissing yours. If he wants to make you feel good, accept that.

lip tips: the kissing details

Dear Sari,

I know everyone says French kissing comes naturally, but I am scared that it won't for me. Once our tongues are in each other's mouths what do I do? And please don't say "just go with the flow," 'cause I want details. Thanks a lot!

Sari Says:

Kissing is something that you just learn by doing, and you don't know what to do until you start. But no, I'm not gonna cop out on you by leaving it at that. Here are some things to try. There is no "right" way to kiss, so, please, understand that the following are just some ideas!

SARI'S LIP TIPS

The Warm-up:

- Let any nervous feelings go away, as much as you can, before you start kissing. The best kisses happen when you really feel at ease. So if you are too freaked out, just wait to kiss some other time, when you are more relaxed.

- If you know you'll be kissing sometime soon, try to avoid chapped lips. Use Blistex or Chapstick if you need to.

- Don't eat tons of garlic or onions before kissing. Your breath should be normal, or else minty-fresh.

- Before you kiss, cuddle up and get close and comfortable with him or her.

The Kiss:

- To start kissing, you can go right to the lips, or if you want, nuzzle up to the other person's neck and, kissing with soft, dry kisses, slowly move up until you get to the lips.

- Keep your lips soft and relaxed. Do not tense up your face at all.

- Close your eyes if you want to feel relaxed and focus just on the kiss.

- Start with closed lips, kissing the other person's closed lips. This will get both of you used to the feeling of the other person's lips on yours.

- Put your hands in a comfortable place, maybe on the person's back or shoulders. Don't grope around too much; focus on how the kissing feels.

- Part your lips slightly, still keeping the kisses soft and gentle.

French Kissing:

- When you are kissing and you feel ready to French kiss, gently open your mouth a tiny bit more (but just a tiny bit).

- Your lips should gently be pressed against each other, like this ( ) not like this ().

- See if the other person also opens his or her mouth a little, too, and gently eases his or her tongue into your mouth. If that happens, then you just kind of let your tongue mingle with theirs . . . and there you have it!
- If you have to put your tongue in the other person's mouth first, open your mouth a little and let your tongue come out just a bit from your slightly parted lips. Do not stick your tongue out, or jam it in his or her mouth. If the other person is okay with this, and does the same, let your tongues mingle. Your tongues just happen to be inside "hanging out" with each other.
- Don't tense up your tongue. It should feel smooth, gentle, and kind of tingly, like the way you feel when you pet a purring cat.
- When you are ready to end the initial kiss, gently close your mouth and pull back a little. You can start kissing all over again at any time.

Finally, remember that the best way to kiss is when you get totally into it, so that you aren't thinking about what you are doing, and you are just enjoying the moment.

Kissing Don'ts

- Don't try to reach your tongue way far back. You're not trying to clean the person's teeth or tonsils!
- Do not open your mouth wide. You do not want to cover the person's chin or nose with your lips.
- Don't stay locked at the mouth. You are not giving CPR!
- Don't slobber a lot. Kissing is moist, but it's not sloppy or slobbery.

you're a great kisser!

Dear Sari,
What do you think makes a great kisser?

Sari Says:
A great kisser is confident. That means that while you are kissing, you are not wondering if you are kissing "correctly." You are sure of yourself, and you are just doing what feels good. Also, a good kisser makes the person he or she is kissing feel comfortable. Both people should feel relaxed and happy. Finally, a good kisser is thrilled to be kissing the person who he or she is kissing.

getting him to kiss

Dear Sari,
My boyfriend is new to dating . . . and kissing. In the hall after school we hug and he gives me a small little kiss and then he walks off. I want something that means something—one that will last a while. But I don't want to hurt his feelings!

Sari Says:
Tell him that you want a little bit more than a little tiny kiss. However, intense making out and really affectionate hugs are usually better in private. So don't pressure him to do more when you're in the hallway at school. A little kiss and hug are the only things that are appropriate at school. But the next time you two are in private, say something like this: "I would love it if we would kiss like this . . . " Then start to kiss him the way you want it to be. He'll probably like it. Just let him know that this is what you want.

- Ice kiss: Put a small ice cube in your mouth, then kiss.
- Chocolate kiss: Put a piece of chocolate in your mouth, and pass it back and forth while you kiss.
- Upside down kiss: One of you holds your head upside down while you kiss.
- Underwater kiss: Kiss underwater in a swimming pool.
- Alphabet kiss: Spell out the alphabet with your tongue on your partner's tongue.
- Word kissing: Anytime you hear a certain word you have to kiss.

magic kingdom mackfest

Dear Sari,

I totally made out with this guy at Disneyworld. I knew him for three hours. We macked down, which was great, but my friend was there with her boyfriend and they haven't even kissed yet. I feel guilty. My friend said it didn't bug her, but I know she was disappointed. I don't want my friend or her boyfriend to think less of me. Got any advice?

Sari Says:

If you feel okay about kissing a guy like that, then it's okay for you to do it. You should not regret what you did or feel guilty about it because it is in the past. However, you can let it shape how you deal with a similar situation in the future. Maybe next time, you could kiss the guy in private, so you don't offend or show off to your friends. Also, if you want to, you can ask a guy for his number so you can wait until you have a date to kiss him. Whatever your friend really thinks about what happened, it won't be a big deal unless it happens all the time. Besides, I'm sure that someday you and she will have a good laugh about the day you kissed at Mickey Mouse's house.

mustache makeout

Dear Sari,

My new boyfriend has a mustache! I don't even know how it's going to feel. Is there any special way I have to kiss him?

Sari Says:

Because a man's mustache grows above his lip—not on his lip—you probably won't notice much of a difference. Unless he has one of those crazy handlebar mustaches and it is so long that it hangs into his mouth. :) Usually when people are kissing, the fleshy part of their lips and the inside of their mouths are involved, not the upper part of the lip near his nose. Of course, if you do feel it, it won't be that big of a deal, just a new sensation. Just kiss as you would kiss any guy.

ring a ding ding

Dear Sari,

I'm 15, and I love my girlfriend, but she has a tongue ring that bothers me and it messes up my kissing ability. The worst thing is that she thinks I'm a terrible kisser because of this. What should I tell her?

Sari Says:

Everyone kisses differently, tongue ring or not. The only way to get someone to kiss the way you like is to ask her to kiss a certain way. Don't try to make excuses, telling her that you are usually a good kisser. Be confident. Just ask her to show you how she likes to be kissed. Then show her how you like to be kissed. If it really is the ring that's causing the problems, you can tell her. Tell her that you are new to the ring thing, and you want her to show you how to kiss around it. Otherwise, ask her to take out the tongue ring, for the sake of your love.

do you speak French?

Dear Sari,
I have been going out with my boyfriend for like two weeks and all we've done is peck—not French. All these peeps are calling us prudes! It is just that my boyfriend is very shy! I told friends to talk to him for me, but nothing has changed!

Sari Says:
You shouldn't be telling your friends to talk to him for you. You need to talk with him yourself. One of the most important parts of a relationship is being able to talk to your partner to improve things. Tell him that you really like kissing him and you think it would be fun if you kissed even more. I know it won't be easy to talk about, but it could help things. Besides just talking about this, you may have to take the lead with him physically. The next time you two kiss, try making the move to Frenching. Gently ease your tongue into his mouth to see if he'll respond.

kissing incompatibility

Dear Sari,
I don't like the way my boyfriend kisses. When we French he like points his tongue and leaves it there. I tried to tell him that I wanted to kiss a different way, like moving our tongues, but he kept saying, "But I like it this way." I want to tell him how to change the way he kisses, but he is really sensitive and I don't want to hurt his feelings.

Sari Says:
You're right, you should avoid hurting his feelings, but you can still keep trying to get him to kiss the way you want. When you're about to start kissing, tell him, "I know that you like kissing one way, but I sometimes

like to kiss another way. Could I please show you the way that I like? It'll be fun—let me show you." Hopefully, he'll say "yes" and you can show him the way you like. Then try to compromise: Sometimes you kiss his way, sometimes he kisses your way. Most of the time when a couple is not immediately compatible, they get used to each other's style of kissing. They often end up blending the ways they kiss into one new style of kissing that is okay (but maybe not "perfect") for both of them. Otherwise, if one of them won't change at all, the other person is forced to deal with it. Hopefully, your guy will change a little. If not, maybe the next guy will be a more compatible kisser for you!

public kisses

Dear Sari,
How do I go about kissing when there are a lot of people around? I mean, I like this guy a lot and I don't mind kissing him when we are alone, but I get this weird feeling when people are around. How can I get past this?

Sari Says:
You don't necessarily need to get past that. Some people simply don't like PDA, Public Displays of Affection. If you don't like it, don't do it! If he starts to kiss you when people are around, if you don't like it, tell him: "I'd love to kiss you later, when we're all alone. That would be so much more romantic!" Then give him a little peck of a kiss and tell him how excited you are to kiss more later. He should get the message.

However, if you really want to kiss in public, the only way to get over feeling shy about something like that is to get more used to doing it. So, in that case, you'd have to kiss him in public *a lot* to get over it. Then you'd be what is called "desensitized" to kissing in public. In other words, you'd get to the point where you'd hardly notice that you were doing it, because you are so used to doing it. It seems like it will either be all or nothing for you.

hickey!

Dear Sari,
What is a hickey? How do you get one??

Sari Says:
A hickey is a bluish, purplish, reddish mark that is caused when someone kisses a person really hard in a particular spot. It is actually a bruise.
It happens when someone is using a lot of suction from his or her
mouth, sucking in while kissing. The suction causes little blood vessels
under the skin to break, thus making a bruise. You can give a hickey (or
get a hickey) anywhere on the body where the skin is tender and sensitive. Often people get (or give) hickeys on the neck, because that is a
place where it feels good to kiss and the skin is very sensitive. Some
people get really excited when they are kissing someone's neck, and
they kiss and suck hard and cause a hickey. For some people it feels
good to get a hickey, for others, it hurts. Some people think it is fun to
have a hickey, because then everyone knows that they were making out.
Other people hate getting a hickey, because it is embarrassing for
people to see it. They are the people you see wearing turtleneck
sweaters in the summer.

kissing constantly

Dear Sari,
If I make out with my boyfriend every night for about two hours would that
be an obsession?

Sari Says:
No, it is totally fine, and not an obsession. Making out every night is fun
and part of getting close to a boyfriend. If you enjoy it, then keep it up,

and do not worry about it at all, even if it is for two hours every night. Of course, at some point you might decide that you want to do nonkissing things with him, like seeing a movie, or just talking about yourselves. That might give your relationship more depth, because you'll actually be talking to each other rather than just kissing all the time. But if you end up kissing, don't worry, it just means that you really like each other and that you like kissing.

peer kissing pressure

Dear Sari,

When I double date to the movies with my best friend, she and her guy spend the *whole* movie making out. My boyfriend and I, however, like to hug and talk and stuff. My friend turns to us and jokes, "C'mon you guys! Make out!" I ask her to stop it. Then, after the movie my friend goes, "Ha ha, did you even *kiss*?" It is so annoying! What do I do?

Sari Says:

Talk to your friend when you two are alone. Tell her that when you ask her to stop joking around about kissing, you're serious. Make sure that she understands that you want her to cut it out. Explain to her that you and he kiss when you both want to, but you also like to talk and touch, not just make out all the time like she and her guy. Hopefully, the next time you go to the movies, she'll behave—mind her own kissing and keep out of yours. Otherwise, if she starts up again, you and your boyfriend should sit somewhere else in the theater, and meet her in the lobby after the movie.

kiss or tell?

Dear Sari,

When I go out with a guy, should I tell him that I have never kissed before? I don't want to sound geeky and say, "I haven't kissed a guy before, so if I mess up, it's not my fault."

Sari Says:

When you meet a guy you want to kiss and the moment for your first smooch is upon you, you'll instantly know what to say or not to say. So don't worry about it so much now. Just be ready to go with your feelings. You definitely don't need to make excuses about the way you kiss, even if it's your first time! A guy should feel honored and thrilled to have you lay your luscious lips on his. Get ready to experience one of the most magical moments of your life.

kissing is safe

Dear Sari,

I thought that there is no way to get AIDS from kissing, even French kissing, but my friend says that I am wrong. Can you get AIDS from kissing?

Sari Says:

You can*not* get AIDS from kissing! You should totally enjoy kissing without worrying. You can French to your heart's content, and you still are not at any risk at all. In order to get HIV, the virus that causes AIDS, you have to get someone's blood, semen, or vaginal secretions into your blood stream. But those are fluids that are not part of kissing, that's why it is safe. For more information about how you can get HIV and AIDS, please read the "Let's Talk About Sex" chapter in this book.

kiss off steroids

Dear Sari,

I was just wondering: If you kiss a guy who takes steroids, does it affect you in any way? Can it get transferred through saliva or anything?

Sari Says:

I'm not a medical doctor, but I believe that the drug can't affect you from saliva or kissing. However, do you realize that steroids can be dangerous and they're illegal unless they are prescribed by a doctor? If you like a guy who is taking steroids, you may want to talk to him about why he is on this drug. If he says he's taking them illegally to build muscle so he's better at sports, tell him it's not worth it! Ask him if he knows about the scary side effects. They include: severe liver problems, heart problems, high blood pressure, severe acne, severe aggressiveness and mood swings, breast enlargement in boys (and decreased breast growth in girls). For more information about steroids, check the drug hotlines in the appendix at the back of this book.

Here's the deal: The other night I was babysitting and my boyfriend came over. So we watched tv with the kids until they had to go to bed. And when they were asleep my boyfriend turned off all the lights. Well everything was fine but when he tried to french me he spit all over my lips and cheeks so I pushed him away and said he was nasty, then he asked why wouldn't I kiss him and I had to give him a lame reason why. Well I guess it was too lame because I haven't heard from him or seen him at all. So what do I do?

Very grossed out

Sari Says:

His slobbering probably was an accident. Now maybe this guy thought that he grossed you out so much that you don't want anything to do with him. He may have been so embarrassed, or felt so hurt after you rejected him, that he is afraid to call you. He might really miss you but is worried that you don't like him anymore, or that you'll reject him again if he calls you. You pushed him away literally and figuratively! If you want to fix your relationship, you have to try to bring him back. Call him and ask if you two can get together. When you see him, just have fun. Go on a date, without worrying about kissing. You need to try to get back on good terms with him before you approach this kissing issue. Then if things get good enough that you start to kiss again, you can say to him, "I love kissing you, and drier kisses are my favorites!" That way, you are telling him to use less spit, but you are saying it in such a nice way that he might not feel hurt by it.

the bottle of love

Dear Sari,

A group of friends and I are going to play "spin the bottle" at a party. Well, I've never had a chance to kiss a guy I like, and at the party, I want to kiss him during the game. So, my question is, is there any way or trick to make the bottle point the way I want it?

Sari Says:

Usually you cannot control where the bottle goes when you spin it—unless you study years and years of physics and apply all the scientific knowledge that you have, but you hardly have time for that before the big night. Here is one trick that might be able to help a little: When the game starts, look at where the bottle points before you spin it and see how far it has to go to get to the guy you want to kiss. The easiest way to get it to go to someone is when the person is not far from where it already points. You can spin the bottle just a tiny bit, a little flick, if he is sitting directly next to where it is pointed. If you have to spin it hard, then there is not a good way to control it. So try to sit next to the guy you like and take your turn when you don't have to spin it far. If it does not work, then I suggest that you find some other time to kiss him that night. The easiest times to kiss a guy are when you are saying "hello" or "good-bye." Just do it kind of quickly. All in one motion, lean in like you might hug him, say, "Bye," then plant a little kiss right on his lips.

boyfriends and girlfriends

Don't you wish that having a boyfriend or girlfriend wasn't so tough? It shouldn't be *that* much different from the kind of relationship you have with your friends, right? You hang out, you do things you both like, you eat pizza and see movies, you talk about school, friends, parents. So, why does it get so complicated?

Well, for starters, you *should* feel as if you are friends. If you don't really have much in common other than having the mutual hots, then your relationship probably isn't going to get too much further than the backseat. But even when you are really crazy about the other person and have tons in common, things can get hairy. You have to deal with friends getting jealous that you're spending lots of time with someone else, your parents worrying about what you're doing with that someone else, balancing your new love thing with school—and these are just the outside factors. Add in lover's quarrels, jealousy, sex, and a slew of other issues that may come up, and you've got enough ingredients to counteract the strongest love potion. So, what's a love-sick fool to do? Never fear, Romeo and Juliet. In this chapter, I'll help you get to the heart of the matter.

are we going out?

Dear Sari,

This guy and I have gone out every weekend for a month. But at school, he acts like we are just buds. Are we really going out, or what?

Sari Says:

You have to ask him. Some people avoid discussing this kind of stuff because they are afraid to commit to a relationship. If that's the case, and he's been avoiding bringing it up, then when you do, you might be disappointed to find that he thought that you and he were just hanging out. However, maybe he really does want a relationship, and the only reason why he did not bring it up is because he was afraid that you may not be interested in really going out with him.

Next time you are together, come right out and say, "Are we going out, or what?" Then keep asking questions until you are clear about what is going on between you two. For example, you could ask him if he is seeing other people, if he expects you not to date anyone else, or you can even ask if he thinks of the two of you as boyfriend and girlfriend. If he says that you are boyfriend and girlfriend, then tell him that he should treat you that way all the time—even at school.

Defining Relationship Lingo

- **Hanging Out:** This is like dating, but without making official, actual dates. At this stage, the couple might not have talked about the fact that they like each other. They are waiting to see if things progress.
- **Dating:** This usually means that two people are going out to dinners or events together. It implies that if the dating keeps up, then they will get into a relationship together.
- **Hooking Up:** If you spend several hours talking with someone you meet at a party and you kiss (or go further, even spend the night), then you "hooked up." It is not as formal as dating, or even as "hanging out."
- **Seeing Each Other:** This is a mild way of saying that you are in a relationship. It's often said when someone is trying to make it sound like it is not a big deal.
- **Going Out:** If two people are "going out," they are in a relationship. It is another way of saying that you are going steady. But be careful with this one. Some people might think that you are going out, but not exclusively boyfriend–girlfriend.
- **Going Steady:** This expression is not the most popular nowadays, but you'll still hear people (especially parents) use it. It means that you are in a relationship.
- **Boyfriend–Girlfriend:** If two people say that they are boyfriend–girlfriend, that means that they have a committed relationship. This expression is the one that leaves no doubt in anyone's mind that you are a couple!

getting to know you

Dear Sari,

My boyfriend and I just started officially going out. This is the beginning of my first relationship. The problem is that I feel like we haven't really gotten to know each other. I want to get to know him without asking a lot of questions that'll make him feel like I'm hassling him. What can I do to spark up a conversation and make the relationship last?

Sari Says:

The best thing to do is to ask him questions, but casually. Instead of firing off a list of twenty questions at him, ask him stuff as it comes up. For example, if you go to a movie, and you are in the theater waiting for the movie to start, ask him to tell you his favorite movies. If you hang out after school, ask him what teachers he likes, what classes he hates, and other school-related stuff. You see what I mean? Ask him lots of things that are relevant to the moment. That way, as more time passes, and you do more things, you will get to know him better.

the right time for gift-giving

Dear Sari,
I got a new boyfriend like one and a half weeks ago. Yesterday I went to the mall and decided to get him a gold chain as a gift. I showed a few friends, and everyone was like, "Why'd you get it for him, you've only been going out for like a week?" Should I give it to him or not?

Sari Says:
That does sound like a major gift to give after only a week and a half. Sometimes giving too big of a gift too soon is not good for a relationship. It might scare him away, or confuse him. Or if you break up, you might be mad that you gave it to him. If I were you, I'd wait to give it to him. Instead, you can do something nice for him, such as give him a card or a flower. Something little like that is an appropriate gift for now. Then save the chain (don't tell him about it), and wait a while to give it to him, maybe for an occasion. Perhaps you can wait until his birthday, or maybe wait until you have been going out six months, so you can say that it's for your "six-month anniversary." If you stay together long enough to give a large gift like the chain to him, then you will be glad that you've been saving the perfect gift for the right time.

Great Gifts to Give

With birthdays, Christmas, Valentine's Day, and your anniversary, you may want to give each other a gift every few months. What are some great gifts to give?

The usual, such as flowers or chocolate, is great. Here are some more ideas for special gifts that won't break the bank:

- Frame a great picture of the two of you.
- Make a mixed tape with all of his favorite songs on it.
- Bake cookies for him, then put them in a tin that you decorated with pictures of things that he likes, including a picture of you two. (By the way, it's perfectly fine to make cookies from a roll of premade dough.)
- Get him a bunch of little gifts that symbolize some of the special things you've done together or things you have in common. (For example, a CD of a band you heard together, or a poster for the first movie that you saw together.)
- Make up a "gift certificate" for things such as a back rub, a day alone together, or even help with his homework.
- Have a radio station play "your" song with a special dedication and ask him to listen.
- Make a cool card. To make it personal, use construction paper, colored doilies, tissue paper, glitter, stickers, buttons, cut-out pictures from other cards or magazines. If you want, include a picture of you two together. Write a few lines about why he is so special to you, or about the good times that you've shared.

not the same around his friends

Dear Sari,

My boyfriend of one month is so sweet when he's only around me, but when he's with his friends, he acts totally different. The topic of sex comes up when his friends are around. He asks me when he'll get some and why I won't give him any now. When we're alone, he tells me he'll wait as long as it takes for me to be ready, if I ever want to have sex with him. The truth is, I'm saving myself for marriage, and I've told him that. Do you think he really wants to have sex with me, or is this some macho guy way that men act around each other? We have not been going out so long that I love him, so if he is not the right guy, I don't want to stay with him. How should I deal with this?

Sari Says:
It sounds more like a macho (and immature) thing that he's saying for the guys' benefit. Yet, because you have only been going out for about a month, this may be an indication that he is not the right guy for you. Before you toss him to the curb, talk with him about this. This beginning stage of a relationship is the best time to make sure that you express how you expect to be treated. Start by being very positive, saying, "One of the things that I like about you is that you are so sweet and support-ive, and you don't try to push me into having sex before I am ready." Then say, "That's why it bothers me when you joke about it in front of your friends." Tell him not to mention sex in front of his friends anymore. He may be doing this because he thinks his friends have some image of him as a guy who should want sex all the time. But the fact is, his friends probably do not even care. Your boyfriend needs to be more sensitive to your feelings and keep your private life private. If he can do that, then he might be a good guy to stay involved with.

Those Three ~~Little~~ Big Words

is this love?

Dear Sari,
My boyfriend and I have been together for a month and a half, and I care about him even more than when we first got together. He says he has never been happier with anyone else, and I feel the same. We only get to see each other once a week, if we're lucky, but we talk on the phone every night. I can seriously see us together in the future. Do you think this is love?

Sari Says:

It sounds as if you two are falling in love. Usually it takes a little bit longer than a month and a half to be sure if you love somebody. After a month and a half, you could feel a strong infatuation for a guy; however, it is probably not complete "love." Labeling what you feel is not the most important thing. What matters most is the way you feel right now. Enjoy your feelings! Whether you and he want to call it "love" or not does not matter. Just enjoy your blossoming relationship.

saying, "i love you"

Dear Sari,
Every time my boyfriend says "I love you," I can't say it back. I want to, but I am too embarrassed. Please help!

Sari Says:
Usually, when someone can't say, "I love you," it means that he or she needs more time in the relationship to feel comfortable enough to say it, and to be sure it is love. I don't think you should push yourself. It is okay if it takes time until you feel ready to say it. Once you feel totally ready (if you ever do), then it is the right time for you to say it. Otherwise, you might not completely mean it. Be patient with yourself and wait until your feelings are in order. Do not say it unless you mean it.

signing, "i love you"

Dear Sari,
I'm 15 years old and I've been going out with this guy for about three weeks (he's the same age). I talk to him on the phone all the time and we email back and forth, as well. We go to the same school, too. But in his emails he always signs them "love," and I think it's way too early for him

to say that. I like him a lot, but I don't think I love him. At least not after only three weeks. Am I just paranoid or something?

Sari Says:

This reminds me of a story from when I was about your age. It was Valentine's Day, and I got a Valentine from a guy named Andy who had a crush on me. But instead of signing the card "Love, Andy" he signed it "Like, Andy." I guess he didn't want to scare me. But in fact, I thought that was the silliest thing I had ever seen—nobody signs a card "Like."

My point is that your guy is probably just avoiding the mistake that my Andy made. Your guy is probably just writing "Love" as a pleasant closing to an email, especially if the email is a little bit flirty. I definitely agree with you that after only three weeks, it is much too soon for him to use the word "love." But this would only be a big problem if he were using it in the sentence, "I love you." When "love" is used as a closing for an email, it is a bit heavy, but he probably does not mean much by it. However, I recommend that you hint that it's not what you have in mind: when you sign your email, do not use "love." Perhaps you could sign your email, "Your email pal," or "Have fun," or, "Talk to you in school," or even just "Bye." Whatever you do, don't sign it "Like." That's just too silly.

saying i love you

Dear Sari,
Should I say "I love you" for the first time on Valentine's Day?

Sari Says:
You should only say "I love you" for the first time when you are sure that's how you feel, and you are sure that your boyfriend or girlfriend will say it back (or if he or she does not say it back, you will not be hurt!). Sometimes on Valentine's Day people feel pressured to say "I love you." That

pressure is bad for a relationship. Forget what day it is! If you want to say "I love you" on Valentine's Day, that's fine, but you don't have to.

does she mean "i love you"?

Dear Sari,

I've been going out with this girl for five months. Every time I say "I love you," to her, I'm not sure if she knows I mean it seriously. She says she loves me, too, but she thinks it's like a "young boyfriend/girlfriend" love, and not like an intimate love. I want her to realize it—and I'm not trying to be mean or anything, but I want her to grow up a bit so she knows that I'm serious and that I'm committed. I know she's committed, too. I just feel like she doesn't really know what I mean when I say, "I love you" to her. I feel like she's not that mature yet, or something like that. What should I do?

Sari Says:

No matter how young you are, you can love someone. But there are different kinds of love. Let her know why you feel that you love her. Instead of just saying, "I love you," be specific. Say things like: "I love the way you look," or "I love the funny things you say," or "I love that you are always there for me." If you really feel like your love for her is as deep as you say, then try to express that.

Then ask her about her feelings toward you. If she does not love you the way you love her, that is not necessarily a sign of immaturity. It might actually be a sign that she *is* mature, and she is just not as in love with you as you are with her. If she feels differently from how you feel, you need to decide if she is the right girl for you. Will you be hurt if she does not love you as much as you love her? Think about that. If you can deal with the fact that your feelings for each other may be at different levels, at least right now, then stay with her—but you may need to tone it down a bit.

love times two

Dear Sari,
I feel very close to telling two different people that I love them both, and then finding out which one loves me, too, and wants to go steady with me. Can you be in love with two people at one time?

Sari Says:
Sort of. . . . What you are feeling for both people is probably not "love," but more like a crush, or "puppy love." If it is real love, it is usually so good that you wouldn't want anyone else. Before you say a word to either of these people, try to sort it out on your own. Decide for yourself who you want to be with, then let the other one down easy, you lovebird, you.

Serious Relationships

balancing school and a relationship

Dear Sari,
I've been with this really great guy for over a year. He just got his report card back, and he did really badly. His dad almost made him call me and break up with me, but his mom told him not to. I feel like it's wrong to be with him when his parents don't want us to be. We can't do anything on the weekends and I don't know what I am supposed to do.

Sari Says:
Of course, this will put a strain on your relationship and limit the time that you spend together. But if you care enough to really want to stay in this relationship, then there are probably some creative ways to handle this period. Ask your boyfriend if you can spend some time with him on the weekends at his place, helping him study. This way, you can spend time

together without feeling guilty about it. You could talk to his mom about all of this if you want—ask her if she thinks there is anything you can do to help him, and let her know that you also want to see him improve in school. If she feels like you are helping him, rather than taking him away from his schoolwork, then she (and maybe even his dad) should feel okay about you two being together.

basketball player

Dear Sari,

I have a boyfriend that talks basketball and plays basketball constantly; we never have time together. For the past few months we haven't done anything . . . well, I played basketball with him one Saturday, but I don't call that spending quality time with yours truly. He tells me I'm caring, beautiful and special . . . but what's *really* special to him? How can I get him to think about me once in a while and my feelings about this? Should I break it off? I'm afraid to talk to him, because I'd offend him. What should I do?!

Sari Says:

This guy is probably not for you—you obviously want a boyfriend who wants to spend time with you. I know that you probably feel funny about breaking up with him because there are some good things about this guy, and because you want a boyfriend. But you should break up with him, because your unfulfilled feelings about your relationship far outweigh your good feelings about it.

If you want to talk with him to give this relationship another chance, then you can. Tell him how you feel, and ask him if he wants to make changes. If he says he'll try, then give him a month or so to show that he can spend more time with you. If he still does not make space for you in his life, then tell him that you want to break up and maybe try to stay friends. I bet that you will find someone more suited for you soon after your break up! Even if you have to go for a while without a boyfriend, you are likely to be happier than being with him; it is better to feel free and alone then to feel ignored by your boyfriend.

Loving Without Losing Yourself

When you get into a serious relationship, do not lose yourself; do not give up your own interests; do not stop talking to your friends. While you need to have time to spend with your partner, you still need to be yourself. If you give up who you really are, then you will not be happy or fulfilled in the long run.

can you still flirt?

Dear Sari,

I have been dating the same guy for about eight months. Things are very serious, and I really like him a lot. But I want to be able to flirt and hang with my friends and talk about other guys. I don't know what to do—I am so confused. Should I break up with him?

Sari Says:

If you had said that you wanted to date other guys, I would say that you should break up with your boyfriend. However, most of what you've told me doesn't indicate that you have to break up with him. You said that you want to hang out with your friends and talk about other guys. These are things that you should be able to do even though you have a boyfriend. You also said that you want to flirt. As long as you do not flirt in front of your boyfriend and as long as you are 100 percent sure that your flirting does not lead to anything or lead another guy on, then occasional harmless flirting is okay. Allow yourself these freedoms and see how it affects your relationship. If you realize that you want the flirting to go further and you actually want to date other people, then there's your answer: You should break up with your boyfriend. Otherwise, there probably isn't any reason to break up with him.

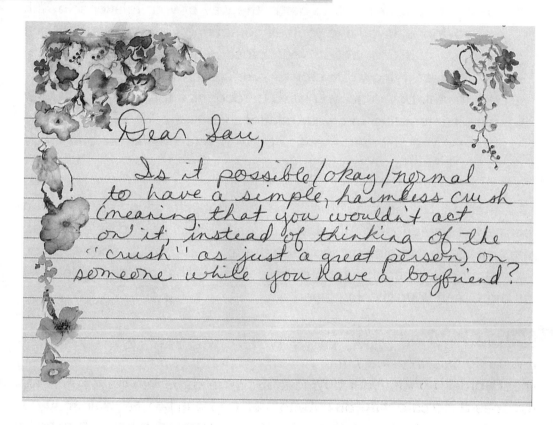

Dear Sari,

Is it possible/okay/normal to have a simple, harmless crush (meaning that you wouldn't act on it, instead of thinking of the "crush" as just a great person) on someone while you have a boyfriend?

Sari Says:

When many people are in a relationship, they are so into their partner that they don't even notice anyone else. But for others, it's normal to have the kind of crush you've described even while in a relationship. It's harmless if you don't act on it, a "look but don't touch" kind of thing. Here are some points to keep in mind:

- Do not let your boyfriend know about your crush. It could make him jealous and hurt, when he has no reason to be.
- Do not blab to your friends about your crush—it could get back to your boyfriend. The crush will have to be a secret only you know.
- Do not allow your crush to get in the way of your relationship with your boyfriend. If you find yourself comparing your boyfriend to your crush, or thinking about your crush when you are with your boyfriend, or trying to be around your crush when you should really be with your boyfriend, you need to recognize these signs that your crush is interfering with your relationship. In that case, you have to decide if you still really want to be with your boyfriend—and if you do, you'll need to get over your crush.

Overall, a little harmless crush that does not last too long is fine when you are in a relationship. But a major crush would be a problem. Keep your crushes to a minimum, and keep them under control; otherwise, you will need to think seriously about the possibility that other guys interest you more than your own boyfriend.

winning over his parents

Dear Sari,
I've been dating a guy for over two years now. His parents walked in on us during a make-out session, and now they hate the idea of us being a couple. This hasn't stopped us that much, but we both don't like the fact that we go behind their back. My parents are completely cool, though. So what should my boyfriend and I do to get our relationship back to the norm with his folks?

Sari Says:
Ask your boyfriend to talk to his parents—just the three of them. He

should try to find out why his parents don't approve of your relationship. Is it because they think that you are too young for a relationship this serious? Or is it just that they still haven't recovered from seeing you making out? During this conversation, your boyfriend could explain that you two are in no hurry, and that for now you just really enjoy being with each other.

Also, he should tell his parents that you'll definitely be more discreet about when and where you kiss from now on! He should explain that he doesn't want to sneak around—so if they want him to always be truthful and open with them, they should accept these things.

Finally, ask your parents if they would be willing to have his parents over for dinner one night. If his parents spend time with your parents, maybe it will help—they'll have someone to talk to who understands your relationship with your boyfriend.

teen marriage?

Dear Sari,

Hi, I'm 17 years old and my boyfriend is 19. We have been together for four years. He asked me if I would marry him. I really love him, but my parents say I'm too young to get married. What do you think I should do?

Sari Says:

People do not get married simply because they are in love and have been together for a long time. People need to have had a very good relationship for years, and (this is very important) they have to want the same things out of life. Unfortunately, many teen marriages end in divorce, because the couple gets married before they really know who they are or what they want out of life. Then when they get older, one or both of them outgrow their spouse. The best marriages are often the ones in which the two people are fully independent adults before they decide to get married.

213

Before people get married, they need to consider lots of things: how they will make money to support themselves, where they both want to live, what else they want to accomplish in their lives besides being a husband or wife, when and if they want to have children, and how they want to raise them.

Then there's the issue of wondering whether there's someone or something better out there for you. Lots of couples who get married as teens have problems, because they start to resent the possibility that they've missed out on a lot in life by marrying so young.

You and your boyfriend need to talk about all of these issues. You should also talk to your parents, his parents, and someone who is outside of the situation, such as a counselor, therapist, or someone from your church.

This is a major decision. Please take time to sort it out. Remember, you can stay boyfriend and girlfriend for as long as you want—you don't have to get married just because it seems like the next step.

worry about him

Dear Sari,
I'm sooo stressed. A few months ago, my boyfriend was in a car accident. He's okay; he just needed a few stitches. Ever since then, I get so paranoid about him driving. I'm scared to death he'll get in another accident. If he says he'll be home at three, and it's 3:05 and he still hasn't called, I flip and break down crying! Whenever he's driving and I'm not with him, I panic and think something's happened. I'm just so paranoid—please help me!

Sari Says:
Your fears are *not* rational. Yes, people sometimes get in car accidents. But this is not something you should worry about every day. You're wor-

rying because it's something you wish you could control. However, you've got to realize that worrying does not help you control the situation. You need to find a way to stop yourself from having these scary thoughts.

When you start worrying, take several deep breaths to calm yourself down. Then tell yourself, "Stop worrying. He's fine." Repeat that over and over to yourself until you can calm down. Then do something else to get your mind off your boyfriend. For instance, when you know he'll be driving, do not allow yourself to watch the clock wondering if he's okay. Instead, read a book, talk to a friend on the phone, do homework, surf the Net, or go out shopping. Any time you start to worry, repeat the process of taking some deep breaths and telling yourself to stop worrying.

Also, if your boyfriend is a good driver (and hopefully he is), remind yourself that he drives safely. The risk of a car accident is much lower if he drives responsibly. If he's not such a good driver, or if he thinks he wants more experience, he could take a driver's ed course as a review. Maybe you could suggest you take the course together, so you can both improve your driving. Improving driving skills can help. Worrying does not help. So stop worrying!

Fighting

Dear Sari,

My boyfriend and I are always fighting. We fight about stupid stuff like what movie to see, or what time he should pick me up. Plus we fight about big things. He gets mad when I go somewhere without him, and doesn't seem to trust me. I'm just worn out from fighting with him every day. But we have been together seven months and I love him. I don't know how to fix things.

Sari Says:

One of the best ways to determine whether or not a relationship is good (and worth staying in or not) is how well a couple works out their problems. It's okay if a couple fights about little things, or even has a big fight once in a while—as long as they know how to resolve the issues. If you and your boyfriend cannot resolve your issues, then you will just keep getting into arguments over and over again. You two may not have much of a future together if you spend most of your time fighting. But before you give up, try the following things to work on your relationship:

- Talk with him about his trust issues. Reassure him that you love him, and that even if you go out without him, you are still thinking of him the entire time. Also, invite your boyfriend to come along more often. Then he'll be able to see that what you do when you go out is far less threatening than he had imagined. Tell him that you want him to trust you more—and ask him to let you know what else you can do that would show you are faithful.

- Talk with him about your communication problem. This won't be the easiest thing in the world, since you often end up fighting when you try to talk. To make it easier, start the conversation at a time when you are less likely to fight, such as when you are both relaxed and happy. First, tell him that you love him and you want to stay with him for a long time. Then let him know that you'd like to figure out a way to stop fighting. Discuss some alternatives to fighting. For example, when one of you gets mad, you could each leave the room for a few minutes and write down what, exactly, is making you mad. Then you could each read what the other person wrote and take another few minutes to find a way to talk about the problem without fighting. You will both need to talk about your *feelings*, rather than just arguing about an issue.

- Also, you will both need to admit that you are wrong at times, or at least that you both need to be more understanding of how to give each other what you need. It is okay to be wrong, and it is helpful to be able to admit that you see the other person's point of view. Don't allow yourselves to fight just for the sake of fighting.

- Finally, be alert to what's going on, so that when a fight starts, one of you remembers to say, "Whoa! Let's stop this—neither of us really wants to be fighting." Then take a "time out." You *can* stop a fight right in the middle, go into separate rooms for a few minutes, then try to talk about the problem.

Hopefully, the more you work at this, the better it will get. If the situation doesn't improve, then you need to consider ending the relationship—you would be better off as just friends.

Dealing with Jealousy

jealousy

Dear Sari,

I am always getting jealous every time my boyfriend talks to another female. I do trust him. But I just always get jealous and wonder if he would cheat. How can I stop?

Sari Says:

If you want a good relationship now, don't waste your time worrying that he might cheat. You say that you trust him, but if you are always worrying when he talks to other girls, you don't trust him.

When you see him talking to girls, tell yourself that he is just being nice and friendly. Tell yourself he has chosen to be with you, not them. Remind yourself that he wants you over every other girl. He should not have to tell you these things—you have to tell yourself! You cannot control the fact that he might talk to other girls once in a while. What you can control is that when you two are together, you're having the best time possible! Try to stop yourself from thinking jealous thoughts by having so much fun with him that that's all you think about.

he's jealous

Dear Sari,
I love my boyfriend with all my heart . . . but he doesn't trust me. I'm an attractive female (or so I'm told). Well, my boyfriend constantly makes comments like, "Oh yeah, I'm sure that you were in the boy's locker room while the entire football team was changing," and "You can count on my girlfriend to flirt with any guy." He says he loves me; I told him how I feel about this and he said he'll stop . . . but he hasn't.

Sari Says:
Sometimes it's flattering when a guy gets jealous. But this sounds downright annoying. Your boyfriend is probably saying these things because he's insecure about being with one of the most attractive girls in school. If he were more confident, he'd know that you only want to be with him, and he wouldn't make dumb comments. In addition to reminding him that you asked him to cut this out, you could also reassure him that you only want to be with him. For example, if he makes some crack about how the football team likes you, say, "Put all the players on the team together, and they still wouldn't be as hot as you are! I only want to be with you!"

Hopefully he'll start to realize that he has nothing to worry about, and stop making such rude comments. But if he doesn't, you should think about getting a new boyfriend—one who only says nice things about you.

female friend

Dear Sari,

My boyfriend has a female friend that he has had feelings for in the past, but not now—or so he says. The problem is, she is at his house 24/7. I don't mind him having her as a friend because I trust him. It's *her* I don't trust. It makes me so uncomfortable that she is always there. He doesn't understand why I feel this way and gets mad at me if I get upset. What can I do to make this better—because it's making our relationship horrible!

Sari Says:

You either have to get used to the friend being there, or you have to talk to your boyfriend to see if he is willing to change things enough that you feel good about it. Tell him that you trust him, but you just don't like sharing him *all* the time. However, since you said that you've already tried talking with him about it, you may simply have to accept the situation as it is. If he is truly trustworthy, he won't let her do anything, no matter what—and you should have nothing to worry about.

In order to stop worrying, try to keep yourself busy when you know that she is over at his place. Get a new hobby, or a new friend, or throw yourself into your schoolwork. Or think of fun things that you and he can do when you get together. That way you won't just be sitting around obsessing about her. Remember that your relationship is about you and *him*—not you and her; not him and her. Do not waste your time—or mind space!—worrying about this girl. Instead, focus on yourself and your boyfriend.

obsessed with his ex

Dear Sari,

How do I stop obsessing about what my boyfriend did with his ex-girlfriend? Even though he no longer sees her or talks to her, *I* think about her all the time. What is this about?

Sari Says:
Wouldn't it be cool if you were the only person who had ever been a part of your boyfriend's life? That's not reality. The fact is that everyone has a past. But it is just that: past. You may be obsessed with it, because of your own issues of feeling replaceable (such as thinking, if he replaced her with me, then what's to say he won't replace me with someone else?). But the fact is that he is with you now, so you need to start living in the present and enjoy him. Get her out of your head. Tell yourself "stop" when you think of her. Then do something fun with him. Do not let some phantom into your relationship.

snoop snoopy snoop

Dear Sari,
How can I stop myself from snooping through my boyfriend's stuff?

Sari Says:
Remind yourself that you should respect him and allow him some privacy. Remember that if he loves you, he would not hide things from you, and you can trust that without snooping. Finally, realize that snooping is dangerous, because if you find something, then you will have to confront him, reveal that you snooped, and deal with the consequences. If you do not find something, then you might end up endlessly looking and looking. Stop the cycle. Fight the urge to snoop!

Dear Sari,

I am in a serious relationship with my boyfriend, and I am starting to doubt some things he says. He has been canceling on me all the time, saying that he has to work at his new job. Then, he told me about three days in a row that he would come pick me up after school. What happened? He said he forgot and fell asleep. Can I trust him? I have no clue if I should believe him or not. I'm totally confused and am in need of help!

Sari Says:

If you trust your guy, now is the time to be supportive and patient. He is going through a busy period and he might just need some time to figure out for himself how he will juggle a job and a girlfriend.

You could talk to him about being more conscientious when you two have plans to get together. Let him know that you trust him and support him, but that you wish he would not break plans at the last minute. You could also tell him that you miss spending time with him, and you want to know if he thinks that his schedule will change soon. Hopefully, it will only be a week or two until he can manage to spend a lot more time with you.

On the other hand, if after a couple of weeks or maybe a month you still aren't spending any time together and he keeps breaking plans, ask your boyfriend if you and he can discuss this problem further. It's possible that his feelings about this relationship have changed, and he is just afraid to tell you.

If your instincts are telling you that his excuses are lame and his stories sound sketchy, then try to get him to explain exactly what he is doing and why he keeps blowing you off. Get him to talk about his feelings about your relationship. Of course, he may get defensive if you confront him. Try to calmly and nicely address the situation by saying something like, "I feel like you and I don't get to spend as much time together as we used to. Is everything okay, or should we talk about our relationship? You can tell me anything." I hope this is just a passing phase, and that he is a trustworthy guy who just needs some time to figure out his schedule!

Long-Distance Relationships

summer distance

Dear Sari,

My boyfriend of nine months recently told me that he is going to be away for the entire summer. Several of my friends are telling me to break off the relationship because it won't work, but then others say if it is strong enough, we will last through the eight weeks. What should I do?

Sari Says:

Don't worry so much about what your friends say. Stay together throughout the summer if that is what both of you want. The week before he goes away, have a long talk about both of your hopes for the relationship over this summer. Ideally, you'll agree that neither of you will date other people and you will trust each other.

Sometimes distance is good for a relationship. "Absence makes the heart grow fonder," as the old saying goes. But as another saying goes, "Out of sight, out of mind." Try to do a good job of keeping in touch with each other to avoid the "out of mind" outcome. Make a deal that you'll talk on the phone once a week and write letters once a week. Communicating like that will strengthen your relationship, because you'll be able to express words and feelings that you'd have trouble expressing in person. The time will go faster than you think it will. Also, keep yourself busy with lots of other friends and activities so you don't feel too sad, depressed, or lonely when he's away.

Dear Sari,
A few months ago, I got into a long-distance relationship with a guy who used to go to my school but then moved 3,000 miles away. His personality is everything I could ever want: sweet, caring, funny, smart. I feel so special when I'm talking to him on Instant Message. But lately, I just think it's better to end it now, no matter how much it will hurt us, than keep it going nowhere, since I may never see him again. What should I do?

Sari Says:
To determine if you should stay with him, think about if your needs are being met. If you need to have a guy around in person, then you're not going to be happy in this long-distance relationship. In that case, you are right that you should cut this off now, since you already know that it's not enough for you. Why tie yourself down if it is wrong for you?

On the other hand, sometimes it is not such a great idea to cut off a relationship that is bringing you a lot of happiness. If being with him—even long distance—makes you happy right now, then maybe you don't need to worry about what will happen in the future. Sometimes it's awesome to live one day at a time.

To help figure out which way to go, make a list of the pros and cons of being with him long distance. If one list outweighs the other, that could help you decide. But if you still find yourself fluctuating between wanting to make it work long distance and cutting him loose, then you may want to consider finding some kind of compromise. You could remain best friends long distance and still send great IMs, but you could also both be allowed to date other people where you live, if that opportunity comes up.

in love with a girl

Dear Sari,

I have fallen in love with my best friend, and she is the same sex as me. All I think about anymore is girls and not guys. I don't think that is normal, so how do I deal with this lesbian problem?

Sari Says:

You *are* normal. Discovering that you may be a lesbian is not a "problem." It is simply a new aspect of who you are that you'll need to get used to. If you suspect your female friend is heterosexual, don't tell her that you have a crush on her—that could ruin your friendship and confuse her. Instead, talk to a counselor about your feelings. You could ask your school counselor or nurse or health teacher if they know of any counselors who see teens for free about "personal identity issues" (if you don't want to say "gay, lesbian, and bisexual counseling"). Or if you don't want to ask at school, there are lots of online resources for gay, lesbian, and bisexual teens. Read the appendix in the back of this book for more information about organizations that can steer you toward support groups in your area.

maybe a lesbian

Dear Sari,

There's a girl who laughs at every joke I make. We wink at each other and stuff. Whenever she sees me in the hallway, she smiles and talks to me. I am not sure if she is flirting or just goofing around. I like her a lot and I would ask her if she likes me, but there is a problem . . . I am a girl, too! A friend asked her what she thought about me, and she said "I love her to death." Are we gay?

Sari Says:

Sometimes people who are the same gender (two girls *or* two boys) can feel very close as friends, and even feel like they are in love with each other, but that does not necessarily mean that they are gay or lesbians. This girl might just really like you and want to be good friends with you.

You need to figure out how you feel about her. Do you feel like you are "just friends," or do you feel attracted to her the way that a boyfriend and girlfriend would feel?

Sometimes teens and preteens feel attracted to members of the same gender, and that does still not automatically mean they are gay. At this age, it may just be a way of exploring your sexuality. However, if after a few years—such as, toward the end of high school—you find that you are attracted to other girls, and never to boys, you might conclude that you are gay. But at this stage of your life, you should probably not label yourself yet.

As far as your friendship with this girl goes, if it feels comfortable hanging around with her, then by all means, go ahead.

maybe gay

Dear Sari,

I don't know how to write about this kind of stuff because I am really quite embarrassed, but I have a real big problem. See, I think I like guys, but I am a guy. It is weird. I don't know what to do. Maybe I am straight, but I don't know. What are the signs of being gay? I don't want to come out of the closet if there really isn't anything to come out of the closet about. I want to tell my parents, but what do I say to them? They will probably disown me or something. Society just doesn't accept gay men. Please help me.

Sari Says:

When someone thinks he is gay, it means that he feels attracted to other men. It's a feeling of wanting to be closer to a guy—more than just a close friendship—it's having a sexual attraction to him. If you are not completely sure that you are gay, talk to a counselor about your feelings. You could ask your school counselor if he or she knows of any professional counselors who see teens about sexual identity. If you don't want to ask at school, there are lots of online resources for gay, lesbian, and bisexual teens. Check the appendix in the back of this book for resources.

Though there is still prejudice out there, society is finally becoming more tolerant of gay people, so don't worry about that for now. Focus on figuring out your own life. Find a counselor to help you talk about your sexual identity and to help you decide if it is time for you to talk with your parents.

breaking up is hard to do

A
h, love. Isn't it grand? The hand-holding, the smooching, the pet names you call each other in private, the cute little gifts you exchange, the endless kisses . . . the breaking up. Hey, wait a minute. Break-up? Who said anything about breaking up? Well, that's pretty much how it goes— one day, everything is as perfect as a new spring morning and then, blammo, you wake up to frost on the ground. Maybe your boyfriend has suddenly started acting a little aloof, or maybe that funny little habit that you always used to think was cute in your girlfriend starts driving you nuts. Whatever it is, relationships *can* end, and at some point, you're going to need to know how to recognize the bitter taste of love gone bad—and when it's time to deposit your significant other in the Ex Files.

Of course, it's never easy to be the dumpee. (Who likes getting his or her heart broken?) But then again, it's not always simple to be the dumper, either. (Who likes to hurt someone who may still love you?) Whichever your situation, there are ways to properly handle it *and* maintain your dignity. I don't have a magic potion that will mend your broken heart, but I can help to recognize when you should be looking for the door—and how to make a graceful exit.

snooping

Dear Sari,

I was snooping in my girlfriend's backpack, and I found a note that started out, "Hey sexy." Is she cheating on me? What do you think I should do?

Sari Says:

You've just pointed out one of the biggest problems with snooping: You have to figure out what to do if you find something. If you ask her about it, it would be obvious that you looked in her backpack without her permission. You'd have to tell her that you snooped, admit to her that it was wrong, and tell her that you are sorry.

However, you might not want to talk to her about it at all. If you ask her about it, and the note turns out to be something totally innocent (it's very possible that a friend of hers was just kidding around), then you are going to be the bad guy in this situation. You'll look like you don't trust her, and you violated her privacy in order to accuse her of something that's not even true.

So maybe you should just try to forget about this. If you have no other reason to suspect that your girlfriend is cheating on you, then you shouldn't accuse her of anything. Trust her and fight the urge to snoop again. On the other hand, if you feel that you have other reasons to be suspicious, then keep your eyes open for anything else that seems fishy (without snooping). Finally, you may want to talk to her about your relationship—without even mentioning what you found. Tell her that you are committed to her 100 percent and you hope that she is committed, too. No matter what you do, respect your girlfriend's privacy—and don't ever snoop again!

is watching strippers cheating?

Dear Sari,

Is it cheating for a guy to watch strippers? My boyfriend of over a year saw strippers with a bunch of his buddies. He thought that I would understand that it didn't mean anything to him. However, I felt betrayed. I am a very conservative person, and my boyfriend and I have not gone very far—so this hurt even more. I said that I would give him a second chance. He truly was sorry and I know that I don't want to break up with him. Did we do the right thing?

Sari Says:

He was right to admit that he saw the strippers, and you were right to talk with him about your feelings. Many women would not want their guys to see strippers, even if they don't consider it "cheating." You did the right thing by letting him know that this is something he shouldn't do, out of respect for you.

However, I do not think you should make the stripper incident into a major issue. You need to let this go. He didn't intend to upset you; he was honest and told you about it, and he apologized. He seems to have no desire to see strippers again, and in fact, it even sounds like he was not into it the one time he did. Now he knows that he shouldn't do this again—and you will know, too. You just have to put this behind you if you want to have a happy relationship with him. It meant nothing to him, so don't let it mean anything else to you.

Dear Sari,

My boyfriend of a year and a half was meeting girls online behind my back. I feel devestated. He denied it for months, then confessed that he has been going into chat rooms for teens who live in our city and emailng with at least three girls who he met there. He told me that he talked on the phone to one of the girls a lot and he sadi he talked to another one of the girls a little, but he swears that he never met any of them in person. I feel like he cheated on me, but he keeps saying that it was not a big deal, and that he did not cheat because he did not meet them in person. WHO IS RIGHT? PLEASE HELP ME.

Sari Says:
Cyber-cheating is cheating. Here's why what your boyfriend did is wrong:

- He lied to you when you asked him about it before.
- He took time away from your relationship to do this.
- He was trying to make plans to get together with at least one of these girls.
- He was portraying himself as single when he'd go into the chat room.
- Phone dates and email can be just as intimate as in-person dates.

If he insists that it should not be called cheating, then tell him that's fine to call it whatever he wants, but it is still very wrong. His deception is grounds to break up with him. If he swears that he will stop emailing with these girls, throw away their phone numbers, change his screen name, and stop going into chat rooms, then maybe you can consider staying with him on a trial basis. But otherwise, you must get out of this relationship if you want a boyfriend who can be faithful to you!

once more chance?

Dear Sari,
I had been dating this girl for eight months, and she cheated on me. Well, it's been a month now and she is asking me to be with her again. She says she won't cheat on me and that I should give her one more chance.

Sari Says:
You have to decide if you want to get back with her. Consider these things:

1. Can you get over the fact that she cheated on you, and can you stop thinking about it?

If you are the obsessive type, then chances are that you will not be able to be with her: you may fixate on the fact that she cheated, and you may not be able to forget it.

2. Can you trust her again?
   If she has explained why she cheated and why it will not happen again, and you can accept what she says, then maybe you can try to trust her again. But if it seems like nothing will change, then you probably will not be able to trust her.

3. Is she, and is this relationship, worth the work?
   Getting back together and improving your relationship will require work. Do you think this person is so "meant for you" that you should work on it? Or would you be better off staying broken up and finding someone whom you are more compatible with?

4. Could you handle it if you broke up again?
   Often when people get back together, the same problems—or worse problems—break them up again. If you two break up again, could you handle the pain? Or would you be better off cutting your losses and staying broken up now?

If you really think that this girl is amazing, and that somehow things between you can be better this time, then get back together. But if there are doubts in your mind, be careful. You do not have to get back with her, and you should not be afraid of being alone. Instead, look forward to meeting someone even better. After all, she hurt you, and you deserve better.

i cheated . . . again!

Dear Sari,
I love my boyfriend so much—I admitted to cheating on him, and after a few tears he forgave me. Then, stupid me, I go out and do it again. Should I tell him?

Sari Says:

What you should tell him is that you do not want to stay in a committed relationship with him! You obviously are not being a good girlfriend to him. You seem to want to be single—so why stay with him? Tell your boyfriend that you cheated again, then tell him that you must break up because you cannot be committed to him. Assure him that it is all your fault, not his. Then, you need to move on, because if you stay with him and cheat, you are just going to hurt him more and more.

However, if you can think of twenty good reasons to stay with him, then maybe you should. And in that case, you *must* stop cheating on him. Of course, if you tell him that you cheated, then you may not have a choice in the matter—he may dump you. So if you really think you want to stay with him and if you do not tell him that you cheated, then you must make a pact with yourself to never, ever do it again. Stop hurting him and break up now—or stop cheating for good.

Signs of Cheating

These are often signs that someone could potentially cheat. The person:
- Cheated in the past.
- Flirts too much.
- Ignores you when you're out with other people.
- Recently changed the way he or she looks or has started talking a lot about new friends whom you don't know.
- Wants to see you less often.
- Has been lying about where he or she has been or what he or she was doing.

he cheated with his ex

Dear Sari,

My boyfriend of two months cheated on me with his ex-girlfriend. The thing that bothered me the most was that he lied to me about it. Not once, but twice—and his ex denied the entire thing. I think he cheated because I wouldn't have sex with him. (He told me that wasn't the reason for his cheating.) My question is, do you think I should break up with him? What should I do?

Sari Says:
If you think that he is worthy of another chance, you could stay with him a little longer to see if he can be faithful to you. However, he lied to you, cheated on you, and seems to be pressuring you to have sex (whether he says he is or not). Those are three strikes against him. Why allow yourself to be hurt by him any more? You deserve a guy who will treat you better.

Another thing: This guy cheated on you early in your relationship. Wouldn't it be great to start a new relationship with a more respectful guy with whom you can have a great time—from the beginning and for many months to come?

Deciding to Break Up or Work It Out

break-up jokes

Dear Sari,
I am currently going out with a guy, but every time I talk to him online, he says he wants to break up. Then he says he is kidding and he would never do anything to hurt me. I need to make our relationship better. What can I do? Please help before something bad ends up happening.

Sari Says:
Joking about breaking up could mean that this guy is confused about whether or not he really wants a committed relationship, or that he has a

bad sense of humor, or maybe that he is just wicked (and I mean wicked "bad" not wicked "good"). Ask him why he says these things. Tell him that you don't think it's funny, it makes you uncomfortable and you want him to stop!

He says he doesn't want to hurt you, but he is hurting you by stressing you out about where you stand with him. Tell him that if he has concerns about your relationship he should tell you, so that you two can talk honestly about it. And if not—if he really wants to be with you—he should not even joke about breaking up. Tell him how much you like him, and that you want to have a good relationship with him. If he, too, wants a good relationship, the step toward making things better is simply having a good time with him. Spend time together, and tell each other more about yourselves to get even closer.

did bad things

Dear Sari,
My boyfriend and I have been going out for almost a year now. We've been through a lot together and I love him very much. My parents used to like him, too, but now they have made me break up with him. He has done some pretty bad things to me, such as cheating on me and verbally and physically hurting me. I can understand why my parents are so mad, but he's set on changing and I really believe that he will. How can I make my parents understand and come around?

Sari Says:
Your parents want the best for you, and they do not want to see you get hurt. They are protecting you from this guy because they know (and deep down you know!) that he is certainly not good enough for you if he is abusive. You deserve to be with a guy who treats you with kindness, respect, and love.

You think he may change, but your parents probably know that it takes a very long time for people to truly change. I understand that you want to give him another chance. After some time passes, if you really feel that he is changing, talk things over with your parents again.

However, to tell you the truth, waiting around for this guy to change might not be the best idea. Right now you probably feel like you cannot live without him—breaking up is so tough, and it leaves you feeling lonely. But consider that you may be way better off without this guy! If, after a little while, you got him out of your mind entirely, you'd be clearing the way for yourself to meet someone new—someone who can love you the way you should be loved. Starting over with someone new may be the best remedy for your situation.

mixed messages

Dear Sari,

I have a girlfriend and we've been going out for almost six months. However, lately I've been feeling weird. Sometimes I feel as though the relationship is as strong as ever, and sometimes I feel the exact opposite. I get mixed messages a lot. Sometimes it seems that I'm the only person in her world, and other times I'm just so unhappy with her that I would rather break up right then. I'm really confused about this.

Sari Says:

You and your girlfriend must be feeling distant from each other. Sometimes when that happens in a relationship two people can stay together if they talk about what they want from the relationship, and from each other. They can work things out by finding new ways to be romantic and add excitement to their relationship. But other times, this feeling of distance is a sign that the relationship is over.

To figure out what to do, first, get together with your girlfriend for a relaxing date; maybe go for ice cream or something. Then tell her that you feel distant from her at times. Ask her if she feels the same way. Talk about what you both want to do about it. If you both think that it is best to move on, then you should break up. But, after talking, you may decide that you both want to work on things and try to stay together. In that case, you'll have to tell your girlfriend every time you feel things are weak in the relationship (and she'll have to tell you every time she thinks things need improvement), and then you'll need to find ways to fix it. It could take a lot of work, so you should both be sure that you want to stay together.

Falling in love with another

Dear Sari,
I have been going out with this guy for four months and I really love him with all my heart and soul. But I have fallen for my best guy friend; I mean, we are made for each other, he's perfect. With my boyfriend I am lacking a whole lot of love, he just never calls me (it's long distance) and he just doesn't show me he cares. But I know he does, and he says he loves me. I just don't know what to do. I am so confused.

Sari Says:
Try to decide if you want to break up with your boyfriend, regardless of the fact that you like your best guy friend. It sounds to me like your boyfriend is not right for you. I know that it feels amazing when a guy says he loves you, but actions speak louder than words—and this guy is not giving you the attention that you need. Since your relationship is long distance, it takes extra effort on both of your parts, and based on what you wrote to me, he is not giving that extra effort. If you want to break up with your boyfriend, it should be for those reasons—not because of your new love interest.

After you break up, then you can decide if your friend is really right for you to get involved with. Make sure that you are willing to risk your friendship by going out with him. (Keep in mind that if you break up with him after going out for a while, it might be very difficult to be friends again.) Also, try to be sure that you didn't start liking your guy friend just because you were trying to get out of your not-so-great relationship with your boyfriend. If you've thought carefully about these issues, and you are sure that you both want to start dating, then go for it.

Get Over It or Get Back Together?

not right for each other

Dear Sari,

I was going out with this girl I really liked. We had been going out for two months. Every weekend we would go see a movie, go to the mall, go to parties or dances. We were always together and happy. Then this girl who I care so much for told me that she had changed in the past few days. She said that she didn't think we were right for each other and that she only wanted to be friends. This is the most painful thing that has ever happened to me. I still love her. She means everything to me. I would do anything to get her back. Please help me. I can't handle this hurt.

Sari Says:

Breaking up is one of the most painful things in the world. You feel lost, lonely, and depressed. But those bad feelings will pass! I promise that you will feel better soon if you try to get your mind off of this and think about other things. Go out with friends, get involved with an activity or sport that you like. Do whatever you can to keep your mind off her and put new things in your life to fill the void that she left. If you feel extremely depressed, talk about this with your close friends or your family.

Sometimes getting your feelings off your chest can help. Whenever you feel ready, start trying to meet new girls to date. Eventually, you will find someone new to fall in love with.

getting back together?

Dear Sari,

My ex and I went out for over a year, and we have been apart for seven months. He has a new girlfriend, but I'm single. He still tells me he loves me and that he misses me. He even went so far as to say that I'm better then his new girlfriend. Well, this last week he and I had sex four times. I told him that he has three choices: he can have me as a friend, he can have me as a girlfriend, or he can't have me. He didn't say anything. Now I think he's left his girlfriend, but I'm not sure. I know it's really messed up, but can you please help me?

Sari Says:

Your ex really only has two choices: he can have you as a girlfriend, or he can't have you at all. It sounds to me as if you two can't successfully have just a friendship right now. You've been too close for too long to be friends. Once people go out for more than a few months (especially if they've had sex) and then break up, it is very difficult for them to take the step backward to being friends again.

You two are still sexually attracted to each other, so a friendship would be too hard. Also, if you were really his friend, then you never would have let him cheat on his new girlfriend. Friends don't do that. If you really think that you and this guy should get back together, give it one more try (only if he did break up with his girlfriend). Otherwise, move on! Stop having sex with him and stay away from him altogether. You can find someone who you like more if—and only if—you make room by getting your ex entirely out of your life.

Dear Sari,

My ex-boyfriend and I broke up a few months ago. It was my doing, for the second time. The circumstances under which I broke up with him are complicated, but let's just say that though we had very few arguments, it felt necessary at the time. I didn't feel he truly cared, though he said he did. Now, I really want him back. . . . We've been together a few times since we broke up, and although he says he still cares for me and likes me, he also says that he couldn't go through a third break-up. I have expressed to him how much I care for him and like him, but he refuses to give me another chance. I want to find some way of getting him back, but people say I criticize him too much and he figures I don't truly like him. I've tried my hardest to be very sweet to him and show him, without being clingy, that I still want him back. Maybe the damage has already been done.

Sari Says:

If he gave you a third chance, that would mean you would have to completely accept him, as he is, for a long time. You'd have to avoid criticizing him; you could never threaten to break up with him.

Right now you are being sweet to him, but if you got back together, would you keep that up? Remember that you broke up with him for good reasons—two times! You probably made the right decision.

Since you've already broken up twice, it sounds as if you are not right for each other. Don't try to get back together just because you miss having a boyfriend.

You're feeling so depressed right now because breaking up is hard and being alone is difficult. But you can and will get over him. When you start to feel depressed about breaking up with your ex, think about all the things that bugged you about him. Those things have not changed, and you will continue to be annoyed by them. He's right to worry that you'd break up with him again if you got back together. Stick with your decision and stay broken up. I bet you'll find someone who's better for you as soon as you get over this relationship.

Feeling for ex

Dear Sari,
The thing is I broke up with my ex to go out with this other guy. Well, things didn't work out and I still have feelings for my ex . . . and tonight he asked me out again. I am scared that things will be weird because I have had second-time relationships before and they never work. But I really want things to work.

Sari Says:
Getting back together with someone usually does not work because the problem that broke you up may occur again—and break you up again. In this case, the problem was that you wanted to date someone else. Do you still need your dating freedom, or can you honestly say that you are 100 percent sure that you do not want to date anyone else and you want to commit to a relationship with your ex? If you are not completely sure, then I do not think that you should get back together with your ex. Why cause him, and you, added pain? Of course, you did write that you really want things to work out with him, and that you know how tough "second-time relationships" can be, so you probably know that you will need to put a lot of work into this if you get back together.

If you want to try to work on it, I suggest that you and your boyfriend talk about the issues in your relationship at least once a week. Be totally honest with him and ask him to be honest with you about all of your feelings. Working on a relationship requires communication and compromises. Of course, you will also need to have fun and create new experiences that you can share together, so your relationship does not turn into all talk.

Dear Sari,

What does being on a "break" *really* mean? My boyfriend and I broke up two weeks ago. Well, two days ago, we kissed in the student parking lot. We are still not together . . . just on a "break" as he says . . . but what does that *really* mean? He says that he still wants to be with me, and that he still really likes me. So am I supposed to just wait around for him? I still have a lot of feelings for him. I don't know what to do. I am really confused.

Sari Says:

Being on a "break" usually means that two people are breaking up for a short period of time (such as a couple of weeks) to find out if they really want to stay together, or if they are better off staying broken up. You should not have to "wait around for him." After being on a break for that brief period of time, you need to decide if you should get back together or not. Now is the time for you two to talk and decide what to do next.

During a break, a couple should try to look for signals that they are ready to get back together, or ready to break up for good. If you start to date or kiss *other* people, that's a good sign that you should break up for good. If you don't want to date anyone else, and you're only kissing each other, those are good signs that you two could get back together.

Talk to him. Tell him that you are ready to get past this and get back together. Explain that to you, your kiss meant that you miss each other, you want to be together and things could work out between you two. Make sure he knows that during this break, you did not date anyone else, and you do not have the desire to date anyone else. Find out if he feels the same way. If not, then you will have to accept the fact that it is best if you break up for good. But since you want to be with him, hopefully he'll agree that it is time you two got back together.

Dear Sari,

My boyfriend and I just broke up a couple days ago and I am so depressed. I don't know whether I should go over to his house, because I don't think I would know what to say. I don't want to start talking about our break-up. Should I not go over, and just lay low until he makes the first move and wants to talk? I mean, if we started talking again, it would make things better. After all, we are only breaking up for a while anyway, we just needed room. So, should I go over there, or not?

Sari Says:

If you are taking a break because you "need room," then you need to have room! I don't think you should go over to this guy's house yet. True, if you're sure you want to get back together, the only way that will happen is if you talk it over with him. However, you both need some time alone right now to make sure that you really are ready to get back together.

Of course you're going to feel depressed—that's natural. To help cope, try keeping a journal about how you're feeling and what you wish you could say to him right now. (This will also help you prepare whatever you might want to say to him when you do talk.) In a few days, give him a call and ask if he's ready to get together. If he is, then have a talk with him and tell him why you are ready to get back together—if you're sure that's what you want. Just in case he does not want to get back together, make sure you have a support system of friends and family whom you can spend time with; this will help you get over him and get past your depression. Whether it works out with him or not, you deserve to be happy.

it's going bad

Dear Sari,

My boyfriend and I were together for over a year and six months; we were so in love. We used to do everything together, and he used to be so sweet, but about around two months ago things started going bad. He started getting really overprotective and he even hit me once. He broke up with me two weeks ago, but he still keeps coming around like he still loves me. I am still too weak to tell him to go away, and I'm not sure if I want him back, but meanwhile I don't know what to do!

Sari Says:

You broke up for good reasons. Now you just need to get some distance from each other so you can both move on. Be strong. Realize that you had a very good relationship for a long time. Cherish the good memories, but also feel secure in knowing that you are doing the right thing by moving on and getting out of what was becoming an abusive relationship.

You must tell him that you need space. Tell him that he's not allowed to stop by your house anymore. I know that you don't want to hurt him, but it will make things worse if you give him the feeling that he might have a chance to get back together with you. Also, spend more time with your friends, or at school activities, so that you'll be too busy to talk to him anyway.

ex keeps calling

Dear Sari,

Me and my ex broke up almost a month ago, but he calls all the time and thinks it will make me jealous if he tells me what he does with his new girlfriend. I think it's annoying because we both have new relationships, and I wish he would leave me alone. How do I tell him that without hurting his feelings?

Sari Says:

Tell him the way you just told me and do not worry about hurting his feelings! His feelings should not matter to you at this point. You have to take care of yourself. He needs to be told that he should not call you often. Let him know that you will call him when you want to talk to him, and if he doesn't hear from you that means you aren't in the mood to talk to him. When you do talk, if he brings up stuff that you don't want to hear about, tell him so. Say, "That should be between you and your girlfriend. Don't tell me about it anymore." Hopefully, he'll respect your wishes. Otherwise, stop talking to him altogether.

Getting Over an Ex

looking for revenge

Dear Sari,

One of my friends and I started dating (very bad idea). He said that he would never hurt me because we have been friends sooo long . . . but he did hurt me worse than anyone ever has. We broke up. I want to get him back for it. I am not just talking "egg his house." I want to do something that will really, really make him mad. Do you have any ideas?

Sari Says:

Have you ever heard the expression, "Success is the best revenge?" It's good advice. When somebody upsets you the way he did, trying to hurt him back is really awful. It's not only immature and petty, it can even be dangerous. What if he then tries to get back at you? Why start a war?

You should be the mature one: Ignore him and move on! The best way to get back at him is by proving you're just fine—happy, in fact—without him. Do not waste your time and energy thinking of something bad to do to him. Instead, think of some good things to do for yourself. Read a good book. Get a great haircut. Buy a new outfit. Have a great time with your friends. Meet a new guy to date. Forget about the jerk who hurt you, and enjoy yourself!

getting past the past

Dear Sari,
I was with my first boyfriend for a very long time. I fell in love with him—and it really was love. Then he cheated on me and broke up with me. It took me one year to fully get over him enough so that I could be with someone else. Now I'm with my new boyfriend. I like him a lot, but I'm scared to like him this much. He tells me he cares for me like no one else he has ever cared for. But I'm so scared to believe him. I don't want to be hurt again, but I don't want to lose my new boyfriend. He is the first person I have liked this much since my first boyfriend. What do I do?

Sari Says:
Keep doing what you are doing. You seem to be getting over the hurt from your ex and developing a strong relationship with your new boyfriend, and that's great!

I understand that you are afraid, but falling in love is always a risk. Sometimes you get hurt, and sometimes it is wonderful and magical, and well worth the risk. In a few weeks or months, as you and your new boyfriend get even closer, you will start to feel safer with him. Trust takes time, and over time you should feel safer about letting yourself fall in love with him.

Of course, there are no guarantees. There is always the chance that you could get hurt again. However, as you start to trust him, you will be able to decide if this is worth the risk. And usually, love is worth the risk. Most importantly, have fun with your new boyfriend. Don't worry so much, and try to get as much out of this relationship as you can.

breaking-up cycle

Dear Sari,

I've gone out with this girl three times in two years. Every time we break up, we're pissed at each other at first, but we're always friends afterwards. Then we get back together, then break up again. We are broken up now. But now there are other girls I like. If I so much as talk to another girl, my ex starts questioning everything I do. What do I do? Is she just jealous, or overprotective?

Sari Says:

You and your ex have created a cycle of breaking up and getting back together. She thinks that as long as you do not meet a new girl to date, then you will eventually get back together with her again. But if you date someone new, that will break the cycle—and that probably scares your ex. You need to help your ex move on, so that you can get on with your life. Here are some things that can help:

- Tell her that you have moved on and you will never get back together.
- Do not spend any time with her for a month or so.
- If you talk with her, do not mention any other girls.
- If she starts questioning you about other girls, don't tell her anything. You shouldn't lie, but it's none of her business; you should change the subject.
- If you do start dating someone, keep her away from your ex and don't hang out with your ex.

Your ex's tendency to be jealous may cause problems in your next relationship, or even with new friendships. You and your ex need to have some space and stay broken up for real—for good.

playing with your ex

Dear Sari,
I broke up with this guy about two months ago. Now we're both in our school musical. We have to work together a lot, but he won't even talk to me. This is his first time in theater so I want him to have a good experience, and I know that he isn't having fun with me being around all the time. I am totally over him now, but I still want to be friends. It is so hard for me to be around him because he is so mad. When I am in a performance, I try to get along with everyone so we can all act our best, but I can't because of him. What should I do? I have tried to talk to him but he keeps walking away and he won't listen to one word I have to say.

Sari Says:
It's often awkward to be around an ex. Usually I would recommend that you talk to him and ask what you can do to make him feel comfortable around you during the play. But since you said he won't listen to you, you don't have many options. You could try to avoid him, or you could even drop out of the play altogether if it's so important to you that he has a good time. But I don't think you should do that!

This really is not your problem. This is something he needs to work out on his own. It's not your responsibility to make sure that he has a good experience in this play. Hopefully, the more time he spends working on the play with you, the more he'll be used to being around you again, and he'll start to act normally. In the meantime, the best thing may be to ignore the way he's behaving—don't let it affect you.

your ex vs. the new guy

Dear Sari,

I was going out with a guy for four months. Then I met another guy in my gym class. I dumped the first guy—*big mistake*—and started going out with the new guy. Now I like the first guy more than I like the new guy. I just can't stop remembering the good, bad, sad, joyous, happy, depressing, romantic, passionate, and all the other times with the first guy. What should I do?

Sari Says:

When you feel like you are still in love with an ex and you have a new boyfriend, it may mean one of two things. Either the guy you are with now is totally wrong for you, and you are fixated on your ex because in comparison you realize that your ex was more right for you. Or the guy you are with is actually right for you, but you are so scared of something so right that you keep thinking that you should go back to something old and familiar—and wrong for you—like your ex.

In order to sort through all this, first you have to stop comparing the new guy to your ex. Pretend that your ex never existed, then ask yourself if you like the new guy. That should help you decide whether or not you should stay with the new guy. Then, you have to do some serious thinking about whether you like your ex right now because you are not happy in your new relationship, or whether you really want to be with your ex again. Keep in mind: There are many more guys out there than just these two. If you are totally single for a while, that might help you meet someone new who you like more than both of these guys.

Dear Sari,

My ex is always telling me how much he likes me and how much he needs to see me. And he tells me to call him, but when I do he won't pick up. He does stuff to me like that all the time. I started going out with this other guy, and all my ex did was bad-mouth me constantly. But the problem is, I still like him so much. He just knows exactly what to say to get me back, and when he has me back, he throws me away. It's like he doesn't want me, but no one else can have me. HELP!

Sari Says:

What you are talking about is very common—when you break up, it's hard to let go of each other, even when you are ready to move on. Someday you and your ex may be able to be friends, but first you have to get over each other. You and he are going to have to take a total break from each other—that means no talking to each other at all. Tell your ex that for two weeks there will be no contact. In fact, you may need to go for a month or a few months without talking to totally get over each other, but for now just start with a two-week period. Tell him that you do not want to hurt him, but you simply need some time to help both of you move on.

You can assure him that someday you want to be friends, but you need to focus on being alone now. When you two broke up, you must have decided that it was the best decision—and you need to work to stick to it. Hopefully, he will respect your request and you can both move on. During this time, you will have to keep yourself busy so that you do not start thinking about calling him. It won't be easy, but over time it will get better.

ex wants to sleep with you

Dear Sari,
My ex-boyfriend wants to cheat on his girlfriend with me. In fact, he even wants to lose his virginity to me. I like him so much, I guess you could even say I love him. But should I let him cheat on his girlfriend?

Sari Says:
If you sleep with him now, I bet you'll get hurt! You'll both be lying, cheating, and sneaking around. Any guy who wants to lose his virginity to you should love you enough to be your boyfriend—not someone else's boyfriend.

Get over your ex and stay away from him completely. Anyway, why in the world would you want to get back together with a guy who wants to cheat on his girlfriend and use you to do it? It's great that you broke up with him, because he sounds like a fool. Stay broken up; don't have sex with him, don't even kiss him. Forget about him. Then find yourself a fantastic boyfriend who knows how to treat you right.

suicide threat!

Dear Sari,

Just recently, I broke up with my boyfriend of three months. We shared everything. We even talked about marrying each other. But time went on, and I guess you could say the fire burned out. I grew apart from him. While we were together, he told a friend that I meant everything to him and without me he would kill himself. He's tried to kill himself before, and I'm really scared. If anything happened to him, I would never forgive myself. I still love him, but just as a friend. He has promised me that he wouldn't do anything dumb, but I think he will. *Help!*

Sari Says:

I understand how much you care about this guy and how scared you must be. Anyone who tried to commit suicide once, as you say he has, might be at risk to try again. However, he is not your personal responsibility. You broke up, and in order to move on—and to help him move on—you need to put some distance between you two. You already talked to him, and he assured you that he was not going to kill himself. Perhaps you are worried about him because you feel guilty about the break-up. Or maybe you are afraid to move on, and you see this as a way you can talk to him and stay close.

I don't think that you should talk to him about this anymore; it might be making things worse. Instead, let the other people in his life help him. Hopefully, he has friends and family who are watching out for him. He will probably be fine.

If you really feel that he is at risk for suicide, however, please tell a school counselor or talk to his parents. For more information about suicide, please call one of the hotlines in the appendix at the back of this book. They can talk to you more about how to handle his suicide threats.

moving past a bad relationship

Dear Sari,

My ex had an outrageous temper. But that was almost a year ago, and now I love someone else and we've been together for about nine and a half months. I truly love him. But it's been hard to share things with him because of the way I was treated in my last relationship. I'm afraid to stand up to him and tell him how I feel because I'm afraid he will get angry with me and even hit me like my ex used to do. I need to know how to get over this and overcome the fear. My heart tells me that he won't hurt me, and he's also told me that. Please help if you can.

Sari Says:

In order to get over this, you need to tell yourself over and over that this guy is not your ex and he will not hurt you. Whenever you start to withdraw from this guy and think about your ex, tell yourself: "He isn't my ex. He will never hurt me. I should not be thinking about my ex now."

Of course, if this new guy (or any guy) ever does anything to you that is at all like what your ex did (yelling at you, hitting you) then break up with him immediately! You should never go through that again. I hope that this new guy is loving and trustworthy. If he is, you will realize that you only should be with guys like him who treat you right.

If you need to talk to someone in depth about your experiences with your ex, please see the appendix in this book for a violence hotline you can call.

boyfriend bailed after divorce

Dear Sari,

My boyfriend just broke up with me because my parents got a divorce. I know it was hard on him when I came to him for support or advice or just a place to stay because my parents were fighting. But I think that he should have stayed with me and tried to help calm me. Instead, I got my own break-up. I think he did the wrong thing, but some of my friends say he did the right thing because I was dumping everything on him.

Sari Says:

It would have been wonderful if your boyfriend had stayed with you and supported you. But if he is not the type of guy who can really be there for you, or if this is not the type of serious relationship that he had in mind, then it was better for him to be honest with you and end the relationship.

Don't blame the break-up on your parents' divorce. He would have broken up with you eventually, no matter what. If it hadn't been the stress of the divorce, it would have been something else: problems with school, or with a friend, or with any number of things that just happen in life. Relationships always have stressful periods. Apparently, this guy only wanted the fun times, not anything serious. Don't worry—you'll find someone who will stay with you for better or for worse. Be patient, and in the meantime try to have fun with your friends and use them as your support system.

dealing with an ex's bisexuality

Dear Sari,

My ex-boyfriend just told me he is bisexual, and I'm really bumming about it. I just want to know if it is my fault that he is gay. When I ask him, he tells me he has liked men for a long time, but I still feel it is my fault. I still have feelings for him, even though when we were going out he cheated on me. I still love him.

Sari Says:

It is impossible to "make" a person become gay or bisexual. People are just the way they are; some people are born gay, lesbian, or bisexual (even if they "come out" later in life). They cannot be changed! You did not make him gay.

As far as your relationship with him goes, I do hope that you can get over your feelings for him. You can love him the way you would love a friend, but don't think about getting back together with him. It sounds as if he was not such a great boyfriend to you, because he cheated on you. If you can be friends with him, that might be cool. However, if your romantic feelings for him don't fade soon, I recommend that you stay away from him for a while, until you are totally over him. Find yourself a new guy—or even a new friend—just to get your mind off this ex.

Finally, I have to bring up the fact that you used the words "my fault." Being gay or bisexual is not a "fault"—homosexuality and bisexuality are not "bad." If you really like this person, be happy that he's now open about his sexual orientation.

Problems with Your Boyfriend's or Girlfriend's Ex

his ex is still around

Dear Sari,

My boyfriend and I have been going out for a year and three months. He told me a while ago that his ex came by to visit his parents. Then he called her and told her not to come around because he doesn't appreciate it. I don't either. She didn't come by for a while. Then just three days ago, she stopped by again. I'm in his life now, and his family is finally getting used to me, but she thinks she's still important to him and his family. What should I do?

Sari Says:

I understand how this would upset you, and I am doubtful that he told her to back off in a way that she understands. He must tell her again to stop coming by. You should not talk with her—this is his responsibility. Also, he should tell his parents that he does not want her coming over. It sounds like they are still making her feel welcome for some reason. Do you know why?

Maybe the more important thing here is that you talk with your boyfriend about the relationship that he wants to have with his ex. Maybe he wants to be friends with her, but he doesn't know how to tell you. If he does want to be friends with her, or if his family still wants to stay close to her, then you have to decide if you can handle this—or if you'd be better off without him (and her).

Break-Up Letter

If you are trying to break up with someone, but the person is not listening to you or is begging to stay together, then try writing him or her a letter. You don't have to make it long; just a few sentences will do. Maybe something like this:

"Dear _____, I loved you when we were together, but now I have moved on and I do not feel that way anymore. I still think that you're a nice person; I just don't want to go out with you again. Maybe someday soon we can be friends, but right now I need some space. So please stop asking me if we can go out again. I am sorry if this hurts, but it would be best if we don't talk for now. I hope you understand."

ex's party

Dear Sari,

I got invited to my ex's birthday party and she also invited my girlfriend of five months. I went out with my ex like two years ago and we were really good friends before and we still are. My girl doesn't want to go to this party for whatever reason, and I don't want my ex to think she's a bitch because she's not.

Sari Says:

I don't think you should go to the party. Your girlfriend's feelings should matter more to you than your ex's feelings. Your girlfriend does not want to go—so don't go.

But just because you don't go to the party doesn't mean that your ex needs to think anything bad about your girlfriend. Just tell your ex that you can't make it. If you want to tell her the truth, tell her that you'd feel more comfortable if you weren't around her when you are with your girlfriend. If she really is your friend, she should understand. If she acts angry or jealous, then she's just acting like an ex—not like a friend! If you don't want to get into all that with her, then just tell her that you have other plans. You'll be doing the right thing by not going. I know that your girlfriend will see that, and I hope your ex can, too.

his ex

Dear Sari,

I met this guy who I really like. We've been hanging out for about a month, and I think he wants to be my boyfriend. He gives me all the right signals and says he likes me. But the problem is that he talks about his ex-girlfriend just a little too much. I mean he doesn't like say that he loves her anymore or anything, and they are *not* even friends now. But he does stuff like says, "Let's go to see this movie, because my ex-girlfriend said I would like it." I was at his house, and there is even a picture of her in his room. He pointed it out, like I wouldn't have noticed it if he did not tell me to look at it. I was wondering why you think he does this, and what I should do. I know he will do it again, but I am too scared to say something to him, because 1) I don't want this to become a big issue between us, and 2) He said he does not want to get back together with her, so maybe I am overreacting. What should I do?

Sari Says:

It is hard to say exactly why he is mentioning her so much. It could be that he is trying to impress you—sort of showing you that he was capable of having a relationship with her, because he wants to have one with you. Or maybe he is just reminiscing about her because he is about to get involved with you. Sometimes when a new relationship is beginning, a person thinks back to the last one because he is experiencing feelings similar to the ones he had when they first met. That's a good thing—it means that he is on the relationship track with you.

The bad side of this is that he is being inconsiderate to you by mentioning her. It is never pleasant to think about your (possible) boyfriend's ex too much or to wonder how you compare to her, and he is making you do just that.

So what should you do? You say that you don't want this to be a big issue between the two of you, but it seems like it is already an issue for *you*. Therefore, you should try to get over it on your own. First, give it more time. He might naturally stop mentioning her so often, once you two are further along in your relationship. But if he keeps mentioning her a lot even after another month, then you can gently say to him, "I've heard a lot about your ex, but since she is not really a part of either of our lives, I would prefer it if you don't mention her so much anymore." Hopefully he'll understand.

Now, when it comes to him having a photo of her in his room—that's another story. That could mean that he has not completely moved on from his ex. Don't let me scare you, though, because it might just be some sort of insecurity that makes him display the picture. If he was with her for a long time, for instance, he probably got used to having the picture there and doesn't yet feel ready to get rid of it. I hope that he does soon, because it is offensive when a guy has a picture of an ex on display, especially since he pointed it out to you! But even though he should put it away, I do not think you should ask him to. He should do that in his own time, without you even mentioning it—then you can be sure he is really over her! If you ask him to get rid of it, then you will never know if he is just doing it for you. However, if things become really serious between you two, and you are still going out three or four months from now and he still hasn't put away the picture, then you could give him a framed picture of the two of you and ask him to put that up instead.

how to break up

Dear Sari,
I've been going out with my guy for a month. It's been cool being with him, but I think I just want to be friends with him now. But I was the person who wanted to go out with him in the first place. How should I break up with him so that he doesn't resent me?

Sari Says:
Whenever you break up with someone, that person will probably be upset, no matter how you handle it. To soften the blow, explain to him that you've always liked him a lot and you still do, you just are not ready to be in a relationship right now. Tell him that you would like it if you still hung out every once in a while, as friends, but that the exclusive relationship should end. That should do it. In time, he'll probably forgive you.

loving being single

Dear Sari,

Please help! I recently broke up with someone. I am all alone *again* for the one day of the year where love matters—Valentine's Day. I'm going to feel like an idiot that I do not have someone special to share such a happy time with. But what I want to know is: How can I brighten my Valentine's Day even though I'm single?

Sari Says:

Here are some great ideas for how to have a fun Valentine's Day alone! In fact, you can try these things any day that you're feeling lonely and need a pick-me-up.

1. Go see a romantic movie by yourself. Take comfort in the fact that real-life love stories are never as good as in the movies!
2. Have a "singles only" party. Play "Spin the Bottle" and "Truth or Dare," and be glad that you're not tied down in a relationship.
3. Give cards and flowers to all of your friends and tell them how much you appreciate their love.
4. Help those who are truly lonely. Visit the elderly in a nursing home or sick kids in the hospital. Make them cards, bring them flowers, or just keep them company.
5. Spend the day with your parents. They need your love, too!
6. Spend the day with a friend who ended a relationship recently. He or she will probably need your support more than ever.
7. Go looking for love! Get a buddy and go browse in bookstores, coffee shops, at the mall, or anywhere you think you might meet some cool people your age who might have things in common with you. Don't be shy—chat up anyone who seems nice and interesting. Bring along a pen and paper so you can write down phone numbers!

8. Go shopping and buy a cute outfit—something that *you* love, rather than something you'd get just to impress a potential date.

9. Spend the day playing with your pet. Fido or Fluffy always wants and appreciates your love. And pets love you right back, unconditionally.

10. Enjoy time with your best friend. Splurge on a fancy dinner together, hang out, or do whatever you both enjoy. Remember that best friends usually outlast most boyfriend–girlfriend relationships.

let's talk about sex

Sex is a big deal. It can be one of the most intimate and beautiful experiences you can share with another person. Or, when rushed into without enough thought and consideration, sex can be emotionally or physically devastating. So what do you *do* about it?

It's important that you have the big facts about the physical repercussions of sex: 1) Sex can lead to unintentional pregnancy; 2) you can transmit or contract various curable and noncurable sexually transmitted diseases (STDs) from having unprotected sex; and 3) one of the ways that HIV, the virus that causes AIDS, is transmitted is through unprotected sex.

Then, besides understanding the physical issues, you have to realize the emotional issues. Sex can give you an amazingly wonderful emotional bond with someone. Yet, it can also cause you major emotional grief. When you have sex with someone, you are sharing a deeply intimate part of yourself, and by making yourself vulnerable in that way, you risk getting hurt.

Because of those biggies, a whole lot of other questions are going to come up. Issues like when to do it, why to do it, how to do it, with whom to do it, sexual positions, orgasms, ejaculation, birth control, masturbation—and that's just scratching the surface.

When you have sex, you can't take it back. But you *can* arm yourself with enough knowledge to make a mature, well-thought-out decision to have (or not to have) sexual relations. Sex is not only like what you see on TV and in the movies, neither is it necessarily like what you hear from various people in your community, school, or church. Think of this chapter as your own personal sex ed class, where you can ask all the questions you want and never feel embarrassed. Let's talk about sex, baby.

Things to Know About Sex, Whether You Are a Virgin or Not

Fun with masturbation

Dear Sari,

Is masturbation good or bad? Can someone do it too much? I've heard some people say that masturbation is bad for you, and other people just make fun of it, like, "Have you been spanking your monkey?" or "Go jerk off!"

Sari says:

Masturbation is the most natural and healthy way to learn about your body and your sexuality and to feel physical pleasure. Most people enjoy masturbation. There is nothing "bad" about masturbation. Some religions (like Catholicism) believe that masturbation is wrong. Some parents teach their children that masturbation is forbidden. Some people hang on to the myths about masturbation, such as it will make hair grow on your palms or ruin your eyesight. The truth is, masturbation will not make hair grow on your palms. It will not ruin your eyesight. It will not make you a bad person.

It is totally fine to masturbate as much as you want, as long as you do it in private and as long as you do not do it so often that it gets in the way of the rest of your life. What I mean is, whether you masturbate once a month, once a week, or once a day—even twice or three times a day—that's fine. However, if you masturbate so much that you cannot make it to school on time or you have no interest in seeing your friends, then you are masturbating too much. It's highly doubtful that masturbation will become a problem for you, however. Most people masturbate and very few find that it interferes with their lives.

You should not feel guilty when you masturbate. Masturbation teaches you how you have an orgasm. It helps you relax. Also, it allows you to feel sexual pleasure risk-free, without any worries about pregnancy or sexually transmitted diseases. Plus, many people like it simply because it's fun. Masturbation is just part of being a healthy sexual person!

talking about sex

Dear Sari:
What's the best way to start a conversation about sex in a relationship without making the other person feel uncomfortable?

Sari Says:
I am glad that you are thinking about this, because talking about sex before you have sex is very important! For some people, talking about sex will be uncomfortable no matter what you say. To make it easier, choose a time when you are both relaxed and you have plenty of time alone together. Then say something to the point, like this: "We've been going out for a while now, and I really like you. I was thinking that it might be good if we talked a little about sex." Then ask whatever questions you are wondering about: "Are you a virgin?", "How far do you want to go with me?", "Do you know how to use a condom?", "Is it okay if we go out and do not have sex?", "If we have sex, what kind of birth control should we use?", "I am a virgin and I do not want to have sex," or whatever it is that you want to talk about. It's likely that the person you're going out with will also be wondering some of these things and will be glad that you raised the issue.

Fingering

Dear Sari,

When I fool around with my girlfriend, I want to finger her, but I don't know what to do. We do not want to have sex at all. We just want to fool around. How do I do it?

Sari Says:

Most girls like it if their clitoris is rubbed with one or two fingers back and forth or in a circular motion. Some girls prefer if you do not rub it with too much pressure, because it can be highly sensitive. Your girlfriend should be able to let you know what she likes; maybe she can touch herself, and you can put your hand over hers so she can show you. Ask her to show you where her clitoris is, if you do not know. It is located slightly above the vaginal opening. Besides clitoral stimulation, some girls like it if you insert a finger or two inside their vagina at the same time. The key here is asking her what she likes.

hand job

Dear Sari,

I want to give my boyfriend a hand job, but I don't know what to do with his penis. I tried once, but he did not seem to do anything. What do I do?

Sari Says:

Usually a guy likes to have his penis rubbed in an up and down motion with your hand wrapped around it. You want to exert some pressure, but do not hold it too tightly. Your hand should be able to move smoothly up and down. Some guys like it if you do this with some kind of lubrication on your hand; others like it dry. All guys like a different amount of pressure and for it to be stimulated in different ways. To learn what your guy likes, ask him to put his hand over yours while you give him a hand job, so he can show you.

everything but intercourse

Dear Sari,
I always hear all of my friends talking about "dry humping" and I have no clue whatsoever what they are talking about. Also, what is "foreplay"? My boyfriend and I want to fool around, but not have sex. Are these things we can do without actually having sex?

Sari Says:
"Dry humping" is a slang expression that refers to when a couple wears clothes (or, at least, underwear) while they are rubbing against each other's bodies in order to feel sexual pleasure, without getting naked. ("Humping" is a slang word that often means a couple rubbing against each other in a sexual way, or having sex. "Dry" means that there is not an exchange of body fluids—for instance, no exchange of the man's ejaculation and the woman's vaginal secretions.)

"Foreplay" means things you do before you have intercourse (the "fore" prefix means before and the "play" part stands for intercourse).

Many couples don't want to have intercourse, but still want to fool around because it can feel good, and it is completely safe sex as long as you keep your clothes on. Ways to be sexual and intimate include: hand holding, massage, kissing on the mouth, French kissing, kissing anywhere on the body, touching each other's bodies (clothed or nude), mutual masturbation, and making each other's bodies feel good in any way you can imagine. Whatever you and your partner are comfortable with doing is totally fine and healthy. Also, being physically intimate in these ways can still be a big deal emotionally. While you do not *technically* lose your virginity from these acts, they are still very meaningful.

stayin' alive?

Dear Sari,
Does the sperm die when it hits the air? I wonder because my girlfriend and I fool around, and I would like to know if I ejaculate on my hand if it stays alive for long.

Sari Says:
When sperm is ejaculated directly inside a woman's vagina during inter-course, it can live inside her for up to five days. However, if sperm is ejaculated anywhere outside her body (like in your hand, or in your underwear, or anywhere on the outside of your or her body), it does not live that long. But it doesn't instantly die when it hits the air, either. If the conditions are warm and moist, the sperm may live for hours, sometimes even longer. So when a man ejaculates (even if it is not inside a woman's body) both the man and woman need to be careful to avoid getting the ejaculate inside the woman's vagina. Although it is rare, it's possible that if a man ejaculated in his hand, for example, then inserted his fingers inside the woman's vagina, she could have live sperm inside her. So if you are fooling around and you ejaculate anywhere (even on your hand), be very careful to keep it away from the inside of her vagina!

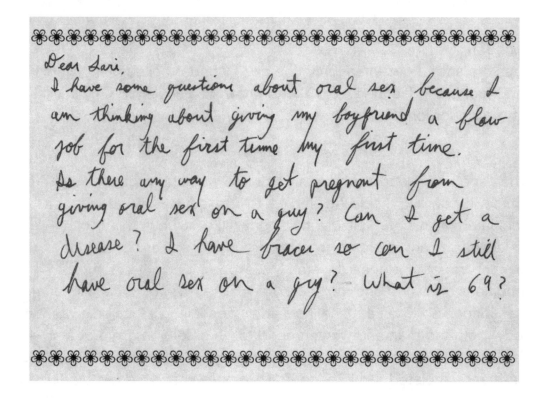

Dear Sari,

I have some questions about oral sex because I am thinking about giving my boyfriend a blow job for the first time my first time.

Is there any way to get pregnant from giving oral sex on a guy? Can I get a disease? I have braces so can I still have oral sex on a guy? What is 69?

Sari Says,

You have lots of good questions, and I'm glad that you are asking them before your first time. You cannot get pregnant from oral sex. In order to get pregnant, sperm in his semen must get inside your vagina. If semen gets into your mouth, there is no way it can travel through your body and into your vagina. However, if a guy ejaculates in your mouth, there's a risk that you could contract sexually transmitted diseases, including HIV, the virus that causes AIDS. If you want to be totally protected from STDs and HIV, the man should use a condom during oral sex. If a woman knows with absolute certainty that her partner has tested HIV-negative and has tested negative for all STDs, she may choose to allow him to ejaculate in her mouth. But if you're not sure whether a guy has any STDs, do not take risks—use a condom the entire time. You can buy condoms, like Durex Colors and Scents, which come in orange, banana, and strawberry.

Braces should not interfere with oral sex, since they are on the outside of your teeth, and you should not be scraping your teeth on the guy's penis anyway. Just to be sure that your braces do not scratch his penis, ask him not to make any sudden movements.

The term 69 means having oral sex on each other at the same time. It is called 69 because if you imagine two people lying side by side with their heads near each other's genitals, their bodies would resemble the number sixty-nine.

how far is too far?

Dear Sari,
How do I know when to stop if I don't want to have sex before marriage? I just am not sure where to draw the line. How far is too far in this case?

Sari Says,
You have to decide for yourself how far you want to go. Some people who want to wait for marriage to have sex will only kiss. Others will touch their partner's body only when they are both clothed, such as giving a massage. Some people will touch when they are both naked, and they may engage in mutual masturbation. Still other people might choose to have oral sex and save only intercourse for marriage. Of course, some people consider oral sex to be even more intimate than intercourse, and those people would never consider having oral sex prior to having intercourse. All this is up to you.

Think about how you feel about kissing—how special must someone be to you before you kiss? Think about how you feel about nudity—is that something to share with someone before marriage? Think about all the different sexual things that people do as foreplay—are these things that you would want to do as a substitute for intercourse, or would you prefer to wait for marriage to do any of them? Finally, if you are still confused, then you may want to talk with someone close to you, maybe even your parents, about their values regarding how far someone can go while still saving sex for marriage. You need to develop your own values about this, but it often helps to have the input of others you respect.

Sex: The First Time

getting on with it?

Dear Sari,

I never really had a steady boyfriend. All my friends have already had sex; they are all like "just find a guy and get on with it." I don't think I'm ready for that kind of commitment yet, but if they all did it, I don't want to feel left out. I'm dating this really sweet guy. He's fun to hang out with and everything. We make out all the time, but when is the right time to have sex with him?

Sari Says:

First of all, your friends might not *all* be having sex. I don't want to say that your friends are lying or anything, but I will say that teens tell me all the time that they sometimes say that they are having sex when they really aren't. In fact, about half of 17-year-olds are still virgins! Some people do not even have sex until they are out of high school.

The longer someone is a virgin, the better. You are showing your maturity by waiting. You should be proud of that. Sex truly is better when you wait until you are older, because you have time to be sure about what you want and to learn more about sex from reading about it, talking about it, and even from making out with guys. You should only have sex when you are ready, not when your friends are ready. It sounds to me like you're having a great time with the guy you're dating now. If he likes you, he will wait for you—or he will be okay with it if you never have sex.

Sex is not something to "just get on with," as your friends say. You shouldn't do it to feel like an adult, or because your friends want you to, or because a guy pressures you. Sex is the most special way to connect with someone you love.

ready for sex?

Dear Sari,
Everyone always says to wait to have sex until you are "ready." How on earth can I know when I am ready?

Sari Says:
If you can answer "yes" to *all* of these questions, then maybe you'll be ready:

- Are you truly in a good relationship with someone you love and trust—someone you want to lose your virginity with?
- Are you able to talk to your partner about all aspects of sex: your relationship, your feelings, pregnancy, birth control and condoms?
- Will you feel okay if this relationship ends after you've lost your virginity with this person?
- Have you learned or read about sex in order to answer questions you have about it?
- If you are a girl, have you gone to a gynecologist for your first exam? (Every girl should do this before the first time they have sex, *or* by age 16, even if she is a virgin.)
- Will you use birth control each time you have sex to prevent pregnancy?

- Will you use condoms properly each time you have sex to prevent sexually transmitted diseases?
- Do you have private times and places to have sex?
- Will it be okay if your parents find out?

Remember—you only have one first time. When you do decide to lose your virginity, you should have given it a lot of thought and had many discussions about it with your partner so you are really sure. Even if you feel ready now, why not wait six more months to be extra sure? You'll still want to have sex in a few months—if it's meant to be. If it isn't meant to be, then you'll know that, and you will be glad that you didn't have sex. Waiting a bit longer will give you more time to make sure you are making the right choice. Throughout your life, you want to be able to look back on the time you lost your virginity without regrets! Sex is precious, and it is the most special way that two people can be close. Save it for the right time in your life and wait until you have the right person to share it with.

Bad Reasons to Have Sex

- You think you need to have sex in order to get your partner to stay with you.
- You think sex will improve a bad relationship.
- All your friends are doing it.
- You want to rebel against your family.
- You think it will make you more mature or cooler.
- You are just curious.

love and sex

Dear Sari,
Do I have to be in love to make love?

Sari Says:

When people who are in love have sex, the sex is more meaningful. It is not *necessary* for people to be in love in order for them to have sex. People have sex for all kinds of reasons, and sometimes love is not their reason. If people choose to have sex in a casual relationship, without love, of course, it is their choice to make. However, it may not be the best choice, especially for your first time. Sex is such an intimate experience that saving it for someone you love makes it amazing. Sex research has found that people enjoy their first sexual experience if they wait until they are older, in a relationship, and they feel like they are in love. So if you want to get the most out of sex, then wait to have sex until you are in love.

the right day for the first time

Dear Sari,

My boyfriend told me that he would wait until I was ready to have sex. Well, I'm ready now. I am wondering should I wait until the end of my period? When is the best time of the month to do that "special thing" with this special guy?

Sari Says:

You should plan to have your first time on a night when you two will feel relaxed and comfortable, have plenty of privacy, and a lot of time. For the first time, it's often best if you can spend the night together alone. In terms of time of month, yes, waiting until you are not having your period is a good idea—only because you will not have to worry about making more of a mess. However, no matter what time of the month it is when you have sex (even if it's during your period), you must use birth control properly! You are always at risk of getting pregnant, so you must always protect yourself.

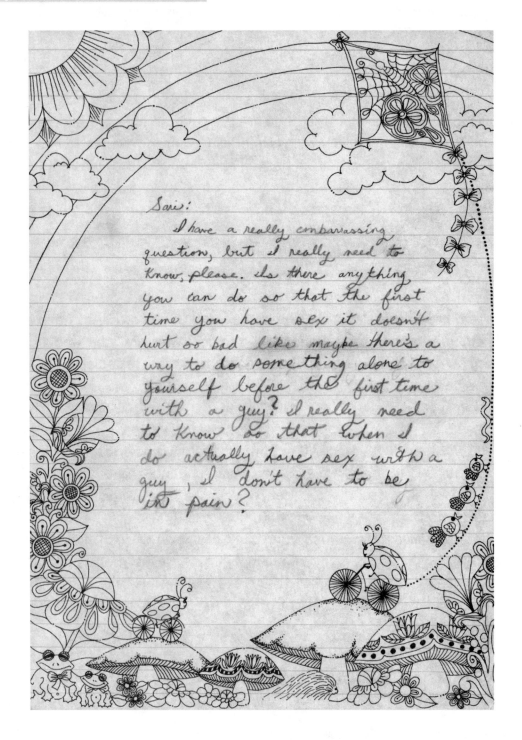

Sari:

I have a really embarrassing question, but I really need to know, please. Is there anything you can do so that the first time you have sex it doesn't hurt so bad like maybe there's a way to do something alone to yourself before the first time with a guy? I really need to know so that when I do actually have sex with a guy, I don't have to be in pain?

Sari Says:

The first time a girl has sex, there is some pain and pressure from the penis being inside her. She might feel the tearing of the small piece of skin in her vagina called the hymen. She may be a little sore and bleed slightly afterward.

However, there are ways that girls can make sex feel more comfortable the first time. If she masturbates regularly, or touches herself before she has sex with a guy, it will help her get to know her body and get used to having something inside it. She could put her finger in her vagina. Also, she could take a close look at her genitals in a hand mirror, to get to know what they look like.

The girl should be relaxed and turned on before sex. If the couple kisses and fools around a lot first, it is usually easier when they do have sex. A good position for her first time is to have the girl lie on her back, with a small pillow under her butt. He must wear a condom. To make the penis go in easier, put some lubrication on the condom and some in her vagina (water-based lube only, like KY Liquid or Astro Glide, which you can get in a drugstore). She must be using birth control, too! Even if he only "puts it in for a second," she could get pregnant.

For her first time, it is usually more comfortable if the guy slides his penis into her vagina gently, rather than thrusting it inside in one push. Once it is in, she might want to ask him to be still for a minute so she can get used to how it feels. Then he can thrust—gently—when they are both ready. As soon as he ejaculates, he must withdraw his penis and take off the condom.

Also, if you're a girl who has not had sex yet and you're thinking about doing so, you should see a gynecologist beforehand. The doctor will examine the inside of your vagina and talk to you about birth control.

But the best way to ensure sex is pleasurable for first time is to wait. Girls who wait to have sex until they are in their late teens (17, 18, 19) report that they had a better first time than girls who had sex for the first time at a younger age. Older girls tend to know their bodies better, and they know more about sex.

Also, girls who have "fooled around" with the same steady boyfriend for six months to a year before they have intercourse with him usually have a better first time. The girl who has fooled around a lot with her steady boyfriend will already have a good idea of what his naked body is like and how it feels to be naked together. Also, many long-term couples who wait to do it until they have been together six months to a year say that their first-time sex was a good experience—because they were in love.

blood and the first time

Dear Sari,

About a week ago I had sex with my boyfriend for the first time, and after we were done I noticed that I was bleeding a little. I know that's normal, but what I want to know is, when we have sex again will I bleed again? How many times does it take for it to stop?

Sari Says:

The reason a girl bleeds the first time she has sex is that the small membrane of skin at the entrance to her vagina tears and then breaks. This small piece of skin, called the hymen (you may have heard it called "cherry," in slang), sometimes doesn't break completely the first time. So it tears a little each time—and bleeds a little each time—until it is completely broken. This could take between one to four times. If you continue to bleed beyond that time, you must see a gynecologist immediately. By the way, every girl who is sexually active must see a gynecologist for an exam, anyway.

no blood the first time

Dear Sari,

I just recently had sex for the first time. It hurt, but I didn't bleed. I don't know why. My boyfriend thinks I might have lied about being a virgin. I don't know what I could do to prove it to him. What is wrong with me?

Sari Says,

There is nothing wrong with you. Near the entrance of the vagina, the thin piece of skin called the hymen rips at some point. Usually, it rips when a girl loses her virginity, which is why it bleeds or hurts. However, for many girls, it might rip when she is riding her bike, riding a horse, or when she uses a tampon. Some girls' hymens are so thin that they don't bleed at all when they break, even during sex. Or it bleeds just a little, so you don't even notice it.

Therefore, there is no way to ever tell for sure whether a girl is a virgin. The only problem here is that your boyfriend is accusing you of lying. He should trust you and believe you. Tell him what I said about how your hymen could have been broken another way, or about how it might be so thin that it just didn't bleed. Then tell him that in the future, he needs to believe you and trust you.

what is a "virgin"?

Dear Sari,

My friend had sex with her first boyfriend. He went inside her, but then she made him get out about four seconds later because she wasn't ready. Her mom told her that she is still a virgin because he didn't actually release anything. But I say she isn't because he went inside her. Who's right?!

Sari Says:

Technically, anyone who has had sexual intercourse (when the penis enters the vagina) is not a virgin—the length of time inside doesn't matter; whether or not the man ejaculated doesn't matter. However, defining someone as a virgin can be much more personal than that, if you want it to be. Some people say that they are virgins just because the first time they had sex was not the kind of experience that they would like to remember as "the first time."

In your friend's case, she may still feel like a virgin because during those four seconds when the guy penetrated her, all she could think about was how to get him out of her. She realized that she was not ready for sex, and she stopped it as quickly as she could. She might think of it as a bad mistake, or even a sort of an accident.

If you want to be totally technical, your friend is not a virgin. But if she considers herself a virgin, then it's fine for her to make that choice. This is nobody else's business, but I'm glad that her mother apparently tried to make her feel better about this.

As her friend, I hope that you will help her feel okay about this, too. Instead of disagreeing with her, tell your friend that if she still considers herself a virgin, then that is her personal choice. Then drop the topic. Allow her to let this pass without debating it, without making it hard on her.

getting him to take "no" for an answer

Dear Sari,

This guy I'm going out with wants to have sex. Whenever we make out, he tries to get me to go further. I don't want to. What should I do?

Sari Says,

Tell him that you do not want to have sex with him. If he tries to convince you to have sex, or starts going too far with you physically, you must tell him "no." Tell him how far you are willing to go and set boundaries that he will not be allowed to cross. Let him know that you have made up your mind, and if he respects you, he should not try to change your mind. Then see how it goes.

You can try to avoid situations in which you have nothing to do but fool around—spend more time going out to movies, dinner, or other events, rather than just hanging out. You should trust him enough—and have discussed this with him enough—that making out won't be an issue because you know that he will only go as far as you want him to go. If he doesn't stop, you must stop seeing him. If he only wants to be with you because he wants to have sex, forget him! You can find someone else who respects you more.

Boys Can Say No

Girls aren't the only ones who say "no" to sex. There are tons of guys who want to wait to have sex. If you're a guy who doesn't want to have sex with someone, don't let her pressure you. If you're a girl, please realize that not all guys want to do it, so don't expect it.

too touchy

Dear Sari,
The guy I am dating keeps trying to grope me. I love him a lot, but he is all hands. Like we went swimming, and he took my bathing suit off, even though I told him to stop, but in the end it was okay, because skinny-dipping was fun. I don't want to keep letting him do things like this; how can I get him to stop?

Sari Says:
You need to talk to your guy and tell him exactly what you want and don't want. Right now, you're giving him mixed signals. On one hand, you're

telling me that you don't want him to touch you in a sexual way. On the other hand, when he did take off your bathing suit, you kept if off and went skinny-dipping. If you don't want him to touch you sexually, you must tell him that before he tries—and if he tries, you've got to tell him "no" and push him away for real, until he stops! If he doesn't listen to you, and he continues to do these things to you, you must walk away from him—fast!

If your boyfriend respects you, he should stop when you ask him to. If he doesn't stop, then no matter how much you say you love him, you should realize that he's trouble. Please be careful. You should never be with anyone who forces you to do anything, and this guy sounds like he's trying to do that. If he doesn't stop, you should break up with him.

is prom night the right time?

Dear Sari,
After the prom, my boyfriend will want to have sex with me. I am a virgin, and we talked about waiting, but now that it is prom, I think maybe it is the right thing to do. Should we have sex after the prom, or wait?

Sari Says:
Some people think that having sex after the prom is basically a require-ment for having a great prom night, or that prom night is the perfect occasion to lose your virginity. But the fact is, you should not feel obli-gated to have sex after the prom. The only reason to have sex is if you are really ready to have sex. "Because it's prom night" is not a good reason to have sex.

You could have much more fun just hanging out with friends after the prom or staying up all night *talking* to your prom date. If you were planning to wait to have sex, don't let the prom change your plans. Keep waiting.

sex as a gift

Dear Sari,

I was thinking about having sex with my new boyfriend on Valentine's Day for his present, but that's kind of a big present. And if I were to get pregnant, I can't be sure that he would stay with me since we just started going out. Even with all of these doubts I still want to. What should I do?

Sari Says:

You should not have sex with him! Losing your virginity as a "present" to someone else is a terrible idea. It should be more like a present to yourself—when you are ready. You do not sound like you are ready to have sex. You will only be ready to have sex when you are responsible to use birth control and condoms. You need to be sure that you will prevent pregnancy before you even think about having sex.

There are many other reasons why you are not ready to have sex, including that you may feel emotionally hurt afterward. The majority of girls are happier when they have their first time with someone they love, have been in a relationship for a long time, and they are older. Please wait to have sex. You will be happier and healthier if you wait.

Instead of sex, you can give him a great card, some candy, an extra-long kiss. If he really likes you, that should be all he expects anyway!

getting the silent treatment after having sex

Dear Sari,

I have a very big problem. I am very much in love with this guy. So I told him how I felt about him, and he said that he liked me, too, but he also likes his freedom. The only problem is about a month ago we had sex. That was my first time, so it meant a lot to me. And now after I told him how I felt, he's been acting very weird around me. We used to talk for hours over the phone, and now he doesn't call me; even at school he only says "hi" once in a great while. I care about him so much, but I don't know what to do.

Sari Says,

Having sex never guarantees love, attention, or even phone calls! It sounds like this guy does not want a relationship with you (he said he wants freedom), and he's keeping his distance from you because he thinks that you want a relationship with him. In order to keep him in your life, you may have to back off. If you do not call him as often, or if you do not seek him out in school, then maybe after a week or so, when you do call, he will be glad to talk with you, or maybe he will even call you.

If giving him space doesn't make things better, then try talking with him. Tell him that you understand that he does not want a committed relationship with you, but you'd like to hang out together still. Make a date to go out with him.

If he does not want to get together at all and cannot handle the fact that you have feelings for him, then you have to realize at some point you and he may be friends, but now is not your time. In that case, you will need to get over him.

As far as the fact that you lost your virginity with him: Try to find a way to feel okay about that for yourself. Having sex with him may have made you feel like you are in love with him, but he may not feel the same way. You cannot get someone to love you, and you have to accept this. Instead of being upset or having regrets about losing your virginity, find a way to feel good about it. Maybe you can tell yourself that you are glad you lost it with a guy who you felt like you loved at the time. Or you can tell yourself that your *next* first time will be with someone who really loves you, someone you've been going out with for many months and who is already in a committed relationship with you!

You have learned a valuable lesson. After you have sex with someone, it can hurt emotionally if the person is not there for you. In the future, you will make your decisions more carefully and wait as long as you can to have sex—until you are completely sure that it is the right person.

too young for sex?

Dear Sari,

I love a boy I've known since I was 6. I am now 13. We had a second-base fling and I was wondering if we should have sex. He wanted to know if I wanted to, and I said that I wasn't sure. What should I do?

Sari Says:

Do not have sex with him. Never have sex if you're unsure whether you want to. At age 13 you are simply not ready. Thirteen-year-olds are too young to fully enjoy sex and to be completely responsible about it: You must go to a gynecologist before you have sex for the first time; you must use birth control and condoms; and in the event that you got pregnant, you must be ready to deal with those consequences. Almost all 13- or 14-year-olds who have had sex say that it was not worth it. They wish they had waited. Please wait!

What Are the "Bases"?

There are many versions of what the "bases" mean. Here are two versions:

First Base: Kissing.

Second Base: Feeling on top of clothes.

Third Base: Feeling under clothes.

Home Run: Kissing and touching while you are both naked.

or

First Base: Kissing.

Second Base: Touching all over, including feeling a girl's breasts or a guy's bulge.

Third Base: Fingering to a girl. Hand job to a guy.

Home Run: Intercourse.

Dear Sari,

If my doctor finds out I'm not a virgin, will he tell my parents? One of my friends got in a lot of trouble because of a doctor. Aren't there laws about confidentiality or something?

Sari Says:

First of all, a doctor can only find out if you are a virgin if you tell the doctor. You might be thinking that a doctor can tell by looking at your hymen, the thin piece of skin inside the entrance to your vagina that tears the first time you have sex. However, the hymen can also tear on its own, not just from having sex. Many virgins' hymens have broken from bike riding, or horse-back riding, or just from a natural process of the body. So your doctor has no physical way of being able to determine if you are a virgin or not.

If you tell your doctor that you are having sex, then your doctor should keep it confidential. Some doctors tell parents personal things about their child, if the child is underage. In my opinion, the doctor should never tell anything, unless you are seriously ill, or if you are putting your health in jeopardy (such as if you are bulimic, or using drugs, or so on). So ask your doctor about confidentiality before you tell anything. Hopefully, your doctor will keep everything absolutely 100 percent confidential. If the doctor does not agree to keep things private, then you might want to find another doctor.

Can You Get Pregnant If . . .

. . . you're in the shower?

Dear Sari,

If you're in a shower with a guy, and he masturbates, but his penis doesn't go near your vagina, can you get pregnant?

Sari Says:

No. To get pregnant, his semen has to get into your vagina. If his penis goes inside your vagina (whether you are in the shower or not) then you could get pregnant. Or if he ejaculated on his hand, and then he inserted his fingers deep inside your vagina, then maybe you'd be at risk. Yet if, as you wrote, all that happened was that he masturbated when you were in the shower together, but your vagina was not in contact with his penis or his semen, there is no way that you can get pregnant.

. . . you have clothes on?

Dear Sari,

My boyfriend and I go through the motions of sex, but with all of our clothes on. Is there a way that some of his sperm could get inside me? I mean, it has to go through four layers of clothing—our underwear and jeans.

Sari Says,

You cannot get pregnant from what you say you are doing. If you don't have sex, and you keep your clothes on—even if the guy ejaculates in his underwear and you have your underwear on—then you will not get pregnant. In order to get pregnant, the man's sperm needs to get inside the woman's vagina. This occurs when a man ejaculates inside a woman while having sex.

What you are doing—going though the motions of sex with your clothes on—will not get you pregnant, because sperm cannot penetrate layers of clothing.

. . . you've never had your period?

Dear Sari,
If you haven't even gotten your first period *ever* yet, you can't get pregnant, right?

Sari Says:
Wrong. You can get pregnant before your first period. The time when a woman is most likely to get pregnant is when she is ovulating, which happens just before she gets her period. Since a woman could begin ovulating anytime, and since she would have her first period shortly after her first ovulation, she would have no way of knowing that she was fertile (i.e., able to get pregnant). That is, if a girl who has not yet had her period ovulates, then has her first period, she never would have known that she was ovulating until her period started. Your first period is the sign that you already ovulated—days or weeks before you got your period. Therefore, if a girl does not want to get pregnant, she must use birth control every time she has sex, whether she has had a period or not!

. . . it's during your period?

Dear Sari,
Can you get pregnant while you are having your period?

Sari Says:
Yes. You must assume that you can get pregnant anytime. It is possible to get pregnant during your period. A women gets pregnant when one of

her eggs is ready to be fertilized by the man's sperm. When a woman is having her period, her body is supposed to be in between the times of the month when the egg is ready—that's why many people think that a woman can't get pregnant during her period.

However, there is some opportunity for a woman to get pregnant during her period. Think of the first day of your period as Day 1 of your cycle. Most women's periods last until Day 5 or Day 7. The most likely time to get pregnant would be between Day 10 and Day 20, because that's when an egg is released inside the woman's body, ready to get fertilized by a man's sperm.

Sperm, however, can live for up to five days inside a woman's body. So if a man's sperm is inside her during or at the end of her period—let's say on Day 7—and her ovulation starts on Day 11, then it would be possible for the sperm to be alive and fertilize the egg, so the woman could get pregnant. Again, that's when ovulation is expected, but it could be early! So if you don't want to get pregnant, do not take any risks, ever. If you have sex, use birth control every time!

. . . the guy pulls out?

Dear Sari,
If my boyfriend and I have sex, and he pulls out without ejaculating inside me, is that a decent way to avoid getting pregnant? We did that, and now I think I am having a pregnancy scare.

Sari Says:
Pulling out (also called withdrawal) is *not* an effective way to avoid getting pregnant. In fact, if you use withdrawal, then there is a big chance that you *will* get pregnant! It does not work well for several reasons. First of all: At least some of the time, the guy may not take his penis out of your vagina in time—either because it feels so good that he wants to

keep going, or because he might not be totally aware when he is about to ejaculate. Second: Before he ejaculates, some sperm are present in the fluid that his penis emits, called "preejaculatory fluid" or "pre-cum." This can get you pregnant! Finally: Withdrawal will not give you any peace of mind whatsoever. You already have a pregnancy scare. If you continue to avoid using birth control, then you will have more scares—not to mention the very good chance that you will get pregnant. That's no way to live. If you use regular birth control, you won't have to worry all the time.

Signs of Pregnancy

Usually, the first sign a woman is pregnant is that she stops having her period. Other signs that a woman may be pregnant are: breast tenderness; tiredness; nausea or vomiting, especially in the mornings.

Birth Control

condoms at any age?

Dear Sari,
I'm just wondering if it is illegal to buy condoms if you're under 18.

Sari Says:
It is *legal* to buy condoms, no matter how old you are! I understand why you're wondering—you have to be 18 to buy certain magazines (like *Playboy*), and you have to be 21 to buy alcohol. But thank goodness you can buy condoms at any age, since condoms protect sexual health and prevent pregnancies. Condoms are very easy to buy, as long as you don't feel embarrassed about it. They're sold in almost every drugstore, supermarket, and even at some newsstands. They cost about $1.50 for three condoms, and you should always buy more

than you think you'll need in case you put one on wrong and need to start over again. If you are sexually active, you need to get used to feeling comfortable buying condoms. Don't worry; the store clerk won't make any comments about it. And you don't need to feel self-conscious—when you buy a box of condoms, be proud that you're smart enough to protect yourself!

the lifespan of a condom

Dear Sari,

I have had a condom in my wallet for like a year. Is it still good? I've like sat on it and everything. Should I get a new one, or stay with the one I have?

Sari Says:

Do not use that condom. You must not keep condoms in your wallet in the future! Heat damages condoms, and all that time that you've spent sitting on the wallet has caused the condom to get hot and to be damaged. You should never store condoms in warm places like your wallet, the glove compartment of a car, a purse, or the bathroom. You need to keep condoms in a cool, dry place, like in the sock drawer of your dresser. Technically, condoms should be kept in a place no colder than fifty degrees F and no hotter than ninety degrees F. If you need to bring them with you on a hot date, then that night you can carry them in a pocket or purse—but only for a couple of hours at the most.

Also, remember that condoms don't last forever. Before you use any condoms that you've had for a while, check the expiration date on the box to make sure they are still good. Most expire about a year after they are purchased. If you can't find the date and you do not know if they are still good, throw them away and buy a new box.

Dear Sari,

My boyfriend and I had sex a few months ago. We were protected and he wants to do it again and I'm okay with it. What is the best type of condom to get?

Sari Says:

The most popular brands of condoms are the best ones to choose—Durex, Lifestyles, and Trojan. Any drugstore or supermarket should have these brands. Don't buy a condom made by some odd little company you've never heard of—you know that you are getting a quality, tested condom if you buy the brand names I've suggested.

You want to get "latex" condoms (most of them are) or "polyurethane" condoms (if you are allergic to latex). Also, most people prefer "lubricated" condoms. You can also choose the color. Many people prefer condoms that are clear, so that they look more natural on the penis. You can choose the texture as well. Standard condoms are smooth, but you can also get them with "ribs," which are tiny raised lines in the latex which a woman can sometimes (but not usually) feel. Also, you can choose the size. The standard condom size is fine for most men, but "large-size" condoms, such as Trojan's Magnum or Durex's Extra Large, are also available. Or, if a guy has a small penis, he can choose a "form-fitting condom."

Try different varieties; eventually, you will find one kind of condom that you like more than the others. Also, make sure that you carefully read the directions in the box about rolling a condom onto a penis. Knowing exactly how to do it can greatly reduce the chance of leakage or breakage.

How to Put on a Condom

1. When the guy is fully erect, and you are both ready to have sex, open the condom package, using your fingers, not your nails or teeth, which can puncture or tear the condom.

2. Look at the condom. Without unrolling it, check to make sure that it will unroll down when it's placed over the penis. You don't want to put it on inside out and then find that it will not roll down, because if you make that mistake, you'll have to throw it away, as it has touched the end of the penis which may have preejaculatory fluid on it.

3. Place the rolled-up condom over the head of the erect penis, leaving a half-inch space at the tip.

4. Roll the condom down over the penis, smoothing out any air bubbles as you go.

5. Once the condom is on, to make sure all the air bubbles are out, run your hand down the length of the penis. Bubbles can cause breakage.

6. After the guy ejaculates in the condom, he should immediately withdraw his penis, then remove the condom, holding the base to prevent leakage.

condom breakage

Dear Sari,

What do you do if a condom breaks during intercourse?

Sari Says,

If a condom breaks during intercourse, the guy needs to pull out immediately. If he has not ejaculated yet, he should just put on a new condom, and it's okay to continue having intercourse. Still, there is a chance that sperm from preejaculatory fluid got into the vagina, so the woman may want to consult her gynecologist about the risk of pregnancy.

If the condom broke after he already ejaculated and semen leaked into the vagina, then he should withdraw his penis immediately and wash with soap and water; the woman can insert a small amount of spermicide (available in foam or jelly at any drugstore). If the woman is worried that she may have gotten pregnant, then she should see her gynecologist immediately. This is why people should always use another method of birth control at the same time as a condom.

Condoms should rarely or never break if they are used properly. If you have problems using condoms, read the directions that come in the box, and also try the following tips to avoid breakage:

- Never unroll the condom before you unroll it on the penis.
- Change the condom during long sessions. The exact amount of time varies (and can be less), but condoms can wear out if sex goes on for more than about thirty minutes.
- Use lubrication. Condoms can break during sex if they dry out. Use a water-based lubricant, such as KY Liquid or Astroglide, which you can buy in any drugstore.
- Be careful that your fingernails don't rip the condom when you are putting it on.
- Check the condom every once in a while during sex by pulling out and looking at it or feeling it to make sure it has not broken.
- Store condoms properly. Keep them in a place that is between 50 degrees and 90 degrees F, which means not in your wallet, car, or anywhere else that is too hot.
- Make sure the expiration date has not passed.
- Change brands if you still have a problem.

how protected are you?

Dear Sari,

If a guy uses a condom, and it doesn't break and nothing goes wrong, then why is there still a chance of the woman becoming pregnant? That just confuses me, because people say "you can get pregnant even if you use protection," and I just don't understand how.

Sari Says:

Every method of birth control has some percentage of failure—meaning that, statistically, the method may occasionally fail. For example: Condoms, when used alone, are about 86 percent effective, which means that 14 percent of the time something could go wrong to make the condom not work properly. If you put a condom on wrong, or the condom breaks, or the guy's penis entered the woman's vagina *before* he put the condom on, then there's a chance the woman could get pregnant. And even if you use the condom perfectly, there is still a slim chance that the condom itself could have something wrong with it.

Birth control pills are 99 percent effective, which means that they don't work only 1 percent of the time. (However, if you forget to take your pill two days in a row or more, then they would not work at all—that is, they'd be 0 percent effective. In that case, you must use a "backup" method of birth control; for instance, condoms.)

The only way to absolutely guarantee that you are not going to get pregnant is to not have sex at all, But combining two methods of birth control makes sex safer. If you take a birth control pill every day at the same time, as prescribed by a doctor, and whenever you have sex use a condom properly also, then you can be *almost* 100 percent sure that you will not get pregnant. Just be very, very careful to always use birth control exactly the way you're supposed to.

condoms under water?

Dear Sari,

If you have sex in the shower with a condom, is the effectiveness of the condom lessened? How about a pool? Or a hot tub?

Sari Says:

Unfortunately, condoms are not designed to be used in water, mostly because it would be too difficult to put them on. If you are in the water fooling around and decide you are ready to have sex, you should get out of the shower/pool/hot tub, dry off (that is, dry off your genitals, so you can correctly put the condom on) and put the condom on. Sure, it will take away some of the spontaneity—but safe sex is worth it!

Female condom

Dear Sari,
What is the female condom, and where can I get it?

Sari Says:
Female condoms are made of sheaths of very thin plastic. Instead of being rolled down over a man's penis the way a regular condom is, the female condom is inserted into the woman's vagina the way a tampon or diaphragm is. It has one plastic ring at the top and one at the bottom. When the female condom is inserted in the vagina, the inside plastic ring stays behind the pubic bone, the plastic tube lines the inside of the vagina, and the outer ring stays outside the vagina. They are not the most effective method of birth control, but female condoms do offer good protection against sexually transmitted infections, including HIV.

Some women do not like using the female condom, because they find it difficult to insert. Also, some women find that, during sex, it bunches up, or the outer ring may slip around, even into the vagina, making them have to stop sex and adjust the female condom. Because of these inconveniences, many women who try the female condom go back to using regular condoms. By the way, you cannot use them with a regular condom, but you should use them with a spermicide for extra protection. Female condoms are available at any drugstore or supermarket that sells condoms. You can usually find them right next to the regular condoms. They cost about $2.50 each (which is more expensive than regular condoms).

Dear Sari,

I'm thinking about sleeping with this guy, but I don't want to tell my mom. My guy and I were thinking about using the Pill, but would I have to have my mom's permission to get it, or can I go to a health clinic by myself? This guy has condoms, but is that enough? I know I want to use protection, I just don't know how to go about getting the Pill without telling my mom!

Sari Says:

If you use condoms alone, then you will have some protection against pregnancy, but not the best protection. Some research has found that using condoms alone is only about 80 percent effective. Other research says they are 90 percent effective. To increase your protection—without having to go to a doctor—you can also use contraceptive foam at the same time that you use condoms. You can buy contraceptive foam in the drugstore; it is usually next to the condoms or near the tampons. It comes with an applicator (it looks sort of like a tampon applicator). To use the foam, you insert the applicator filled with foam inside your vagina right before you have sex. When used together, condoms and foam are about 90 percent effective. (Don't trust the foam alone, without condoms, because some research has found that by itself foam is only about 70 percent effective.)

However, even using condoms with foam is still not as much protection as using birth control pills. Birth control pills are about 99 percent effective (if you follow the directions very carefully). Yes, you can go to a health clinic or Planned Parenthood on your own to get on the Pill—without your mother knowing. You do not need your mom's consent for a doctor to prescribe birth control pills for you. Just keep in mind that if you really do not want your mother to find out, you will have to hide your pills from her. (This is not always easy, since you have to take a pill at the same time every single day, without ever missing one.)

birth control pill side effects

Dear Sari,
I want to take birth control pills, but would like to know what side effects they have.

Sari Says:
Birth control pills sometimes have very mild side effects, such as a five-pound weight gain or loss, breast tenderness, mood swings, and head-aches. However, if a woman is taking the right type of birth control pills for her body, she may have no side effects at all. Birth control pills come in different brands, different dosages, and different combinations of hor-mones—there are many types to choose from.

When you see the doctor in order to get on birth control pills, you will start on the type of pill that the doctor feels is best for you. But, if you have any side effects, the doctor may switch you to a different type of pill. He or she will try to find the pill for you that doesn't cause side effects. Also, when a woman is on the Pill, she must not smoke, since that can cause other very serious complications, including cardiovascular problems.

low-dose birth control pills

Dear Sari,
I am taking a birth control pill that the doctor said is the lowest dosage of hormone available. Wouldn't that make it easier for me to get pregnant than a higher dose? Please help, I don't want to get pregnant.

Sari Says:

There are many different brands of birth control pills that use different doses of hormones. Yet the type of pill and the amount of hormones it contains does not matter at all when it comes to pregnancy prevention. All birth control pills work the same way. Low-dose pills such as those you're taking (these include the brand names Alesse, Ortho-tri-cyclen, and Ortho-novum, to name just a few) work exactly the same as higher-dose pills.

Most people today are given low-dose pills because they have fewer side effects than high-dose pills. Higher-dose pills, which used to be the only pills available, often cause problems such as bleeding between periods, weight gain, and headaches.

Your doctor has put you on the right pill for your body—that's your doctor's job! Your job now is to take the pill at exactly the same time every single day in order to be fully protected. For more information, talk to your doctor, and read the little pamphlet that comes in each pack of your pills. Also, if you want to be extra safe and protect against AIDS and STDs, use condoms in addition to the birth control pill.

the pill and cancer

Dear Sari,
Do birth control pills cause breast cancer?

Sari Says:

The most recent research about birth control pills shows that they do not increase the risk of breast cancer. Some older studies had shown that they might increase your chances of getting breast cancer, but those studies were shown to be inconclusive. In fact, research suggests birth control pills actually reduce the risk of cervical cancer and endometrial cancer. For more information about birth control pills and cancer, talk to your doctor.

depo-provera

Dear Sari,
What is the Depo-Provera shot? What are the side effects?

Sari Says:
Depo-Provera is a method of birth control that uses hormones to regulate a woman's menstrual cycle and prevent pregnancy. It is given by a doctor as a shot in the butt or arm once every twelve weeks, and the woman is over 99 percent protected against pregnancy for those twelve weeks. (However, she is not protected from sexually transmitted diseases, so you should still use condoms.)

Depo-Provera has some difficult side effects. Irregular bleeding is the most common side effect. Periods become fewer and lighter for most women. Most women will have no periods after five years of use. Other women will have longer and heavier periods. It may take a year for periods to start up again after a woman stops using it. In some cases, it also causes increased appetite and weight gain, headaches, sore breasts, nausea, nervousness, dizziness, depression, rashes or spotty darkening of skin, hair loss and increased facial or body hair. If these side effects occur, then this may not be the best method of birth control for you, and you should ask your doctor if you should switch to something else—such as birth control pills.

morning after

Dear Sari,
Please tell me about the "morning-after pill." I think I need it. Where can I get it? Does it have to be prescribed by a doctor, or is it over-the-counter?

Sari Says:

The "morning-after pill," also called "emergency contraception," is a series of hormone pills that a doctor can prescribe a woman to take up to seventy-two hours (three days) after having had unprotected sexual intercourse. If an egg was fertilized as a result of unprotected intercourse, then the morning-after pill will dislodge the fertilized egg from the uterus, so that she will no longer be pregnant. This is not considered a standard method of birth control—it is only an emergency measure.

The morning-after pill has many side effects, such as severe nausea, dizziness, and heavy cramping and bleeding. It must be taken under close medical supervision.

There is no simple solution to having unprotected sex. That's why you should use birth control every single time you have sex! For more information, check the relevant organizations listed in the appendix at the back of this book.

RU-486

Dear Sari,

What is this abortion pill that I heard about in the news? Can anyone just go and get it, and then the baby they are carrying dies? Please explain this pill to me.

Sari Says:

The abortion pill that you heard about is called RU-486. It has been used in Europe for years, and it is now approved for use in the United States. If a woman gets pregnant and decides she wants to have an abortion, she can take RU-486 to end the pregnancy, instead of having a surgical abortion. The "abortion pill" actually refers to the process of taking three medications over the course of one or two weeks. It must be prescribed by a doctor; it's also available at Planned Parenthood clinics. It can only be taken up to seven weeks after a woman gets pregnant. This is when the product of conception is still in its embryonic state.

If a woman chooses this abortion method, she would see her doctor, who would first give her a shot of methotrexate. This causes the embryo to detach from the wall of the uterus. Then the doctor would give her a pill of mifepristone, which helps the walls of the uterus shed some more lining (this normally happens only when a woman has her period). A few days later, the doctor would give her a third medication called miso-prostol, which causes the fetal tissue to be expelled through the vagina. About twelve days later, the woman must see the doctor a third time to confirm that the abortion was successful. Women experience heavy bleeding, cramping, pain, and nausea or vomiting when the fetus is chemically aborted from the body; many who have used RU-486 say it's somewhat like having a very bad period. Having an abortion with RU-486 instead of surgery still requires at least two visits to a doctor and costs about the same as a surgical abortion: $200 to $350 dollars at a clinic such as Planned Parenthood.

Supporters of RU-486 are very pleased that the pills are now avail-able, because it is much easier, safer, and more private to have an abor-tion with RU-486 than with surgical abortion. Opponents feel this procedure makes it too easy and "casual" to have abortions. Yet, it is never easy for a woman to decide to have an abortion. Taking RU-486 may make the *procedure* easier than having surgery, but it does not make the emotional issues any easier at all.

If you are considering having an abortion, I recommend that you see a counselor to talk about your options and decide whether carrying the baby to term or abortion (whether it's surgical or RU-486) is the best thing for you.

unprotected sex

Dear Sari,

My boyfriend and I had sex—the first time with a condom, the second and third without, but he did pull out. Yeah, I know we shouldn't have even done that, but it happened and I know what could happen. Anyway my question is: I don't have regular periods, so I never know when they're coming. After we had sex, I never got it. It's been a month and now I am having some light spotting. Should I just wait it out? Please help me out! I don't know who else to ask; I don't have anyone.

Sari Says:

You know that you absolutely need to be using condoms and birth control, so I will spare you a huge lecture, but I will point out that part of the reason why birth control is so important is that it helps you avoid all the stress you're experiencing right now. You should go see a gynecologist. Any girl who is sexually active should see one anyway, and now is a great time for you to go since you have some questions that are really best answered by a doctor: 1) Could I be pregnant?, and 2) What birth control can I use on a regular basis?

You can either ask one of your parents to take you to a doctor, or you can make an appointment at a Planned Parenthood in your area (you don't even have to tell your parents to do that). Once you start going to a gynecologist, you'll have a doctor whom you can call and ask any of these questions at any time.

Dear Sari,

If I took a home pregnancy test a month after having unprotected sex, would the results be accurate—how long do you have to wait?

Sari Says,

Most home pregnancy tests can indicate whether you are pregnant fourteen days after conception. When a woman has regular periods, fourteen days after conception is usually right around the time when she would be having the first or second day of her period. So for a woman with regular periods, she could try the pregnancy test when her period is about two days late. But if you are irregular, just go by the date that you had sex and take the test at least fourteen days after that if you want to test yourself at home.

The more accurate urine test that a doctor does can detect if you are pregnant after about ten days since the day that you had unprotected sex. If the doctor does a blood test, it can determine if you are pregnant seven days after you had unprotected sex. I really recommend that you see a doctor. That way you can also talk to the doctor about your birth control choices. Perhaps you will want to have the doctor prescribe birth control pills for you, so you will be protected from getting pregnant.

wants a baby!

Dear Sari,

My mom just told me that we are moving in two months, and I really don't want to. I am with a great guy now and I am so happy. The only thing to do is get pregnant, that way we will have to stay here with the father. How can I tell my mom that I wanna have a baby?

Sari Says:

Get real and stop thinking this way! Having a baby is probably the biggest event in a woman's life. There are good reasons to have a child and there are terrible reasons to have a child. Good reasons: If you're married, in love, financially stable, and you and your spouse want to start a family; you are emotionally able to take care of a child for the rest of his or her life. A terrible reason to have a child: Because you think it will help fix something else in your life even though you are not at all ready to support a child.

One of the worst reasons to have a child is because you are afraid of moving with your mom! Think about it. What if you get pregnant, and you still have to move? What if your boyfriend dumps you after you get pregnant, because he or his family gets so upset about it? What would this do to your relationship with your mom? What about your life? Don't you want to keep having fun, dating, and doing all the regular stuff that teens get to do? Would you be able to finish school?

Think about the child. Is it fair to bring a baby into this world for your own selfish reasons? You cannot support a baby now. Do you know that a baby needs constant attention—twenty-four hours a day, every day—from its mother? Do you have any idea how much it costs to have a baby? The hospital bills alone are about $3,000 if your insurance does not cover it. Then the first year of the baby's life will cost at least $10,000 to $15,000 with food, diapers, clothes, and doctor visits, not to mention your own expenses. Do you have that kind of money? What about love and marriage? Wouldn't you want to wait until you are happily married to have a baby with your future husband?

I understand that you are feeling desperate about the move. But you are not thinking straight. Don't even consider getting pregnant now. Instead, talk to your mom about other options. Maybe you have a friend or relative in the area with whom you could live. But if she says that you must move, be brave: Move and make the best of it. Do not get pregnant!

preg and period

Dear Sari,
Can you get your period while you are pregnant?

Sari Says:
A woman stops having her period when she is pregnant. Here's a basic explanation: When a woman is not pregnant, each month, the lining of her uterus builds up. Then, once her body realizes that she is not pregnant, that lining is shed, resulting in the woman having her period. When a woman is pregnant, her uterine lining keeps increasing, without shedding, to accommodate the fertilized egg. A pregnant woman doesn't get her period during her entire pregnancy.

However, sometimes when a woman gets pregnant, she may bleed a little once in a while during the pregnancy because of other things that are going on in her reproductive system. It is *not* a period; she may have a bit of light blood flow, or spotting. (This most often occurs six weeks after the last period once she is pregnant, when the fertilized egg implants into the wall of the uterus.) If a woman experiences heavy bleeding during her pregnancy, then she must see a doctor.

If you asked this question because you think you might be pregnant, but you are having regular periods (two months in a row), then you most likely are not pregnant. However, I am not a doctor and I can't tell if you are pregnant. If you want to check yourself, you could take a home pregnancy test, available at any drugstore. The best way to find out for sure whether you are pregnant is to get tested by a doctor.

more unprotected sex

Dear Sari,
I just had unprotected sex with my girlfriend. I think I wiped the semen out in time, I just don't know. So if she's pregnant, what should I do—from

a guy's perspective? We don't want to have kids, so should we have an abortion? My parents aren't aware that I am sexually active. Would our parents know if she got an abortion? Do we need insurance and stuff like that? Is there any money involved? Should I even be worried about this? I'm going so paranoid.

Sari Says:

If you have unprotected sex, you should be worried about it! This is why you must use condoms and birth control every time you have sex. Once you ejaculate inside a woman during sex, the fact that you "wiped out" the semen afterward does not make a difference. The second you ejaculated inside her, your sperm traveled right up toward her ovaries.

In terms of what happens next: If your girlfriend thinks she might be pregnant, she should see a doctor or take a home pregnancy test. As for the guy's role in all this: Right now, be supportive and talk to your girl-friend a lot about this. Make sure that she finds out right away whether she is pregnant. If she is not, then all you have to worry about is using protection next time.

If she is, then you two have to discuss your values about abortion. Hopefully, you two will agree on what you'd like to do. Having an abortion costs between $250 and $500 at most clinics, including Planned Parenthood. Some insurance companies will cover the costs, others will not. If you do not have that kind of money, some clinics will let you pay with an installment plan, a little money per week, until it is paid off. But no matter what, it will cost you at least a couple of hundred dollars.

Telling a parent is not required in many states—but it is required in some states. In fact, twenty-six states do require a girl under 18 to get a parent's permission before she can have an abortion. In those states, if she does not want to tell her parents, the only way she can avoid it is if she appears before a judge who then decides whether she is mature enough to make her own decision about abortion.

To find out about the laws in your state, and about abortions in general, call Planned Parenthood. And remember: From now on, *always* use birth control and condoms.

Sexually Transmitted Diseases

what are STDs?

Dear Sari,
I keep hearing that if I have sex, I have to be careful of STDs. What are they and how dangerous are they?

Sari Says:
STD stands for "sexually transmitted disease," which means a disease or an infection that can be passed from one person to another while they have sexual intercourse or oral sex. Sometimes they are also called "STI" for "sexually transmitted infection," and a long time ago, they used to be called "VD" for "venereal disease."

Some of the most common STDs are: chlamydia, genital warts, gonorrhea, herpes, syphilis, and HIV (the virus that causes AIDS). You can be cured of some STDs. For example, chlamydia and gonorrhea can be treated by a doctor and can go away. Other STDs, such as herpes, genital warts, and syphilis, can last your whole life once you get them. AIDS can be life-threatening. Herpes, genital warts, and HIV can all be passed on for the rest of your life to other people whom you have sex with. All STDs, if not treated, may cause more serious problems, such as infertility.

The only way to keep yourself from catching STDs is to practice "safer sex" when you have sex. That means that you *must use condoms* every time you have sex. Also, a doctor can test you to make sure that you do not have any STDs. For more information about STDs, call one of the hotlines listed in the appendix in the back of this book.

genital warts

Dear Sari,
If someone gets genital warts from having sex, can't the warts just be removed? What exactly is genital warts, and is it serious?

Sari Says:
Genital warts, also called Human Papaloma Virus, is a virus that causes warty bumps on or in your genital area. It can be contracted from having unprotected sex with someone who has the virus. The person may or may not have visible warts, so you may not know that the person has it.

If you get genital warts, the warts can be removed through slightly painful procedures that a doctor performs, such as cutting them off, using acid to burn them off, freezing them off, or using a laser to remove them. However, because the virus stays in your system forever, the warts may reappear and need to be removed again and again. Genital warts is more than just a nuisance. This virus can be very dangerous, because some strains of it can cause cervical cancer in woman, which is why it is an extremely serious disease.

spread of herpes

Dear Sari,
Can someone get herpes from kissing someone with a cold sore? If the person has oral sex on me, would I get herpes down there?

Sari Says:
There are two types of the herpes virus: Type-1, which often causes cold sores on the mouth and does not necessarily affect the genitals, and Type-2, which causes genital sores that can be spread during intercourse.

It is possible to spread herpes Type-1 or Type-2 to either the mouth or the genitals. Any time herpes sores are present on the mouth, avoid contact. Any time herpes sores are on the genitals, you should not have sex because you can infect your sex partner, even if you use a condom. Once the sores are gone, you can resume sexual activity. The sores can be treated, and someone with herpes can consult a doctor for treatment and more information.

simple steps for preventing STDs

Dear Sari,
I need to know if you can get HIV or any other STDs from unprotected sexual contact, even when it is not completely having sex—like when the penis is put in the vagina, but nothing happens and it is taken out?

Sari Says,
Yes. You can get certain sexually transmitted diseases from skin-to-skin contact, or penis–vagina sexual contact, even if the man does not ejaculate. These STDs include herpes and genital warts. Some other STDs (such as chlamydia, syphilis, gonorrhea, and HIV, the virus that causes AIDS) are carried in semen, blood, or vaginal secretions. In order to get those STDs, the infected person's blood, semen, or vaginal secretions must enter your body—from having intercourse or oral sex, for instance. Since a man may secrete some semen before he ejaculates, it is possible to get those STDs from penis–vagina contact even if the man does not fully ejaculate. If you ever have any abnormal discharge, pain, itching, bumps, or sores, then see a doctor to find out if it is an STD and which STD it could be. Because some STDs do not have noticeable symptoms, getting tested is a good idea. But remember: The only way to prevent any STD is to use condoms every time you have any sexual contact. Use condoms!

STDs and virgins

Dear Sari,
Can you get STDs or any other diseases if both partners are virgins?

Sari Says:
You cannot get a sexually transmitted disease from someone who does not have a sexually transmitted disease! If someone has not had any sexual contact (intercourse or heavy petting) at all, then you can be sure that the person does not have anything that he or she could have caught from sexual activity.

Sometimes, however, one partner might lie to the other, saying that he or she is a virgin, or that he or she does not have any diseases, when that is not actually true. Another possibility: Two partners might both start out as virgins, but if one cheats on the other, that could bring an STD into the relationship. That's why the only ways to be sure that you don't catch anything is to either not have sex at all, or use condoms correctly every time you have sex.

AIDS transmission

Dear Sari,
I know you can get AIDS from sexual intercourse, and that AIDS is transmitted through the blood and other fluids. Can you get AIDS from say, oral sex? Kissing? Are there any other possible ways to get AIDS?

Sari Says:
HIV, the virus that causes AIDS, is present in three body fluids: blood, semen, and vaginal secretions. In order to get HIV, infected blood, semen, or vaginal secretions needs to get into your bloodstream. The ways it can get into your bloodstream are through any cut or scrape, or

through the microscopic openings in your "mucous membranes," such as the inside lining of the vagina, the rectal tract, and the skin on the penis. It is easiest to get HIV from penis–vagina intercourse or anal intercourse.

It is possible to get it from oral sex, but not highly likely. In order to get HIV from oral sex, blood, semen, or vaginal secretions must get into a cut in your mouth, a canker sore, or maybe a part where your gums are open (for example, from brushing teeth). That could happen.

In order to prevent getting HIV, you must use condoms every time you have intercourse. No exceptions! To protect yourself during oral sex, you should use condoms on the man, or a piece of latex (called a dental dam) over the woman's vulva. If you decide not to use protection during oral sex, then be careful that you don't let any semen or vaginal secretions get into your mouth. (You can lick around the area, just not on it.)

You cannot get AIDS from kissing! Also, you cannot get it from swimming, sharing food or eating utensils, hugging, holding hands, or from a toilet seat.

HIV Testing

If you have had unprotected sex and you are worried that you may have contracted HIV, the virus that causes AIDS, then you can get a free anonymous test at many local testing centers. Check out the AIDS hotline phone numbers in the appendix at the end of this book.

it's history

Dear Sari,
I was just wondering if it is my current boyfriend's right to know who I have had sex with in the past. I have been tested and don't have any STDs.

Sari Says,
No one has a "right" to know whom you've had sex with. It is your choice

if you want to tell him. You may want to tell your boyfriend about your ex-boyfriends just so he knows a bit about your past relationships. However, who you've had sex with is your personal business. As long as you are using condoms to prevent STDs every time you have sex with your new boyfriend, then you do not need to tell him anything.

If you do not want to tell him about your sexual past, but he still feels that it is very important to him to know about it, then you could ask him if you could compromise. Maybe you could tell him how many people you've had sex with, but not their names or the details. By the way, a recent study found that almost half of the women surveyed, 47 percent, had lied to a man by telling him that they have had fewer sexual partners than they actually had. It is just as common for men to lie about the number of partners that they have had. This just goes to show why you should use condoms every time you have sex, no matter what your partner says.

It only takes one episode of unprotected sex to get an STD. Safe sex is not affected by how many people you have had sex with—only by whether or not one of the partners has an STD. Therefore, if someone contracted an STD, it doesn't matter if that person had sex with one person or a hundred people. So there is no good reason to tell all about your sexual past.

Rape

this is rape

Dear Sari,
I went to a friend's house to say good-bye to him before he goes off to college. I had never kissed him before, but I kissed him good-bye. Then he kept kissing me at first really gently, but when I told him to stop he kept kissing and touching me. I begged him to let me go, but I couldn't control the situation. The next thing I knew, he'd ripped off my sundress

and, well, he forced himself into me for a few moments until I could push him off of me. I can't say it's rape, though—because I went along with it in the beginning, you know? After I started crying and he let me go, he said he was sorry, and I threw on some clothes and left. It was awful, but I know that I can get past it—as long as I'm not pregnant. I know he didn't finish inside me—but there's a chance I'm pregnant, huh? I'd be so grateful for any advice.

Sari Says,

What happened to you is horrible. The fact is, you were raped. When someone you know (no matter how much you like him) forces you to have sex, it's called date rape, or acquaintance rape. Even though you "went along with it at the beginning," you were resisting sex and telling him "no"—and yet he did not stop. If you tell a man to stop and he still forces himself on you, that is rape.

You need to find someone to talk to about this. You can talk to a counselor over the phone by calling one of the rape hotline numbers you will find listed in the appendix in the back of this book. Getting over this may not be as easy as you think. I hope you can get help to sort out your feelings and understand that you did nothing wrong—you did *not* "ask for it." This guy is a bad, dangerous person.

As far as whether you could have gotten pregnant, the risk is lower since he did not ejaculate inside you. However, it would still be a good idea if you got a pregnancy test just to be sure. You could use the kind that you buy in a drugstore, but I suggest that you go to a gynecologist instead. Also, since he did not use a condom, you need to ask the gynecologist to test you for sexually transmitted diseases. Please talk to a counselor, a parent, or an adult friend about what this man did to you.

getting over rape

Dear Sari,
I am going out with this guy that I love so much. When we are together we really hit it off. The only problem is, a couple years ago I was raped. I still have bad dreams about it at night. I love my boyfriend and the time has come where he wants to have sex, but I don't know if I'm over that horrible experience. What should I do?

Sari Says,
Rape is a traumatic experience that, sadly, stays with you for years. You do not have to tell your boyfriend that you were raped—only do so if you want to and you think it will help your relationship. You should, however, tell him that you want to wait to have sex until you are ready. In the meantime, you could really benefit from therapy to help you overcome the nightmares and fears that occur as a result of rape, and to help you figure out how to talk with your boyfriend if you want to tell him. For more information call one of the rape hotlines listed in the appendix at the end of this book.

Having Sex

acting differently during sex

Dear Sari,
My boyfriend says that during sex I act differently from how I usually act. What does this mean? Am I doing something wrong?

Sari Says:
You are not doing anything wrong. Your boyfriend may just be seeing another aspect of who you are. Having sex is one of the most intimate

things you can do with someone. He is getting to know you in a way that few people ever will. Everyone has a public personality—you know, the way you behave at school, or around your friends or a boyfriend. But everyone also has a private personality, which is what you reveal to him in deeply intimate moments such as during sex. That could be what he means—he is seeing a different side of you.

When people are being sexual, they often show different aspects of their personalities. Sometimes people seem more shy during sex, because they are naked and they may feel vulnerable or become quiet and self-conscious. Other people feel wild during sex, letting loose, saying sexual things, and being totally adventurous. Do you think that you show him different sides of yourself when you are with him? The only way you can truly find out what your boyfriend means is to ask him! Talk about it.

how long should sex last?

Dear Sari:
How long is sex supposed to last? I know there's no set time, but I was just wondering, is an hour considered long? Average? What does it depend on?

Sari Says:
As you say, there is no set amount of time for sex. Actually, sexual intercourse is usually the briefest part of sex, and all the other stuff ("foreplay") takes longer.

Sometimes the whole thing lasts only a couple of minutes; other times, it could last an hour or more. For example, a couple may start out kissing for fifteen minutes, touch and kiss each other's bodies for twenty minutes, have intercourse for ten minutes, then cuddle for fifteen minutes. But this is just an example. Sure, sex play could last an hour, but it could just as easily last three minutes.

The bottom line is: Don't worry about how long it should last. When someone becomes sexually active, they usually find that sex play lasts as long as he or she and his or her partner want it to last.

discovering sexual positions

Dear Sari,
My girlfriend and I were both virgins when we started having sex. We are very responsible: We always use protection, and our parents even know that we are sexually active. The problem is we have orgasms, but sex seems the same all the time. Like I put it in, when I am on top, and that's it. How do I know what positions we are supposed to be in during sex?

Sari Says,
These are some basic sexual positions:

- Man on top, also called "missionary," in which the woman is lying on her back with the man on top of her.
- Woman on top, in which the man is on his back, and the woman is on top.
- Side by side, in which both people are on their sides facing each other.
- From behind, also called "doggie style," in which the man enters the woman's vagina from behind, when she is either bending over, or lying on her stomach.
- Standing, when both people are standing up.
- Sitting, when they are sitting face-to-face.

Then there are endless varieties of these positions. Such as you can have sex from behind while you are lying on your sides in a "spoon" position. Or you can have sex with the man standing up and the woman lying on the edge of the bed. If you want variations, it's all a matter of playing around and seeing what feels good.

having more fun during sex

Dear Sari,
I have had sex with two different guys. With the first guy, sex was sort of boring, but I figured it was just me, because he was my first. But now, with my new boyfriend, I also feel like sex is not exciting. I just wait for it to be over. Shouldn't sex feel really, really good and be more exciting?! Why is this happening? How can sex be fun for me?

Sari Says:
Before some people have sex, the image that they have of it may be like what they have heard people talk about, or bits of sex that they have seen in movies (R-rated movies, or even in porn). They might think that sex is going to be some wild acrobatic act, in which two people contort their bodies into all kinds of wild positions. The fact is that sometimes sex is as exciting as it seems in movies, but most of the time it is not.

However, I am not just going to tell you that your expectations may be too high. Probably there is more to it than that. You may not be letting yourself go and getting into it. You can move around, try different positions, talk, laugh, and go wild to have more fun. It may not be like in the movies, but it will be more exciting if you get into the act. Also, you may not be getting turned on enough to start with. Next time, ask your boyfriend for a back massage, then to kiss your body all over, before you start having sex. That could get you more into having sex.

never had an orgasm

Dear Sari,
I am a 16-year-old girl and I have never had an orgasm at all ever. I am

not sexually active, but I have tried masturbating. I just do not know how can I start having orgasms.

Sari Says:
All women can have orgasms, and you will with some practice. Orgasms originate from stimulation that you give to your clitoris. Take a look at your vulva in a hand mirror to see where your clitoris is located. Your clitoris is there for only one reason: To give you pleasure. When you are looking at it, believe that it can and will help you have an orgasm. Once you know where it is, the next thing to figure out is how to stimulate it to make yourself feel the best. Some women also like stimulation in their vagina. So you can explore whatever feels good.

To do this, lie down and allow yourself to feel totally relaxed. Then start masturbating by touching your clitoris. Try rubbing it in a circular motion, or back and forth, or any way that feels good. If you want to, you can put a finger in your vagina. Massage the entire area, if you'd like. Touch your breasts, or neck, or legs, or anywhere that feels good. Enjoy all the feelings. When you feel as if your body is reaching some peak of sexual excitement, don't stop. Keep touching yourself, then you may be able to roll those feelings beyond where you have taken them before into the feelings of orgasm.

In order to have an orgasm, you need to let yourself go entirely. You can't try to control your body. You cannot worry about how you will look when you have an orgasm, or what sounds will come out of your mouth or body.

If you often come close but fail to climax, you may be trying too hard. To have an orgasm, you have to lose control and let your body do whatever it is going to do. Let the feelings flow over you and you may orgasm faster than if you are "trying."

how to have orgasms during sex

Dear Sari,
I am an 18-year-old girl, and I have been having sex with my boyfriend for

one year. I have orgasms when I play with myself, but I have never had an orgasm during sex. How can I do that?

Sari Says:

It is difficult for many woman to reach orgasm during intercourse, because they are not always getting the stimulation they need for it during sex. You see, most women have orgasms from stimulation of their clitoris—not from stimulation inside their vagina alone.

Think about the motion that a man uses to have an orgasm when he is masturbating: It is a back and forth motion on his penis. That's the same motion that is used during thrusting during intercourse. That's why it is easy for men to come during sex.

Women, on the other hand, usually use a circular motion to stimulate their clitoris during masturbation. That's why, during intercourse, many women must have clitoral stimulation in order to have an orgasm (not just the back and forth motion of thrusting).

For a woman to have an orgasm more easily during sex, she may want to try being on top. When the woman is on top during sex, as she thrusts, she can rub her clitoris against the base of the man's penis or his pubic area. This can help give her the friction and motion she needs for an orgasm.

If you want to try to have orgasms in any position during sex, you can experiment with using your hand to stimulate your clitoris during intercourse. For example, if he is on top inside you, when you want to have an orgasm, just slip your hand down between your two bodies and masturbate your clitoris until you orgasm. Or if your partner wants to help you enjoy sex and reach orgasm, he can use his hand to stimulate your clitoris.

If you both talk about it, and you show him how you stimulate yourself when you masturbate, then you should be able to figure out together how you can have orgasms during sex. Finally, let yourself go during sex and allow your body to have an orgasm. Since you know how to do it when you masturbate, you should be well on your way to having orgasms during sex.

coming when he wants

Dear Sari,

Help! I am a 17-year-old guy, and when I have sex, I ejaculate before I want to. Just a minute or two after I enter my girlfriend. How can I slow down?

Sari Says:

It is extremely common for young guys to ejaculate before they want to. Sex is so new and exciting that it can be tough to get control. But the fact is that you can learn how to feel in control of when you are going to ejaculate, without missing out on any pleasure. Here's one activity you can try.

To control ejaculation, a guy must be able to recognize the feeling before "the point of no return" and reduce his sexual arousal just enough that he does not reach that point until he is ready. Guys can learn how to pinpoint their level of sexual excitement and keep it at a level that will give their partners pleasure, without coming.

Your sexual excitement increases as you get closer to orgasm. Think of it as being on a scale from 0 to 10. Zero means you don't feel any arousal. Ten is what you feel during orgasm. Try to get your body and mind to stay at an even level of excitement during sex (around level 7 or 8) without getting to the point of no return, which would be around level 9. You can practice this technique while you're masturbating:

- When you feel yourself getting close to orgasm, label that feeling in your mind with an appropriate number.
- When you feel like you're getting close to level 8 of arousal, try to take it down a notch, remaining at 7 so you don't lose control and reach level 9, which would put you on the brink of orgasm.

- The best way to do this is to stop masturbating when you reach about level 8; then start again when your excitement gets down to about 5 or 6. You should practice this daily or at least several times each week, so that you eventually can masturbate for about thirty minutes without ejaculating until you're ready.
- Once you've mastered these counting skills, you can try the same sort of thing during intercourse with the one you love.

A couple of last tips: Condoms can decrease sensitivity a little bit, so wear a condom when you have sex. Also, many guys last longer if they have already ejaculated once first; try masturbating (or mutual masturbation) before you have sex, then have sex shortly after when you get aroused again.

Look at Your Vagina

Girls should all become familiar with what their vaginas look like. When you're sure that you have privacy, get undressed from the waist down. Lie down on your back with your knees bent and your legs open. Then take a hand mirror and place it near your vagina. Angle it so that you can see your vagina in the mirror. You might need to prop your head up to see better. Take note of what's what: your vagina, clitoris, and so on.

what's the G-spot?

Dear Sari,
I heard that to make a girl feel really good, I should touch her G-spot when I finger her. Then I asked my girlfriend, and she told me that is not true and the G-spot does not exist. What's the deal?

Sari Says:
The G-spot does exist—it's simply the name of an area in the female

body. This area is about two inches up on the inner upper wall of the vagina between the back of the pubic bone and the front of the cervix. In this area, there is a bundle of nerve endings that may be more sensitive than the rest of the vagina. I say it "may be more sensitive," because some women feel nothing when their G-spot is stimulated. Therefore, the question isn't really "Does it exist?" but "Does it do anything?"

Even though every women has a G-spot, not every woman has the same response to its stimulation. Some women claim that pressure on that spot produces sexual arousal, while many women feel nothing at all if it is stimulated. The only way to find out if a woman feels anything good from G-spot stimulation is by trying to stimulate that area. Repeatedly rub the flat of your fingertip against the G-spot area on the upper, inner wall of the vagina using a "come here" motion. If she feels any stronger sensations, such as the feeling of getting closer to orgasm, then her G-spot feels good to her, and you may want to stimulate it. If she feels nothing, that is also normal, and you should not force the issue anymore.

Dear Reader,

You've now reached the end of this book . . . almost. While I've answered all sorts of questions that teens have asked me, there may be more questions that YOU have. That's where the next few pages come in. Following is a list of resources where you can get help for your specific situation. Take advantage of all these resources. It's your life, and you should make the most awesome life you can for yourself. Always ask for help when you need to figure out how to navigate your way through the tough times—then the good times will be back again in no time.

I hope I've helped you with this book, and I wish you all the best for total happiness!

Sari

TO SEND QUESTIONS TO SARI LOCKER:
Mail:
Sari Locker
P.O. Box 20258
New York, NY 10021

E-mail through the web site:
www.sarisays.com

The following numbers are all 24 hours (unless specified), confidential, and toll free.

GENERAL TEEN CRISIS HOTLINES
Teen Helpline 1-800-621-4000 (Operated by the National Runaway Switchboard)

Youth Crisis Hotline 1-800-784-2433 (Operated by National Hopeline Network)

Teen Line 1-800-522-8336 (noon–midnight MT)

Teen Crisis Line 1-800-448-3000 (Operated by Girls and Boys Club)

BIRTH CONTROL, DOCTOR'S VISITS, SEXUALITY QUESTIONS
Planned Parenthood
1-800-230-PLAN (1-800-230-7562)
www.plannedparenthood.org

National AIDS and STD Hotline (Operated by the Centers for Disease Control and Prevention)
1-800-342-AIDS (1-800-342-2437)

ABUSE ASSISTANCE
Child Abuse or Sexual Abuse

1-800-4-A-CHILD (1-800-422-4453)
RAPE, ABUSE, INCEST
1-800-656-HOPE

GAY, LESBIAN, BISEXUAL SUPPORT
Gay and Lesbian National Hotline
1-888-843-4564
Monday–Friday 4 P.M.–midnight, and Saturday noon–5 P.M. EST
Parents and Friends of Gays and Lesbians
202-638-4200 (located in Washington, DC)
www.pflag.org

ADOPTION INFORMATION, PARENT SEARCH
International Soundex Reunion Registry
775-882-7755

American Adoption Congress
202-483-3399
www.americanadoptioncongress.org

EATING DISORDERS
American Anorexia/Bulimia Association
212-575-6200
www.aabainc.org

National Eating Disorders Organization
918-481-4044

Anorexia Nervosa and Related Eating Disorders
541-344-1144

DRUG OR ALCOHOL ABUSE
Drug and Alcohol Abuse Referral Hotline
1- 800-821-4357

Drug and Alcohol Abuse in Families
1-800-736-9805
www.familiesanonymous.org

National Clearinghouse for Alcohol and Drug Information
1-800-729-6686
www.health.org/catalog

CUTTING
Self-Abuse Finally Ends
1-800-DONT-CUT (1-800-366-8282)
www.selfinjury.com